The Politics of Global Tax Governance

Why has global tax governance been politicized and how can we explain the varying intensity and content of public debates? This book offers an integrated theory of the politicization of international institutions and a detailed account of how the institutional design and policy output of tax governance by the EU and OECD have developed over time.

Offering the first in-depth empirical analysis to compare politicization across international institutions, it blends institutionalist explanations that focus on the growing authority of international institutions, and sociological and political economy approaches that take into account domestic context.

Exploring why and how international institutions have become increasingly contested in the 21st century, this book will be of particular interest to the scholars of the transfer of authority from the nation-state to international institutions, and the societal repercussions and political struggles that connect these processes. Researchers in the fields of political science, international relations, sociology, and political communication will also find it useful and insightful.

Henning Schmidtke is a Research Fellow at the German Institute of Global and Area Studies (GIGA), Hamburg. His research interests include the formation, design, and behavior of international organizations and the contentious politics around them. His work has appeared in the *Review of International Organizations, Review of International Studies,* and *West European Politics.*

Global Governance

Series Editor: John J. Kirton
University of Toronto, Canada

Global governance is growing rapidly to meet the compounding challenges of a globalized 21st-century world. Many issues once dealt with largely at the local, national or regional level are now going global, in the economic, social and political-security domains. In response, new and renewed intergovernmental institutions are arising and adapting, multilevel governance is expanding, and sub-national actors are playing a greater role, and create complex combinations and private-partnerships to this end.

This series focuses on the new dynamics of global governance in the 21st century by:

- Addressing the changes in the structure, operation and impact of individual intergovernmental institutions, above all their innovative responses to the growing global challenges they confront.
- Exploring how they affect, are affected by and relate to non-state actors of global relevance and reach.
- Examining the processes of cooperation, competition and convergence among international institutions and the many global governance gaps where global challenges such as terrorism, transnational crime and energy do not confront powerful international institutions devoted to their control.
- Dealing with how global institutions govern the links among key issues such as climate change and health.

In all cases, it focuses on the central questions of how global governance institutions and processes generate the effective, legitimate, accountable results required to govern today's interconnected, complex, uncertain and crisis-ridden world.

The G20
Evolution, Interrelationships, Documentation
2nd edition
Peter I. Hajnal

The Politics of Global Tax Governance
Henning Schmidtke

For more information about this series, please visit: https://www.routledge.com/Global-Governance/book-series/ASHSER1420

The Politics of Global Tax Governance

Henning Schmidtke

Routledge
Taylor & Francis Group
LONDON AND NEW YORK

First published 2019
by Routledge
2 Park Square, Milton Park, Abingdon, Oxon OX14 4RN

and by Routledge
52 Vanderbilt Avenue, New York, NY 10017

Routledge is an imprint of the Taylor & Francis Group, an informa business

First issued in paperback 2021

British Library Cataloguing-in-Publication Data
A catalogue record for this book is available from the British Library

Library of Congress Cataloging-in-Publication Data
Names: Schmidtke, Henning, author.
Title: The politics of global tax governance / Henning Schmidtke.
Description: Abingdon, Oxon ; New York, NY : Routledge, 2019. | Series: Global governance | Includes bibliographical references and index.
Identifiers: LCCN 2018054221 | ISBN 9781138540842 (hardback)
Subjects: LCSH: Taxation—International cooperation. | Taxation—Political aspects. | International finance. | International relations.
Classification: LCC HJ2305 .S36 2019 | DDC 336.2—dc23
LC record available at https://lccn.loc.gov/2018054221

ISBN: 978-1-138-54084-2 (hbk)
ISBN: 978-1-03-209377-2 (pbk)
ISBN: 978-1-351-01243-0 (ebk)

Typeset in Times New Roman
by Apex CoVantage, LLC

For my parents

Contents

Figures

Tables

Acknowledgments

Many people contributed to this book. My family and friends made it possible in the first place by encouraging my curiosity and being patient with the time-consuming process of discussing these questions. My parents have provided unwavering support since I began being a student of political science. My friends have been remarkably tolerant of my fascination with international institutions and their politicization.

Colleagues at several institutions enriched this project. Early on, the intellectual dynamism of the University of Bremen and the Jacobs University – especially colleagues from the Collaborative Research Center 597 "Transformations of the State" – helped me with many aspects to my work. My mentors Philipp Genschel, Frank Nullmeier, and Michael Zürn were incredibly generous with their time and insightful feedback. Across departments, faculty and students have supported my work. I am especially grateful to Jennifer Gronau, Achim Kemmerling, Peter Mayer, Martin Nonhoff, Steffen Schneider, Laura Seelkopf, Daniel Seikel, Sebastian Streb, Irina Wiegand, and Dieter Wolf.

I am also grateful for the support of the University of St. Gallen and the TUM (Technical University Munich) School of Governance. Extensive comments from people such as Eugénia da Conceicao-Heldt, Pieter de Wilde, Klaus Dingwerth, Matthias Ecker-Erhardt, Dominic Hoeglinger, Liesbet Hooghe, Achim Hurrelmann, Swen Hutter, Anna Leupold, Gary Marks, Christian Rauh, and Arndt Wonka immensely improved the manuscript during this time.

Last but certainly not least, people affiliated with Routledge have worked hard to bring this book to a wide audience. I am especially grateful to editor Rob Sorsby and to editorial assistant Claire Maloney for their faith in this project and their patience with my pace of work.

Henning Schmidtke
Bremen, September 2018

1 Exploring the causes and consequences of international institutions' politicization

Global governance has undergone a fundamental transformation in the past few decades. While international institutions were long the exclusive preserve of a small circle of elites, the past 20–30 years have witnessed the disappearance of the traditional separation between the *high* politics of international affairs and *low* domestic politics, giving citizens, civil society organizations (CSOs), business associations, multinational corporations, and social movements a more prominent role. Increasingly, non-governmental actors, especially from the Global North, engage with the institutional design, decision-making, and policy output of global governance arrangements.

This broad societal politicization spans many areas of global governance. The European Union (EU) has been going through a series of crises of public confidence, which culminated in the public rejections of the European constitutional treaty in referendums in France and the Netherlands in 2005, violent protests against European austerity measures during the Euro crisis in many southern European countries, and most recently the "Brexit" referendum in 2016. Other major international institutions, such as the World Bank, the International Monetary Fund (IMF), or the Group of Eight (G8) and Group of Twenty (G20) have also experienced episodes of protest and broad public contestation. An absolute absence of public interest and controversy over issues of global governance is today exceedingly rare. The western permissive consensus under which insulated elites were able to cut international deals has given way to a new era of constraining dissensus in which political elites must look over their shoulders when negotiating issues of global governance (Hooghe and Marks, 2009: 5; Zürn, 2018).

The ambition of this book is to offer a systematic theoretical and empirical account of this development in the issue area of global tax governance. Guided by the questions of where, when, and why global tax governance has become a substantially more controversial issue of public debate, it aims to provide a historically comprehensive analysis of the politicization of international institutions. Understanding the causes of politicization in times of rising populist sentiments against international integration is central to the theory and practice of global governance (Lake, 2018). Once we can explain why, where, and when citizens, CSOs, business actors, and political parties engage with the issue of global tax governance, we can get traction on other pertinent questions of today. Does politicization shift the balance of power between political actors and thus change the course of international cooperation and integration towards more or less authority delegation to the international level? How does the growing engagement of broader levels of western populations affect global governance outcomes? Can these developments help ameliorate the alleged democratic deficit and thus bolster the legitimacy of international institutions?

The book aims to make three contributions to the existing literature. To begin with, it provides the first detailed account of how the institutional design and policy output of global tax governance by the EU and the Organization for Economic Cooperation and Development (OECD) – two crucial international organizations (IOs) in the area of taxation – have developed over time. I show that European tax governance has expanded substantially, despite a stable formal mandate, whereas the OECD's authority has largely stagnated. These crucial differences in the formal mandate, institutional design, and tax policy output of both organizations set the stage for their varied politicization. As I show in detail in Chapter 4, the EU's growing authority and tax policy output have triggered a continuously accelerating politicization. By contrast, the less-intrusive institutional design and tax policy output of the OECD have contributed to a less strong and more episodic politicization pattern.

Furthermore, the book is empirically comprehensive through its historical comparative approach. While existing contributions to the study of international institutions' politicization mainly consist of case studies focusing on most recent episodes of public opposition to the EU, this book provides the first in-depth empirical analysis that compares politicization across international institutions, time, and space. In this exercise, it draws on a fine-grained content analytical tool that combines political claims and political valuation analysis to trace debates about global tax governance in the quality press of three European democracies (Germany, Ireland, and Switzerland) from 1981 to 2011. This long-term historical comparative approach is unique in the present literature, although it is a necessary precondition for a sound empirical analysis of politicization (Zürn, 2016). The comparison of politicization patterns across international institutions helps to gauge the explanatory power of approaches focusing on the varying political authority of international institutions. Here, the different institutional design of the EU and the OECD, and the development of both organizations' tax policy output over time, constitute an ideal comparison. The analysis of the politics of global tax governance in three European democracies reveals that global tax governance shapes substantively different patterns of politicization at the national level. A country's positions in international tax competition and the varying mobilization of cosmopolitan citizens and nationalist globophobes explain why the intensity, tone, and content of public debates vary strongly across national debates. As I show in detail in Chapter 5, the populations of low-tax countries tend to react strongly to international tax policies that threaten their economic growth models and national identity. The comparison between high-tax countries such as Germany and low-tax countries such as Switzerland

and Ireland help to uncover the crucial conditioning effects of national contexts on politicization patterns.

Finally, the book is theoretically ambitious, developing and testing a comprehensive theory of politicization. The book's main theoretical claim is that present explanatory approaches have to be integrated into a comprehensive theory of politicization rather than being treated as competing explanations (Zürn, 2016). I propose a theory that views the growing political authority of international institutions as the driving force of their politicization, while domestic economic and cultural contexts are the crucial conditioning variables which determine the strength of the political authority effect on the national level. By blending institutionalist explanations that focus on the growing authority of international institutions (Hooghe and Marks, 2009; Rauh, 2016; Zürn, 2018) and sociological and political economy theories that take into account domestic context (Eichenberg and Dalton, 2007; De Wilde et al., 2016; Hutter et al., 2016), the book sheds light on why and how international institutions become increasingly contested in the twenty-first century. Only if it is understood that the changing nature of international institutions and their growing authority interact with country-specific mobilization potentials it is possible to explain the varying patterns of politicization.

My argument can be summarized in three main points. First, I demonstrate the politics of global tax governance have indeed undergone a far-reaching transformation. Public attention to the issue, controversy in public debates, and the plurality of actors involved have grown over time. The period of the most dramatic change has been the late 1990s, and there is no indication that the politicization of global tax governance will go away anytime soon. The room for maneuver for political elites in the area of global taxation has decreased. As the public becomes more aware of global tax governance and its implications, political elites can be expected to become more careful in taking this public scrutiny into account. At the same time, levels and patterns of politicization have proven to vary strongly across international institutions, over time, and across countries.

Second, I argue that this variation in the politicization of tax governance is mainly explained by a combination of three factors: the transfer of political authority from the national to the international level, domestic economic context, and domestic cultural context. The principal driver of global tax governance's politicization has been the shift of political authority from national to international institutions and the exercise of this authority by IOs. The substantial increase of politicization surrounding the expansion of formal authority and tax legislation at the EU and the less-strong politicization of the OECD, where authority transfers and tax legislation have been less intrusive, shows that western public spheres are sensitive to authority shifts. They react with more attention, higher controversy, and a diversification of the actors who voice their views in the media.

Yet, these institutional effects do not unfold in a vacuum. Rather they interact with domestic economic and cultural contexts. A country's positions in international tax competition and the varying mobilization of cosmopolitan citizens, nationalist globophobes, and mobilizing actors, such as political parties, explain why the intensity, tone, and content of public debates vary strongly across countries and over time. The recipe for a strong politicization of global tax governance consists of an international institution with strong formal authority, a broad and frequent tax policy output, a domestic economic growth model tailored towards tax competition, and a high share of cosmopolitans and nationalist globophobes activated by mobilizing political actors in a given population.

Third, I conclude that the emergence of political authority beyond the nation-state has different implications for citizens according to their cultural and economic situations and perceptions. The question of whether these developments will result in more responsive politics of global tax governance because international institutions and national governments are forced to take a broader set of preferences into account or in less responsive tax governance because international bureaucrats and national governments react to politicization by shielding their negotiations from public scrutiny cannot be conclusively answered by this book. However, some informed speculation is warranted. Taking into account the complex nature of politicization, concerted strategies of shielding global tax governance from public scrutiny appear to be difficult to implement. First, politicization varies substantially across countries. This cross-country variation implies that both national governments and international institutions are confronted with different strategic environments. While some governments are haunted by public scrutiny and demand for more or less international cooperation in taxation, other governments are less constrained by public scrutiny. Clearly, this situation transforms the nature of the game considerably and may decrease the chances of international cooperation altogether; but whether governments and international institutions are able to implement common shielding strategies under these conditions is questionable at best. Second, the temporal variation of politicization processes makes coordinated shielding mechanisms even less likely. As politicization does not follow a single temporal sequence but emerges sometimes already during negotiation processes, and at other times only years after legal enactment of major treaties or specific policies, politicization processes appear to be beyond the control of political elites. While it may be possible to design and cover authority transfer during the phase of negotiation and implementation (Schimmelfennig, 2014; Genschel and Jachtenfuchs, 2018), the outcomes of these changes are difficult to control and may spur politicization even years after legal enactment.

Beyond its conclusions on the politicization of international institutions, the book carries implications for three ongoing debates in International Relations (IR) theory. First, it speaks to research on the institutional design and policy output of international institutions. The results of the book challenge the assumption that design decisions are made by a narrow circle of political elites in isolation from the concerns and demands of their populations (Jupille et al., 2013; Johnson, 2014; Koremenos, 2016). Rather such elite negotiations take place in an increasingly politicized environment: negotiators and policy-makers need to take into account both the normative and economic demands of the public. Second, the book's results carry implications for the broader literature on transnational activism and influence in global governance (Della Porta, 2007; Della Porta and Caiani, 2009; Tarrow, 2012), showing that the mobilization of civil society actors is neither constant across countries nor over time. Finally, the book engages with the normative debate on democratic responsiveness and legitimacy of global governance institutions, highlighting that public debate and contestation as a fundamental precondition for global democracy has emerged over the past decades (Keohane et al., 2009; Scholte, 2011).

The puzzle: the politicization of international institutions

The past decades have witnessed a continuous transformation in the dominant modes of global governance, from interstate cooperation – negotiated, managed, and implemented by small circles of political elites around national governments – to more complex modes of governance involving transnational, supranational, and subnational actors previously at the margins of global governance (Abbott et al., 2016; Hooghe et al., 2017). International institutions have opened up to transnational actors, giving participation rights in their decision-making (Tallberg et al., 2013); they have begun to orchestrate various non-governmental actors in working towards their governance targets (Abbott et al., 2015); and they have changed their institutional designs to become more accountable, democratically inclusive, and transparent (Grigorescu, 2015).

These developments have taken place within a radically altered political environment. In the past, political elites had taken decisions of international cooperation in closed circles, outside the spotlight of public scrutiny (Lindberg and Scheingold, 1970). The vast majority of citizens and CSOs did not care about the issues of global governance, and to the very limited extent they that they did, they provided latent support (Aldrich et al., 1989; Holsti, 1992). During this era of permissive consensus, political elites enjoyed largely unrestricted freedoms of choice on the purpose, design, and performance of international institutions. Neither the policy output of global governance arrangements nor their general legitimacy was fundamentally challenged. During the past decades, however, this permissive consensus has been replaced by a far more complicated environment for international decision-making, involving a growing salience of global governance issues, a polarization of respective opinions, and an expansion of the actors and audiences engaged in monitoring and influencing international affairs (Zürn, 2018). As Jeffrey Laurenti put it in a *New York Times* newspaper article almost two decades ago: "The old priesthood cannot keep the unwashed laity from the altar of international relations any longer" (*New York Times*, 23 September 1996).

While the EU, with its failed constitutional referenda and most the recent decision of the United Kingdom (UK) to leave the EU, is often portrayed as the poster child of this politicization of international institutions (Hooghe and Marks, 2009; Hobolt and Tilley, 2014; Hutter et al., 2016), scholars from different research areas have shown that the EU is clearly not the only global governance arrangement confronted with heightened public salience and controversy, and that failed referenda are only one set of empirical observations that demonstrate this radical shift (Zürn et al., 2012).

First, in the field of party politics, Hanspeter Kriesi and colleagues (2008, 2012) have taken up the politicization of international institutions from a political-cleavage perspective (Lipset and Rokkan, 1967). Their research shows that in Western Europe a new political cleavage between those in favor of international integration and those opposed to it – the integration/demarcation cleavage – transforms the electoral space and provides growing room for controversial debates about international institutions (see also Vowles and Xezonakis, 2016). Similarly, scholars from the field of European integration have begun to analyze the politicization of the EU in the electoral space (Bartolini, 2005; Otjes and Katsanidou, 2017). Since Cees Van der Eijk and Mark Franklin's (2004; 2007) thesis that the issue of European integration is a "sleeping giant" for European party politics, scholars have started to investigate the rise of Eurosceptic parties (Kriesi and Pappas, 2015; van Kessel, 2015; de Vries, 2018) and how European Parliament (EP) elections have become less of a second-order event over time (Clark and Rohrschneider, 2009; Hassing Nielsen and Franklin, 2017). In this context, Sara Hobolt and colleagues (2009: 112) show, for instance, that the EU is becoming a more salient issue for the electorate. Furthermore, under the heading of political agenda-setting (Baumgarnter et al., 2006), scholars have shown that the EU and other international institutions rank considerably higher on party agendas (Green-Pedersen, 2012; Ecker-Ehrhardt, 2014) and in parliamentary debates (Wonka, 2016; Rauh and de Wilde, 2017).

Second, research on individual attitude formation, political mobilization, and participation outside of the electoral arena has become increasingly interested in the question of what individual citizens know about international institutions, how they are perceived, and whether their activities become targets of public contention. As regards the micro-level of individual attitude formation, European integration scholars have been following the changes in public support for the EU for quite some time. Building mostly on survey data, this strand of the literature demonstrates that trust in the EU has been decreasing over the past decade (Down and Wilson, 2008; Hobolt, 2012; Usherwood and Startin, 2013). Relatedly, it could be shown that citizens hold meaningful individual attitudes on other international institutions (Furia, 2005; Ecker-Ehrhardt, 2012; Schlipphak, 2015) and care about the legitimacy of global governance arrangements more than they did in the past (Dellmuth and Tallberg, 2015; Hurrelmann and Schneider, 2015).

Finally, scholars from the field of civil society participation and contentious politics have shown that transnational movements and CSOs increasingly address and protest international institutions (O'Brien et al., 2000; Bandy and Jackie, 2005; Tarrow, 2005). This strand of literature reveals that formal cooperation between international institutions and civil society (Tallberg et al., 2013; Abbott et al., 2015) and public protests and civil society campaigns against international institutions have grown in number and intensity (Imig and Tarrow, 2000; Gronau et al., 2009). Research on public debates on international institutions in the media comes to similar conclusions. Scholars focusing on the European public sphere have shown that issues of EU governance attract ever-growing media attention and spur controversial public debates (Risse, 2015; Hoegliner, 2016).

Research from the field of political communication reveals that the salience and contestation of international institutions in the news (Walgrave et al., 2008) and online media (Pelc, 2013) have also risen over the past decade. The literature on the empirical legitimacy of international institutions has discovered similar trends towards an increasing politicization of international institutions (Schneider et al., 2007; Nullmeier et al., 2010; Schmidtke and Nullmeier, 2011).

This wealth of empirical data showing that international institutions are no longer the preserve of political elites but have moved into the spotlight of public scrutiny and contestation present us with a set of puzzles. First, why has the salience of and controversy over international institutions in public debates grown so strongly over the past decades? Since the end of World War II, international cooperation and the creation of international institutions to foster this cooperation have been able to build on a broad societal consensus. Western societies accepted the formation of the post-war governance structure as a viable way to prevent the world from the horrors of the past and to establish a stable and prosperous system. Why citizens in western societies have changed their mind so radically is the starting puzzle for this book.

Second, what explains the remarkable speed with which politicization processes have taken place? The social norms and values that have underpinned the long-standing permissive consensus on international cooperation do not change quickly but take time to transform. Similarly, party and media systems, respective political cleavages, and the resulting forms of political mobilization are rather resistant to change. Once in place, these political configurations tend to become self-reinforcing by structuring actors' expectations, increasing adaptation costs, and generating positive feedback effects that lock-in the status quo for extended periods of path-dependence (Rixen et al., 2016; Fioretos, 2017). Yet, these expectations of stability notwithstanding, we have witnessed a dramatic politicization of international institutions over the past few decades.

Third, why does the politicization of international institutions vary extensively across multiple dimensions? Why have some international institutions become highly politicized, but not others? How can we explain that periods of strong salience and controversy alternate with periods of relative calm and disinterest? Finally, why are international institutions a considerably more conflictual issue in some western countries than in others?

This book takes up these puzzles and questions. Focusing explicitly on the politicization of global tax governance in German, Irish, and Swiss public debates, I seek to explain where, when, and why actors outside the narrow circle of political elites around national governments have become more interested in this area of global governance.

Research design: a comparative historical analysis

This book is a theory-developing exercise with the goal of theorizing the varied politicization of global tax governance in particular and of international institutions more generally. My intention is not necessarily to offer entirely new arguments but to show how existing theoretical approaches can be combined into a more complete explanation of varying levels and patterns of politicization across international institutions, countries, and over time. The inadequacy of the widely shared logic of competing rather than complementary theories explaining cross-institutionally and cross-nationally varying levels and patterns of politicization warrants a deductive-inductive case study research design (George and Bennett, 2005: 19–21; Gerring, 2007: Chapter 3).

The empirical analysis aims to explore how exactly these factors play out in the politics of global tax governance as an interesting, information-rich, and typical case of the politicization of international institutions more generally. The research design is tailored to the task of probing the explanatory power of my theory of politicization and of theorizing the interaction effects between institutional and domestic context factors. This explanatory nature of the endeavor and the need to systematically collect qualitative data on the public debates about global tax governance, the transformation of the international institutions involved in this issue area and their tax policies output, as well as the domestic economic and cultural contexts, makes a comparative historical case study design (Lijphart, 1971; Mahoney and Rueschemeyer, 2003) a suitable compromise between an individual case study and the quantitative analysis of the politicization of a wide array of international institutions in many countries.

The book analyzes the politicization of global tax governance for two main reasons. First, global tax governance and its politicization is an important but understudied element of an increasingly globalized world. Historically, taxation has been of high political salience since the early days of the nation-state due to its redistributive nature (Genschel, 2005; Martin et al., 2009). Taxes made the state, and the state made taxes (Norberg and Hoffman, 1994: 303). However, forces of globalization increasingly challenge nation-states' ability to extract and deploy resources. Due to the increasing mobility of goods, services, and capital, the perceived need to go beyond unilateral or bilateral governance of taxation has never been more pronounced (Zucmann, 2015). Taxation is no longer the prerogative of individual nation-states. Rather cooperation between nation-states, international institutions, and private actors has become necessary to overcome complex international cooperation and coordination problems inherent to taxation (Palan, 2002; Braithwaite, 2003; Rixen, 2011). More recently, these transformations have led to more ambitious global tax governance. Spearheaded by the EU's engagement in virtually all important ways of taxation and the OECD's efforts to regulate tax competition and prevent the kind of tax avoidance and evasion of the global rich that cyclically erupt in large public scandals (Elbra and Mikler, 2016), such as the 2013 Paradise Papers or the 2016 Panama Papers Investigations (Kerzner and Chodikoff, 2016; Alldridge, 2017). As a result, the globalization of taxation (Paris, 2003), its governance, and its societal and political repercussions constitute a field of research that deserves more scholarly attention.

Second, from a research design perspective global tax governance constitutes a pertinent case because it is likely to yield varying levels and patterns of politicization across international institutions and over time. The dynamic transformation of global tax governance over the course of the past few decades provides for substantial variance of the explanatory factors highlighted by my theory of politicization. Beginning in the 1920s, when technical experts of the League of Nations first discussed how international commerce affected taxation and how problems of double taxation could be solved, global tax governance has become an issue for many international institutions. Ranging from the United Nations (UN), the World Trade Organization (WTO), the G8, and the G20, to the OECD and many regional institutions like the EU or the Nordic Convention on Mutual Assistance in Tax Matters, the number of international institutions involved in global tax governance and the scope and level of their authority have grown substantially over time (Lesage and Van de Graaf, 2013). The wide range of international institutions involved in global tax governance enables me to compare levels and patterns of politicization across different international institutions while keeping the issue area and its specificities constant. Furthermore, the specific nature of global tax governance – a regulatory field with distributive consequences (Rixen and Zangl, 2013: 371–373) – fosters the external validity of my results because this type of issue area is neither an extremely strong nor weak case of politicization. This design breaks with previous politicization scholarship, which is dominated by accounts of the most prominent IOs, notably the EU, and their overall politicization.

More specifically, the qualitative analysis consists of two carefully selected comparative historical case studies. They draw on a rich variety of primary and secondary sources, including large-scale newspaper content analysis data, surveys, official documents, and existing empirical research. The first set of case studies compares politicization processes across two international institutions, namely tax governance by the EU and the OECD from 1981 to 2011. These institutions have been selected for two reasons. First, they are two major players in the field of global tax governance. The OECD is the key international institution in the context of global income tax governance (Rixen, 2008) and some even attribute a "state-like role in international tax policy" to it (Sharman, 2012: 19). Although other global institutions such as the WTO, the UN, the World Bank, and the IMF have shaped international tax rules, the OECD is generally recognized as the most influential international institution in the field of global income tax governance (Kerzner and Chodikoff, 2016). The EU's role in taxation is even more prominent (Genschel, 2002). Although EU membership is more restricted than that of the OECD, the EU can be considered to shape global tax governance more than any other international institution. Its legally binding tax policy output encompasses direct as well as indirect taxation and ranges from loose coordination of tax administration to the strict harmonization of tax rates (Radaelli, 1997; Genschel and Jachtenfuchs, 2011; Genschel and Schwarz, 2011).

Second, the different dynamics of both institutions' authority in global tax governance and their policy output make them an optimal choice for the empirical analysis of how the transfer of political authority to the international sphere spurs politicization. The EU's political authority has increased substantially over the course of the past decades. While a similar trend of growing authority can also be noted for the OECD, the gap between both institutions widens over time because the OECD's authority expansion is considerably weaker than the EU's. Consequently, the comparison within and across both institutions provides substantial variance of their political authority and thus facilitates an in-depth analysis of the causal nexus between international institutions' authority and their politicization.

The second set of case studies traces the politicization of EU tax governance in Germany, Ireland, and Switzerland from 1981 to 2011 to deepen the insights gained from the first historical comparison and to get even closer to the causal mechanisms that link politicization, international authority, and domestic context. In the spirit of the most similar systems design (Gerring, 2007: 131–139), these countries are similar in many important respects and differ in terms of domestic economic and cultural context. All three countries are established liberal democracies with consolidated political institutions and party systems. They belong to the economically most developed and internationally most integrated countries in the world and are thus strongly affected by the globalization of taxation. Although the selected countries have varying preferences as regards the specific content and direction of global tax governance due to their different comparative (dis-)advantages in tax competition,[1] the high degree to which they are affected by the growing supply and demand for global tax governance is an important scope condition for the comparison.

Within these scope conditions, the selection of countries maximizes the variance of the explanatory factors highlighted by my theory of politicization. I have selected countries that vary in terms of the level of authority transferred to the EU. The selection of Germany (a founding member of the EU that has not opted out of any major step of European integration), Ireland (an accession country that has opted out of a number of integration steps), and Switzerland (which is not a formal member of the EU, but which is nonetheless considerably integrated with the EU via bilateral treaties) represents the entire spectrum of levels of integration. Furthermore, the economic and cultural contexts in these countries vary as well. Switzerland has built a strong reputation for its low corporate and individual tax rates, and it is a country of strong polarization between cosmopolitans and nationalist globophobes. Less radically than in Switzerland, Ireland's economic development is also tied to tax competition and low corporate tax rates – yet the mobilization potential of cosmopolitans and globophobes is lower than in Switzerland. While the German cultural context is similar to the Irish case, its economic context is remarkably different. Germany represents large, high-tax countries, which potentially lose rather than win in tax competition.

The argument in brief: authority transfer, domestic economic and cultural context

The book establishes two prominent patterns in the politicization of global tax governance. First, the politicization of global tax governance that began in the 1980s and has intensified only more recently in 1990s takes place across the EU and the OECD, and shows no signs of ending. Based on a comprehensive analysis of newspaper articles that either evaluate the politics of global tax governance (valuation analysis) or put forward claims on how to change and improve governance (claims analysis), I can corroborate the existence of far-reaching politicization of global tax governance. The public salience of global tax governance has increased significantly over time. This mounting visibility is the basis of the politicization process. If an issue is essentially not visible in the public arena, it cannot become politicized because it does not exist on the public agenda. Similarly, the data show that the number of affective statements on global tax governance and, thus, the controversy in public debate has increased. Finally, I show that the plurality of actors involved in public debate about global tax governance has also grown over time. Actors outside of national governments dominate the discussions over the entire time period. Instead of becoming more important over time, speakers outside the narrow elite circles have been important since the 1980s. In association with executive actors, they push the issue on the public agenda.

Second, the patterns of variation in politicization across international institutions and countries have been remarkably stable over time. While politicization has expanded across the board, early differences have proven highly resilient over time. Politicization has been much stronger for the EU than for the OECD. Measured across countries, politicization is also growing invariably, but with different temporal patterns and content. The German case is marked by a constantly growing politicization with a strong focus on cosmopolitan problem-solving frames. In Ireland, politicization emerged during the 2000s, and public debate focuses mainly on the preservation of national sovereignty. In Switzerland, the debate is less consistant and is marked by episodes of politicization that focus mainly on the preservation of national sovereignty.

What accounts for these patterns in the politicization of global tax governance? The book assesses the interaction of three explanations that have so far often been treated as alternative rather than complementary. The empirical findings largely confirm my integrated theory of politicization. The main claim of the book is that the transfer of authority from national to international institutions drives politicization, but this effect is strongly conditioned by domestic economic and cultural contexts. While political economy research suggests that authority transfers become politicized due to their economic implications, more society-centered theories claim that socio-cultural concerns – that is, exclusive nationalism and cosmopolitanism – shape country-specific patterns of politicization. The combination of these three perspectives helps us to understand why, when, and how global tax governance has become politicized over the past decades. The results of the three case studies on the politicization of EU tax governance in Germany, Ireland, and Switzerland show that the recipe for a strong politicization of European tax governance consists of formal authority transfer, broad and frequent EU tax legislation, which targets economically sensitive areas, and a high share of cosmopolitans and nationalist globophobes in a given population. Formal authority transfer is the key driver of politicization. Its effect is intertwined with EU tax legislation. While much of the current literature on politicization focuses exclusively on formal authority transfers, my analysis implies not only that national mass media reacts to major treaty revisions but also that politicization is shaped by the policy output of international institutions. Even in issue areas like taxation, in which EU formal authority is still low, we observe politicization driven by the interaction of formal authority transfer and policy output. The cases of Ireland and Switzerland show that the key condition for politicization is that EU tax legislation targets areas which are of pronounced national economic or cultural importance. The growing political authority of international institutions has, thus, different implications for country-specific patterns of politicization. Although formal authority transfer and EU tax legislation have similar effects on the German and Irish tax systems – and to some extent also on Switzerland – the varying timing, level, and content of politicization in the three countries can be understood only with a view to national economic and cultural contexts.

The implications: institutional design, transnational mobilization, and democratic legitimacy

What are the implications of these results for our understanding of global governance? I identify three important areas of IR research for which my findings carry consequences.

To begin with, this book engages with the literature on *international institutional design and policy output.* While existing research in the field assumes that both design and policy decisions in international institutions are driven by the rational cost-benefit calculations of narrow policy elites isolated from the concerns and demands of their populations (Lundgren et al., 2018), the results of this book uncover a different picture. My findings reveal an increasing politicization of international institutions in the area of global tax governance and, thus, challenge the broadly held assumption that public demands can be ignored for explaining international institutional design and policy output. Although I do not trace how exactly public debates feature in negotiations on international institutions, I argue that politicization is highly likely to constrain such negotiations (Rauh, 2016). First, governments will ask the question of whether the political opportunity costs created by public scrutiny and controversy diminish the gains from transferring authority to international institutions. If strong public resistance is expected, for instance, because the envisioned international institutions target national growth models or issues of high cultural value, less authority transfer may result. The most recent episodes of politicization in relation to the Transatlantic Trade and Investment Partnership (TTIP) illustrate this relationship (de Ville and Siles-Brügge, 2017). Both the United States (US) and many European countries agreed that a court of arbitration and protection of foreign investment would be a cost-efficient solution to the question of how to guarantee compliance with the agreement. Yet, many European citizens did not like the idea of delegating this authority to a supranational court and, thus, losing parts of their national sovereignty. The result was mass protests across European capitals, which contributed to the current standstill in TTIP negotiations.

Second, the outcome of negotiations on institutional design features is also likely to be affected by politicization. My results on the varied nature of politicization across countries and over time imply that national governments and international institutions are confronted with different strategic environments. While some governments are haunted by public scrutiny and specific demands, other governments may be less constrained by public scrutiny. Clearly, this situation transforms negotiation processes considerably and may decrease the chances of international cooperation altogether.

Second, the book's results carry implications for the literature on transnational activism and influence in global governance, showing that the mobilization of civil society actors is neither constant across countries nor over time. This insight is highly important for the research trying to explain the creation and transformation of transnational political movements. It shows that next to factors of political opportunity, the mobilization of transnational movements challenging international institutions may also be driven by the interaction of international institutions' authority and domestic context. Consequently, the question of who participates in such movements may have to do with the domestic contexts from which individual actors come.

Finally, the book engages with the normative debate on democratic responsiveness and legitimacy of global governance institutions, highlighting that public debate and contestation as a fundamental precondition for global democracy has emerged over the past decades.

Plan of the book

This introduction is followed by five chapters. Chapter 2 presents the theoretical argument. I start by introducing, separately, the institutionalist explanation of politicization and the two society-based approaches of post-functionalism and modernization theory. I show that, individually, all three explanations – despite their analytical value – have difficulty in explaining the varied nature of politicization. The second part of the chapter integrates the three accounts into a theory of politicization capable of explaining different politicization patterns across institutions, time, and space. I describe the general theoretical logic, identify testable hypotheses, and outline the observable implications of my theory.

The empirical Chapters 3 to 5 constitute the centerpiece of the book. Using a three-stage empirical analysis, they probe the explanatory power of my theory of politicization and specify the causal links spelled out in Chapter 2. Chapter 3 showcases the dataset and politicization indicators. It, first, introduces the three key components of politicization, that is, the salience of global tax governance in the media, the polarization of positions taken in these debates, and the plurality of actors who contribute to them. It presents the operationalization and measurement of these variables. The chapter shows that global tax governance has experienced strong politicization since the 1980s. Salience, polarization, and the plurality of actors commenting and evaluating the politics of global tax governance have expanded substantially over time. This indicates that global tax governance no longer flies under the radar of public scrutiny. Yet, the data also indicate that this politicization is not the result of a continuous trend. Rather, public debate on global tax governance is characterized by issue attention cycles.

Turning to the explanation of these results, Chapter 4 probes the explanatory power of the growing political authority of international institutions active in the field of taxation. To this end, I disaggregate the data and compare the politicization patterns of OECD and EU tax governance. The chapter shows that a complex interaction between the growing formal authority of both institutions and their tax policy output accounts for politicization over time and for variance across institutions. The data reveal that the level of political authority formally vested in international institutions and the policies following from this authority drive the process of politicization and lead to a more intensive politicization of EU tax governance than for the OECD.

Finally, Chapter 5 probes my theory of politicization by disaggregating the data further. In this chapter, I provide three in-depth case studies on the politicization of EU tax governance in Germany, Ireland, and Switzerland and compare the respective politicization processes across countries. The results corroborate my theory of politicization. Driven by an interaction of increasing formal authority and a growing frequency of tax legislation and conditioned by varying national contexts, politicization follows substantially different trajectories in the three analyzed public debates. The data show that cross-country variance is shaped by national economic and socio-cultural contexts. The more national economic growth models come under pressure from EU tax governance and the stronger the conflict between exclusive nationalists and cosmopolitans in a given country, the stronger is the politicization of EU tax governance. Furthermore, I demonstrate that economic and cultural conditions shape the content and evaluative thrust of public debates. The politicization of global tax governance is by no means a linear process across national publics but unfolds in specific national trajectories.

Chapter 6 concludes the book by summarizing the main findings. Overall, the recipe for a strong politicization of international institutions consists of (a) formal authority transfer to the international level, (b) broad and frequent policy output on the international level, which (c) targets economically sensitive areas, and (d) a high share of cosmopolitans and exclusive nationalists in a given country to mobilize the resulting concerns over the impact of this legislation on economic well-being and cultural self-determination. In addition, Chapter 6 discusses the generalizability of my results and outlines their implications for research on international institutions' design and behavior as well as for the study of contentious politics, and transnational democracy and legitimacy.

Note

1 Small countries enjoy competitive advantages as regards the link between tax base and tax rate. They are likely to profit from international tax competition whereas large countries are potential losers (Kanbur and Keen, 1993).

References

Abbott, K. W., Genschel, P., Snidal, D. and Zangl, B. (eds.) 2015. *International Organizations as Orchestrators*, Cambridge: Cambridge University Press.

Abbott, K. W., Green, J. F. and Keohane, R. O. 2016. Organizational Ecology and Institutional Change in Global Governance. *International Organization*, 70, 247–277.

Aldrich, J. H., Sullivan, J. L. and Borgida, E. 1989. Foreign Affairs and Issue Voting: Do Presidential Candidates "Waltz Before a Blind Audience?". *American Political Science Review*, 83, 123–141.

Alldridge, P. 2017. *Criminal Justice and Taxation*, Oxford: Oxford University Press.

Bandy, J. and Jackie, S. (eds.) 2005. *Coalitions Across Borders: Transnational Protest and the Neoliberal Order*, Lanham: Rowman & Littlefield.

Bartolini, S. 2005. *Restructuring Europe: Centre Formation, System Formation, System Building, and Political Structuring Between the Nation State and the European Union*, Oxford: Oxford University Press.

Baumgarnter, F., Green-Pedersen, C. and Jones, B. 2006. Comparative Studies of Policy Agendas. *Journal of European Public Policy*, 13, 959–974.

Braithwaite, V. (ed.) 2003. *Taxing Democracy: Understanding Tax Avoidance and Evasion*, Oxon: Routledge.

Clark, N. and Rohrschneider, R. 2009. Second-Order Elections Versus First-Order Thinking: How Voters Perceive the Representation Process in a Multi-Layered System of Governance. *Journal of European Integration*, 31, 645–664.

Della Porta, D. (ed.) 2007. *Global Justice Movement: Cross-national and Transnational Perspectives*, Oxon: Routledge.

Della Porta, D. and Caiani, M. 2009. *Social Movements and Europeanization*, Oxford: Oxford University Press.

Dellmuth, L. M. and Tallberg, J. 2015. The Social Legitimacy of International Organizations: Interest Representation, Institutional Performance, and Confidence Extrapolation in the United Nations. *Review of International Studies*, 41, 451–475.

De Ville, F. and Siles-Brügge, G. 2017. Why TTIP Is a Game-changer and Its Critics Have a Point. *Journal of European Public Policy*, 24, 1491–1505.

De Vries, C. E. 2018. *Euroscepticism and the Future of European Integration*, Oxford: Oxford University Press.

De Wilde, P., Leupold, A. and Schmidtke, H. 2016. Introduction: The Differentiated Politicisation of European Governance. *West European Politics*, 39, 3–22.

Down, I. and Wilson, C. 2008. From "Permissive Consensus" to "Constraining Dissensus": A Polarizing Union? *Acta Politica*, 43, 26–49.

Ecker-Ehrhardt, M. 2012. Cosmopolitan Politicization: How Perceptions of Interdependence Foster Citizens' Expectations in International Institutions. *European Journal of International Relations*, 18, 481–508.

Ecker-Ehrhardt, M. 2014. Why Parties Politicise International Institutions: On Globalization Backlash and Authority Contestation. *Review of International Political Economy*, 21, 1275–1312.

Eichenberg, R. C. and Dalton, R. J. 2007. Post-Maastricht Blues: The Transformation of Citizen Support for European Integration, 1973–2004. *Acta Politica*, 42, 128–152.

Elbra, A. and Mikler, J. 2016. Paying a "Fair Share": Multinational Corporations' Perspectives on Taxation. *Global Policy*, 8, 181–190.

Fioretos, O. (ed.) 2017. *International Politics and Institutions in Time*, Oxford: Oxford University Press.

Furia, P. A. 2005. Global Citizenship, Anyone? Cosmopolitanism, Privilege and Public Opinion. *Global Society*, 19, 331–359.

Genschel, P. 2002. *Steuerwettbewerb und Steuerharmonisierung in der Europäischen Union*, Frankfurt a.M.: Campus.

Genschel, P. 2005. Globalisation and the Transformation of the "Tax State". *In:* Leibfried, S. and Zürn, M. (eds.) *Transformation of the State*? Cambridge: Cambridge University Press.

Genschel, P. and Jachtenfuchs, M. 2011. How the European Union Constrains the State: Multilevel Governance of Taxation. *European Journal of Political Research*, 50, 293–294.

Genschel, P. and Jachtenfuchs, M. 2018. From Market Integration to Core State Powers: The Eurozone Crisis, the Refugee Crisis and Integration Theory. *Journal of Common Market Studies*, 56, 178–196.

Genschel, P. and Schwarz, P. 2011. Tax Competition: A Literature Review. *Socio-Economic Review*, 9, 339–370.

George, A. L. and Bennett, A. 2005. *Case Studies and Theory Development in the Social Sciences*, Cambridge, MA: MIT Press.

Gerring, J. 2007. *Case Study Research: Principles and Practices*, Cambridge: Cambridge University Press.

Green-Pedersen, C. 2012. A Giant Fast Asleep? Paty Incentives and Politicisation of European Integration. *Political Studies*, 60, 115–130.

Grigorescu, A. 2015. *Democratic Intergovernmental Organizations? Normative Pressures and Decision-Making Rules*, Cambridge: Cambridge University Press.

Gronau, J., Nonhoff, M. and Nullmeier, F. 2009. Spiele ohne Brot: Die Legitimitätskrise der G8. *Leviathan*, 37, 117–143.

Hassing Nielsen, J. and Franklin, M. N. (eds.) 2017. *The Eurosceptic 2014 European Parliament Election*, London: Palgrave Macmillan.

Hobolt, S. B. 2012. Public Opinion and Integration. *In:* Jones, E., Menon, A. and Weatherill, S. (eds.) *Oxford Handbook of the European Union*, Oxford: Oxford University Press.

Hobolt, S. B., Spoon, J.-J. and Tilley, J. 2009. A Vote Against Europe? Explaining Defection at the 1999 and 2004 European Parliament Elections. *British Journal of Political Science*, 39, 93–115.

Hobolt, S. B. and Tilley, J. 2014. *Blaming Europe? Responsibility Without Accountability in the European Union*, Oxford: Oxford University Press.

Hoegliner, D. 2016. *Politicizing European Integration – Struggling With the Awakening Giant*, Basingstoke: Palgrave Macmillan.

Holsti, O. R. 1992. Public Opinion and Foreign Policy: Challenges to the Almond-Lippmann Consensus Mershon Series: Research Programs and Debates. *International Studies Quarterly*, 36, 439–466.

Hooghe, L. and Marks, G. 2009. A Postfunctionalist Theory of European Integration: From Permissive Consensus to Constraining Dissensus. *British Journal of Political Science*, 39, 1–23.

Hooghe, L., Marks, G., Lenz, T., Bezuijen, J., Ceka, B. and Derderyan, S. 2017. *Measuring International Authority: A Postfunctionalist Theory of Governance*, Vol. IV, Oxford: Oxford University Press.

Hurrelmann, A. and Schneider, S. (eds.) 2015. *The Legitimacy of Regional Integration in Europe and the Americas*, Basingstoke: Palgrave Macmillan.

Hutter, S., Grande, E. and Kriesi, H. (eds.) 2016. *Politicising Europe: Integration and Mass Politics*, Cambridge: Cambridge University Press.

Imig, D. and Tarrow, S. 2000. Political Contention in a Europeanising Polity. *West European Politics*, 23, 73–93.

Johnson, T. 2014. *Organizational Progeny: Why Governments Are Losing Control Over the Proliferating Structures of Global Governance*, Oxford: Oxford University Press.

Jupille, J., Mattli, W. and Snidal, D. 2013. *Institutional Choice and Global Commerce*, Cambridge: Cambridge University Press.

Kanbur, R. and Keen, M. 1993. Jeux Sans Frontièrs: Tax Competition and Tax Coordination When Countries Differ in Size. *American Economic Review*, 83, 877–892.

Keohane, R. O., Macedo, S. and Moravcsik, A. 2009. Democracy-Enhancing Multilateralism. *International Organization*, 63, 1–31.

Kerzner, D. S. and Chodikoff, D. W. 2016. *International Tax Evasion in the Global Information Age*, Basingstoke: Palgrave Macmillan.

Koremenos, B. 2016. *The Continent of International Law: Explaining Agreement Design*, Cambridge: Cambridge University Press.

Kriesi, H., Grande, E., Dolezal, M., Helbling, M., Höglinger, D., Hutter, S. and Wüest, B. 2012. *Political Conflict in Western Europe*, Cambridge: Cambridge University Press.

Kriesi, H., Grande, E., Lachat, R., Dolezal, M., Bornschier, S. and Frey, T. 2008. *West European Politics in the Age of Globalization*, Cambridge: Cambridge University Press.

Kriesi, H. and Pappas, T. S. (eds.) 2015. *European Populism in the Shadow of the Great Recession*, Colchester: ECPR Press.

Lake, D. A. 2018. International Legitimacy Lost? Rule and Resistance When America Is First. *Perspectives on Politics*, 16, 6.

Lesage, D. and Van De Graaf, T. 2013. Thriving in Complexity? The OECD System's Role in Energy and Taxation. *Global Governance*, 19, 83–92.

Lijphart, A. 1971. Comparative Politics and the Comparative Method. *American Political Science Review*, 65, 682–693.

Lindberg, L. N. and Scheingold, S. A. 1970. *Europe's Would-Be Polity: Patterns of Change in the European Community*, Englewood Cliffs: Prentice-Hall.

Lipset, S. and Rokkan, S. (eds.) 1967. *Cleavage Structures, Party Systems, and Voter Alignments*, New York: The Free Press.

Lundgren, M., Squatrito, T. and Tallberg, J. 2018. Stability and Change in International Policy-making: A Punctuated Equilibrium Approach. *Review of International Organizations*, 13, 547–572.

Mahoney, J. and Rueschemeyer, D. 2003. Comparative Historical Analysis: Achievements and Agendas. *In:* Mahoney, J. and Rueschemeyer, D. (eds.) *Comparative Historical Analysis in the Social Sciences*, Cambridge: Cambridge University Press.

Martin, I., Mehrotra, A. K. and Prasad, M. (eds.) 2009. *The New Fiscal Sociology: Taxation in Comparative and Historical Perspective*, Cambridge: Cambridge University Press.

Norberg, K. and Hoffman, P. T. 1994. Conclusion. *In:* Norberg, K. and Hoffman, P. T. (eds.) *Fiscal Crises, Liberty, and Representative Government*, Stanford: Stanford University Press.

Nullmeier, F., Biegoń, D., Gronau, J., Nonhoff, M., Schmidtke, H. and Schneider, S. 2010. *Prekäre Legitimitäten: Rechtfertigung von Herrschaft in der postnationalen Konstellation*, Frankfurt a.M.: Campus.

O'Brien, R., Goetz, A. M., Scholte, J. A. and Williams, M. 2000. *Contesting Global Governance: Multilateral Economic Institutions and Global Social Movements*, Cambridge: Cambridge University Press.

Otjes, S. and Katsanidou, A. 2017. Beyond Kriesiland: EU Integration as a Super Issue After the Eurocrisis. *European Journal of Political Research*, 56, 301–319.

Palan, R. 2002. Tax Havens and the Commercialization of State Sovereignty. *International Organization*, 56, 151–176.
Paris, R. 2003. The Globalization of Taxation? Electronic Commerce and the Transformation of the State. *International Studies Quarterly*, 47, 153–182.
Pelc, K. J. 2013. Googling the WTO: What Search Engine Data Tell Us About the Political Economy of Institutions. *International Organization*, 67, 629–655.
Radaelli, C. M. 1997. *The Politics of Corporate Taxation in the European Union: Knowledge and International Policy Agendas*, London: Routledge.
Rauh, C. 2016. *A Responsive Technocracy? EU Politicisation and the Consumer Policies of the European Commission*, Colchester: ECPR Press.
Rauh, C. and De Wilde, P. 2017. The Opposition Deficit in EU Accountability: Evidence From Over 20 Years of Plenary Debate in Four Member States. *European Journal of Political Research*, 57, 194–216.
Risse, T. (ed.) 2015. *European Public Spheres: Politics Is Back*, Oxford: Oxford University Press.
Rixen, T. 2008. *The Political Economy of International Tax Governance*, Basingstoke: Palgrave Macmillan.
Rixen, T. 2011. From Double Tax Avoidance to Tax Competition: Explaining the Institutional Trajectory of International Tax Governance. *Review of International Political Economy*, 18, 197–227.
Rixen, T., Viola, L. A. and Zürn, M. (eds.) 2016. *Historical Institutionalism & International Relations: Explaining Institutional Development in World Politics*, Oxford: Oxford University Press.
Rixen, T. and Zangl, B. 2013. The Politicization of International Economic Institutions in US Public Debates. *Review of International Organizations*, 8, 363–387.
Schimmelfennig, F. 2014. European Integration in the Euro Crisis: The Limits of Postfunctionalism. *Journal of European Integration*, 36, 321–337.
Schlipphak, B. 2015. Measuring Attitudes Towards Regional Organizations Outside Europe. *Review of International Organizations*, 10, 351–375.
Schmidtke, H. and Nullmeier, F. 2011. Political Valuation Analysis and the Legitimacy of International Organizations. *German Policy Studies*, 7, 117–153.
Schneider, S., Nullmeier, F. and Hurrelmann, A. 2007. Exploring the Communicative Dimension of Legitimacy: Text Analytical Approaches. *In:* Hurrelmann, A., Schneider, S. and Steffek, J. (eds.) *Legitimacy in an Age of Global Politics*, Basingstoke: Palgrave Macmillan.
Scholte, J. A. (ed.) 2011. *Building Global Democracy? Civil Society and Accountable Global Governance*, Cambridge: Cambridge University Press.
Sharman, J. C. 2012. Seeing Like the OECD on Tax. *New Political Economy*, 17, 17–33.
Tallberg, J., Sommerer, T., Squatrito, T. and Jönsson, C. 2013. *The Opening Up of International Organizations*, Cambridge: Cambridge University Press.
Tarrow, S. G. 2005. *The New Transnational Activism*, Cambridge: Cambridge University Press.
Tarrow, S. G. 2012. *Strangers at the Gates: Movements and States in Contentious Politics*, Cambridge: Cambridge University Press.
Usherwood, S. and Startin, N. 2013. Euroscepticism as a Persistent Phenomenon. *Journal of Common Market Studies*, 51, 1–16.
Van Der Eijk, C. and Franklin, M. N. 2004. Potential for Contestation on European Matters at National Elections in Europe. *In:* Marks, G. and Steenbergen, M. R. (eds.) *European Integration and Political Conflict*, Cambridge: Cambridge University Press.

Van Der Eijk, C. and Franklin, M. N. 2007. The Sleeping Giant: Potential for Political Mobilization of Disaffection with European Integration. *In:* Van Der Burg, W. and Van Der Eijk, C. (eds.) *European Elections and Domestic Politics: Lessons From the Past and Scenarios for the Future*, Notre Dame: University of Notre Dame Press.

Van Kessel, S. 2015. *Populist Parties in Europe*, Basingstoke: Palgrave Macmillan.

Vowles, J. and Xezonakis, G. (eds.) 2016. *Globalization and Domestic Politics: Parties, Elections, and Public Opinion*, Oxford: Oxford University Press.

Walgrave, S., Soroka, S. and Nuytemans, M. 2008. The Mass Media's Political Agenda-Setting Power. *Comparative Political Studies*, 41, 814–836.

Wonka, A. 2016. The Party Politics of the Euro Crisis in the German Bundestag: Frames, Positions and Salience. *West European Politics*, 39, 125–144.

Zucmann, G. 2015. *The Hidden Wealth of Nations: The Scourge of Tax Havens*, Chicago: Chicago University Press.

Zürn, M. 2016. Opening Up Europe: Next Steps in Politicisation Research. *West European Politics*, 39, 164–182.

Zürn, M. 2018. *A Theory of Global Governance: Authority, Legitimacy, and Contestation*, Oxford: Oxford University Press.

Zürn, M., Binder, M. and Ecker-Erhardt, M. 2012. International Authority and Its Politicization. *International Theory*, 4, 69–106.

2 A theory of politicization

Driving forces and conditioning contexts

Why have international institutions become politicized over the past decades? How can we explain this rather recent phenomenon, its specific timing, and variance across institutions and countries? With the theoretical and political implications outlined in the introduction, these questions have begun to attract the attention of European integration and IR scholars from diverse theoretical perspectives, highlighting a number of factors to explain why public debate and controversy surrounding international institutions have begun to rise only during the past decade or two. Essentially, this strand of explanatory literature features two basic approaches, which are frequently treated as competing (Zürn et al., 2012; Ecker-Ehrhardt, 2014; De Wilde et al., 2016) rather than complementary explanations. In this chapter, I develop a novel theoretical framework for explaining politicization, integrating these perspectives. I introduce this framework in three steps. First, I conceptualize the politicization of international institutions (dependent variable). Second, I outline the two most prominent explanations and their variants. Finally, I combine these explanations into an integrated theory of politicization. This theoretical synthesis lays the groundwork for the subsequent empirical chapters of the book, where I assess the explanatory power of individual explanatory factors and their combination.

The two prominent explanations discussed in the literature are anchored in different theoretical traditions and form the core of distinct explanations of the politicization of international institutions. For each, I describe the general theoretical logic, identify testable hypotheses, and outline observable implications. While both explanations are formulated as explanations for why international institutions' politicization grows, they can just as well explain the opposite dynamic of declining politicization. Finally, I integrate both perspectives to close their individual blind spots and develop a theory of politicization that can explain variance across institutions, time, and space.

First, an institutionalist explanation focuses on the political authority of international institutions as the driving force of politicization (Zürn et al., 2012). From this perspective, scholars highlight that due to changing institutional design the political authority of international institutions has reached a critical level that puts them frequently in the position to make binding decisions on matters relating to states' domestic jurisdiction, even if those decisions are contrary to a state's own preferences (Cooper et al., 2008: 254; Genschel and Zangl, 2014: 4–8; Zürn, 2018). In particular, the level of political authority vested in international institutions has grown because of the pooling of decision-making powers among states and the delegation of authority to supranational bureaucracies, parliaments, and judicial bodies (Alter, 2014; Hooghe et al., 2017; Rocabert et al., 2018). In addition to the higher level of political authority, the scope of international institutions' authority has increased because they have become involved in an expanding number of issue areas. Today, the tentacles of international institutions delve into almost every aspect of domestic policy-making (Barnett and Finnemore, 2004: 1). This combination of the growing scope and level of political authority of international institutions is hypothesized to account for the politicization of these institutions because citizens are more frequently confronted with the direct effects of international decision-making. Citizens interpret international institutions no longer as the sum of national preferences, but as important independent actors whose activities have direct implications for their lives. Once-remote objects of orientation move closer to citizens because they experience the effects of international institutions on their everyday lives more than ever before. From an institutionalist point of view, this growing intrusiveness and visibility of international institutions provide the basis for their politicization.

In contrast, the second strand of literature focuses on domestic economic and cultural contexts, respective mobilization potentials, and the crucial role of mobilization political actors (Hoeglinger, 2016; Hutter et al., 2016). As I will demonstrate over the course of this chapter, this society-based explanation (Rixen and Zangl, 2013: 367) also starts – although implicitly – from the premise of a growing scope and level of political authority of international institutions and adds two conflicting cultural developments as conditioning variables. One camp of scholars (Deutsch et al., 1957; Ecker-Ehrhardt, 2012) highlights the emergence of cosmopolitan values and the so-called skill revolution in established democracies (Koehn and Rosenau, 2002) as a crucial condition for politicization. This modernization perspective is rooted in the observation that due to processes of societal modernization (Zürn, 2004; Inglehart and Welzel, 2005) citizens have become transnationally connected (Favell, 2008; Mau et al., 2008; Favell, 2009) and that these processes have triggered a skill revolution that enhances the "transnational competencies" of individuals and their identification with cosmopolitan values (Beck and Grande, 2007; Jung, 2008; Kuhn, 2011). These competencies and values provide individuals with the necessary cognitive abilities and identity to recognize global interdependencies and to grasp the complexity of international politics (Koehn and Rosenau, 2002; Hainmueller and Hiscox, 2006). This cognitive mobilization increases both the public awareness of and the identification with international institutions and contributes thus to their politicization.

By the same token, the second camp of researchers focuses on the group of exclusive nationalists as potential drivers of politicization processes. These globophobes feel threatened by the growing political authority of international institutions and therefore start engaging more critically with them (Burgoon, 2009). This post-functionalist perspective – first formulated by Liesbet Hooghe and Gary

Marks (2009) in the context of the growing constraining dissensus on European integration – emphasizes that citizens holding a rather exclusive national identity oppose the political authority of international institutions (Hooghe and Marks, 2004; Hooghe and Marks, 2005; Hooghe and Marks, 2009) and are, thus, likely to be mobilized be right-wing and populist parties. In contrast to cosmopolitan politicization, this nationalist variant depends more strongly on the activities of mobilization actors (Kriesi et al., 2012; Hoeglinger, 2016; Castanho Silva, 2018).

While both the institutionalist perspective and the cosmopolitan and post-functionalist variations of the society-based approach have already been demonstrated to enhance our understanding of the politicization of international institutions, the remainder of this chapter shows that their full explanatory potential is realized only by integrating both explanations. Rooted in the "new interdependence" literature (Farrell and Newman, 2014), I suggest a theory of politicization that views the scope and level of the political authority of international institutions as the driving force of politicization. Domestic context is the crucial conditioning variable, shaping the strength of the political authority effect in different domestic settings. To arrive at this integrated theory, the chapter is organized in four sections. First, I specify the dependent variable. I spell out what I mean by the politicization of global tax governance, emphasizing that the politicization of international institutions is a multi-dimensional phenomenon subdivided into three principal components. In the two subsequent two sections, I outline the institutional and society-centered explanations in more detail. I present the general logic of both explanations, specify the causal chains that link explanatory factors to the politicization of international institutions, and detail their individual observable implications. The fourth section demonstrates how both explanations can be integrated into a more comprehensive theory of politicization. I show how the approaches are interrelated and which combinations of institutional design and mobilization potentials lead to higher/lower levels of politicization and specific patters of public debate. This final section paves the way for the subsequent empirical analysis of the politicization of global tax governance.

Conceptualizing the politicization of global tax governance

The analytical focus of this book is the politicization of global tax governance. In this section, I specify this dependent variable in two steps. First, I provide a specific definition of the concept. Second, I describe how I conceptualize its three operationalizing components: salience, controversy, and plurality.

I define the politicization of global tax governance as a process that increases the salience and controversy in the public sphere surrounding international institutions that are active in the field of taxation (for similar definitions see Zürn et al., 2012: 71; Ecker-Ehrhardt, 2014: 1; De Wilde et al., 2016). This usage of the concept excludes static approaches, defining politicization as a status rather than a process and the transformation of the inner workings of institutions – that is, institutional politicization (Peters and Pierre, 2004). Instead, I focus on the societal processes that lead to an increasing intensity and conflict of public debates on global tax governance and the widening of the group of individual and collective actors mobilizing and participating in these debates. In other words, "politicization is given if issues that did not catch the eye of the general public previously are debated in the public sphere" (Rixen and Zangl, 2013: 365). At the core of this definition is the salience and controversy of global tax governance in public debates. The essential meaning of the concept, as it is applied in this book, is captured by the notion that global tax governance becomes politicized as it is targeted by controversial public evaluations and demands.

Moving to the second step in my conceptualization of the politicization of global tax governance, I distinguish between three operationalizing components of politicization: salience, controversy, and plurality (Hutter and Grande, 2014: 1003; De Wilde et al., 2016: 4). The first component is the salience of an issue. Does the level of public debate on global tax governance increase over time? Only if the public takes note of global tax governance and describes, discusses, or evaluates it actively, can it be expected to become politicized. In other words, the basic condition to be met for the politicization of global tax governance deals with the intensity of the public debate. This level of discussion increases over time for the politicization of global tax governance (see also Green-Pedersen, 2012: 177; Statham and Trenz, 2013: 4). If nobody voices concerns about global tax governance, its "politicization remains inhibited" (De Wilde, 2011: 567), even if interested actors hold different opinions and demands.

The second component is the controversy of public debate on global tax governance. Do individual evaluations of global tax governance in public debate become more plural (Down and Wilson, 2008: 26; Hooghe and Marks, 2012: 841)? For politicization to occur, there need to be at least two different opinions on the issue. The increase of salience alone is not sufficient for politicization. The second criterion to be met is that actors increasingly voice their demands and opinions in public and evaluate global tax governance. Only if participants of public debate formulate normative evaluations and reveal conflicting attitudes towards an issue can it be considered to be controversial and thus politicized. This growing controversy on global tax governance should not be equated with generally more opposition and less support for international institutions. Contrary to much of the literature on the politicization of European integration (Checkel and Katzenstein, 2009; Hoegliner, 2016; Hutter et al., 2016), I do not argue that politicization has exclusively negative effects like the rise of new populist nationalist, xenophobic parties. Rather, I understand politicization as a process that gives both supporters and opponents of international institutions the opportunity to voice their arguments, ideas, and concerns. From this point of view, politicization may bring about opposition – but it may just as well create support and demand for a stronger harmonization of national tax systems via international institutions.

The third component is the plurality of the debate on global tax governance. Does the number of participants and mobilizing actors in an increasingly salient and controversial debate increase (Zürn et al., 2012: 72; Hutter and Grande, 2014: 1004)? My focus on public debate implies that the exchange of arguments has to take place among actors outside the narrow circle of political elites. Only if national political executives become less dominant as speakers and representatives of political parties, civil society, and lay people are included, the final criterion of politicization is met. This public resonance differentiates politicization from intergovernmental bargains and lobbying (De Wilde, 2011: 568). While conflicts between national political executives about international institutions and their occasional public salience are a basic feature of global governance, politicization refers to debates that involve a variety of additional agents of politicization like representatives of CSOs, unions, movements, or individual citizens.

In sum, global tax governance should be accompanied by a growing publicly visible exchange of conflicting views communicated by a broad array of actors. The three components of politicization – salience, controversy, and plurality – are mutually interdependent. The politicization process is complete if all three components are present. While the public salience of global tax governance is clearly the precondition for politicization because both controversy and plurality are only observable when a public debate develops, public salience alone is not sufficient. Theoretically, an issue can be salient but non-controversial. To put it bluntly: just because everybody frequently talks about the weather, this does not mean that the weather is a particularly politicized issue. Similarly, controversy and plurality are mutually interrelated because the exchange of conflicting arguments requires at least two agents of politicization.

The institutionalist explanation: rising international authority

Building on this specification of my dependent variable, I turn to the explanation of the politicization of global tax governance. The first explanation of politicization emphasizes the growing authority of international institutions as a driving force. This institutionalist perspective depicts the undermining of executive multilateralism, characterizing the international politics of the post-war era (Zürn, 2004), and the continuous pooling and delegation of political authority at the international level as the central driving force of the politicization of international institutions (Zürn et al., 2012; Zürn and Ecker-Ehrhardt, 2013; Zürn, 2018). While the post-war international system was based on a reciprocal at-the-border coordination of international issues by national representatives and thus left national authority largely unaffected (Ruggie, 1992: 572), two structural transformations of the international system have challenged this mode of international politics and are hypothesized to account for the politicization of international institutions.

The first important factor is the increasing scope of international institutions' authority (Ecker-Ehrhardt, 2014: 7; Hooghe et al., 2017). International institutions become politicized because they expand their reach beyond the classical areas of international coordination toward new issue areas and in turn affect a larger group of actors (Schmitter, 1969: 166). By the same token, the number of issue areas in which international institutions are expected to act and to solve global problems beyond the reach of individual states also increases due to the growing number of such global problems (Hale et al., 2013; Zürn, 2013: 33). Consequently, the activities of international institutions are no longer restricted to a limited number of issue areas that solely require the reciprocal at-the-border coordination of national policies. Rather, international institutions have begun and are expected to intervene in beyond-the-border issue areas and even in core state powers like security, fiscal, and administrative policy (Genschel and Jachtenfuchs, 2014: 9). These interventions restrict national sovereignty more strongly and affect more directly the lives of a growing population. As today's international institutions "work extensively in domestic governance issues, overseeing matters that once used to be the prerogatives of states" (Barnett and Finnemore, 2004: 1) and are, therefore, increasingly influential in issue areas that affect the welfare of individuals around the globe, citizens experience the effects of international institutions on their everyday lives more than in the past. The poster child of this development is clearly the EU, whose policies affect almost every aspect of the everyday life of its citizens (Pollack, 1994; Leuffen et al., 2013). This growing importance and visibility of international institutions in combination with a growing array of global cooperation problems provide the basis for politicization. Because international institutions are more and more recognized as independent agents that have the potential to shape political outcomes in a diverse range of issue areas they attract growing attention and controversial public debate (Ecker-Ehrhardt, 2012). In other words, the increasing issue scope of international institutions creates incentives for individuals and collective actors to engage with global governance (Tarrow, 2001: 14; Coleman and Wayland, 2006: 244).

The second factor highlighted by the institutionalist explanation is the rising level of international institutions' authority (Zürn et al., 2012: 90–95). This argument is premised on the observation that the decision-making procedures of international institutions are changing. As a consequence of the broadening scope of international institutions, political competencies once rooted in the nation-state are increasingly transferred to the international level. By delegating tasks like agenda-setting, monitoring, dispute settlement, or even direct rule implementation to supranational bureaucracies, parliaments, and judicial bodies, and by pooling national sovereignty in the collective decision-making procedures of international institutions, states intended to restore their capacity to govern in a globalized world and to provide international institutions with the means to regulate an ever more interdependent world (Keohane et al., 2009: 4).[1] As a result, the level of authority of many of today's international institutions goes well beyond intergovernmental coordination. International institutions independently perform a wide range of policy tasks (Hawkins et al., 2006; Abbott and Snidal, 2010), are engaged in supranational dispute settlement (Alter, 2014; Tallberg and McCall Smith, 2014), and apply increasingly supranational decision-making procedures (Blake and Payton, 2015; Hooghe et al., 2017). This transfer of political authority to international institutions is hypothesized to trigger their politicization because it provides them with independent agency, making them a more important target of public legitimacy demands (Nullmeier et al., 2010; Grande and Hutter, 2016). Because international institutions' political authority has reached a critical level – putting them frequently in the position to make binding decisions on matters relating to states' domestic jurisdiction even if those decisions are contrary to a state's own preferences (Cooper et al., 2008: 254) – they shape the lives of a growing number of citizens. Consequently, they will be perceived as politically independent actors and become the target of public support, criticism, and demand.

In essence, the institutionalist explanation highlights the transformation and empowerment of international institutions as the main driver of their politicization. A widening audience or clientele becomes involved in the critical evaluation of international institutions because they begin to comprehend the rising scope and level of international authority. While international institutions in the past decades were simply too small, too irrelevant, and too weak to become politicized, their empowerment over the past decades helped to lift them beyond this veil of invisibility. Today's international institutions play roles that are more and more comparable to national political institutions and are thus increasingly exposed to public debates.

In the literature, this argument is often reduced to a focus on formal changes in the scope and level of international institutions' authority (Rixen and Zangl, 2013; Ecker-Ehrhardt, 2014; Grande and Hutter, 2016). I move beyond this focus in two ways: first, a more comprehensive understanding of authority should not only take into account formal rules but also the policy output of international institutions. It is evident that treaties, constitutions, conventions, protocols, and rules of procedure guide the conduct of international institutions and are thus an important determinant of politicization. However, this formal authority is only half the story. Only if formal rules are put to work on the ground, resulting in policy output relevant to the broader public, politicization can be expected to follow. Second, I explore whether and to what extent politicization is shaped by the expansion of international institutions into specific policies. Along the lines of Theodore Lowi's (1964) distinction between distributive, regulatory, and redistributive policies, it can, for instance, be expected that international institutions engaged in redistribution are more likely to become politicized than purely regulatory institutions (Pollack, 1994: 112; Rittberger et al., 2014: 195). This suggests a more nuanced understanding of political authority, taking into account the interaction of formal rules and policy output as the driving force of politicization.

I now turn to the specific empirical implications of the institutionalist explanation. What kind of variance is predicted across institutions, countries, and over time? Does the institutionalist explanation expect specific patterns of politicization? What exactly can be expected to become the bone of public contention (object of politicization) and what kind of arguments or normative criteria (criteria of politicization) are likely to shape public evaluations and demands? While most of the current literature is mainly interested in levels of politicization, I argue that the specific framing of public debates on international institutions is of crucial relevance for understanding the driving forces of politicization. Building on the twofold transformation of the scope and level of international institutions' authority, proponents of the institutionalist perspective differentiate two causal mechanisms that shape specific patterns of politicization across institutions, space, and time.

The first mechanism refers to the widening scope of international institutions. Due to a growing number of complex global political problems, international institutions process an expanding amount of issues related to these interdependencies of a globalizing world. Consequently, public attention and demand for solutions are also transferred to the international level, which, in turn, leads to a politicization of international institutions' output. This notion of "output politicization" (Ecker-Ehrhardt and Wessels, 2013: 47–51) provides a first reference for the specification of the particular pattern of politicization. In terms of the objects of politicization, it points to the classical differentiation between policy, politics, and polity (Bartolini, 2005: 355; Mair, 2007: 3; Zürn et al., 2012: 98). If politicization is indeed driven by the growing scope of international institutions, this should be reflected in an emphasis on policy output (Hurrelmann et al., 2012) rather than decision-making (politics dimension) or the institutions themselves (polity dimension). Similarly, politicization patterns can be expected to zero in on a specific set of criteria of politicization. Here, a useful organizing distinction is provided by Fritz Scharpf's (1999) typology of input and output legitimacy. Following this distinction, I assume that public debates on international institutions can discuss whether decision-making is fair and democratic or actors can evaluate the quality of a decision in terms of effectiveness or contribution to the common good. As output politicization emphasizes the increasing relevance of international institutions' output, I conjecture that politicization criteria are likely to emphasize the quality of international policies and their consequences. In sum, I expect the increasing scope of international institutions' authority to shape a pattern of politicization that discusses international institutions' policies (object of politicization) on the basis of output criteria (criteria of politicization) or what Frank Wendler (2014: 550) calls problem-solving debates.

The second mechanism identified by the institutionalist explanation refers to the growing level of international institutions' authority. Here, "input politicization" (Ecker-Ehrhardt and Wessels, 2013: 43–46) proposes that higher levels of political authority shape public debates in which individuals transfer criteria of legitimate authority from national contexts to the international level (Keohane et al., 2009; Keohane, 2011; Zürn, 2018). This mechanism suggests that the migration of political decision-making to international institutions results in mounting demand for inclusive, transparent, and responsive procedures. Because decisions are no longer taken by consensus among all affected states but by majoritarian procedures (Blake and Payton, 2015), public demand for transparency and accountability increases (Ecker-Ehrhardt, 2014: 9). As regards the object of politicization, growing levels of authority should, therefore, result in a more pronounced emphasis on the polity and politics dimension. The evaluation of these politicization objects should be framed in terms of criteria of politicization that focus on input rather than on output. Instead of asking for the effectiveness of international decisions, these legitimacy debates (Wendler, 2014: 550) should primarily be framed in terms of democratic values such as transparency, responsiveness, or accountability.

Table 2.1 Observable implications of institutionalist theory

Level of variance	*Level of politicization*	*Pattern of politicization*
Across institutions	With higher level or scope of authority, levels of politicization are likely to be higher	Higher scope of authority implies *problem-solving debates*, higher level implies *legitimacy debates*
Over time	With growing level or scope of authority, levels of politicization are likely to grow	Growing scope of authority implies a shift toward *problem-solving debates*, growing level implies a shift towards *legitimacy debates*
Across countries	With higher level or scope of authority, levels of politicization are likely to be higher	Higher scope of authority implies *problem-solving debates*, higher level implies *legitimacy debates*

In sum, the institutionalist explanation emphasizes that varying levels and patterns of politicization over time and institutions are likely to be shaped by the scope and level of international institutions' authority. Although less explicit, the explanation also predicts variance of the dependent variable across countries. Table 2.1 summarizes the observable implications.

First, the level of politicization is likely to vary across institutions according to the scope and level of authority. Powerful institutions interfering deeply with national sovereignty, like the EU, which dictates a wide array of rules to its member states, should be exposed to higher levels of politicization than weaker institutions like the OECD, which focuses on a smaller number of issue areas and has only limited independent political authority. Theoretically, the institutionalist perspective seems to be indifferent to the relative importance of input and output politicization. Institutions with a broad scope but low level of authority may well become strongly politicized and vice versa. A case in point is the G8, which has a comparatively broad scope but a low level of authority because decisions are taken by consensus and are non-binding (Dobson, 2007; Gstöhl, 2007). Whether processes of input and output politicization are cumulative, implying that institutions that are equipped with a broad scope and a high level of political authority yield the highest levels of politicization, or whether they are rather substitutive is an open empirical question.

Second, the level of politicization is also likely to vary over time. As the growth of the scope and level of international institutions' authority is frequently portrayed as a rather recent phenomenon that has emerged during the 1980s and 1990s (Lenz et al., 2015), the institutionalist explanation suggests that first signs of politicization should have been observable since the 1980s and the level of politicization should follow varying levels of authority over time. Clearly, this expectation does not imply a mechanistic nexus, linking authority transfer directly to politicization processes. Rather, I expect that the complex interaction between policy output and formal authority results in three different temporal sequences of politicization. A direct sequence, in which mounting formal authority and policy output result in increasing politicization levels, is one plausible scenario. It appears similarly plausible that politicization precedes formal authority transfers because public debates are not only interested in the results of political processes but also in the process itself. In this scenario, a major treaty revision, which expands the scope of an international institution or changes decision-making procedures, or a prominent policy decision changes public debate much earlier because the decision-making process itself and potential alternatives are debated even before formal implementation. Yet, politicization could also come with a considerable time lag. Here, increasing formal authority or policy output is initially not recognized by the public but as soon as outcomes become visible, the level of politicization increases.

Third, the level of politicization is likely to vary across countries because the authority of an institution may have a varying impact on different countries (Oppermann and Vierig, 2009; Oppermann and Vierig, 2011: 5). Most generally, the degree of an institution's authority over a country is conditioned by membership. If a country is a formal member of the institution, it is directly bound by respective decisions. In this case, the authority of an institution is strong and direct. Non-members, by contrast, are only indirectly affected if international institutions' decisions entail externalities on them. The general distinction of (non-)membership implies a clear differentiation of levels of politicization across members and non-members (Grande and Hutter, 2016). Research on differentiated European integration (Schimmelfennig et al., 2015) and the fuzzy boundaries of other international institutions (Kux and Sverdrup, 2000; Koch, 2009), reveals a continuum between membership and non-members. While most advanced in the EU, where formal members opt out of specific policies, whereas non-members opt in, differentiated integration is a common feature of many international institutions that operate outreach mechanisms to include non-members or grant escape and withdrawal clauses to members (Koremenos, 2016: Ch. 5). As a result, I expect levels of politicization to vary according to a country's specific degree of integration into a given international institution. At one end of this continuous scale, we find full members of a given institution which are subject to the full level of international authority. The level of politicization should be comparably high in these countries. At the other end, we find countries that are neither members of the institution nor in any other form associated with it and that are not even indirectly affected by the institution's decisions. In this case, the level of politicization should be comparably low.

Finally, the institutionalist explanation implies clear patterns of politicization. For institutions characterized by a growing level of authority, an intensifying public debate on international decision-making procedures (object of politicization) dominated by arguments on their input (criteria of politicization) – that is, a legitimacy debate – should be observable. Institutions marked by a broad scope should be accompanied by a pattern of politicization that emphasizes policies (object of politicization) and output criteria of politicization. A mixture of both patterns is likely in cases that combine both a broad scope and high level of authority.

Society-centered explanations: domestic economic and cultural context

The empirical starting point of the society-centered explanation is the observation that not all strong and influential institutions are always politicized. Hence, society-centered explanations ask for the conditions under which the growing authority of international institutions translates into politicization (Zürn, 2013: 33; Hutter et al., 2016). Coming from a broadly constructivist perspective, I argue that both the post-functionalist theory put forward by Hooghe and Marks (2009) and the modernization perspective building on the work by Ronald Inglehart and Christian Welzel (2005) – commonly regarded as alternative rather than complementary explanations of politicization – point to the missing part of the puzzle. Both explanations highlight that domestic economic and cultural contexts condition the politicizing effect of the growing authority of international institutions. In the words of Juan Diez Medrano (2003: 249), I claim that national "cultures act like differently shaped curved mirrors that exaggerate or shrink the dimensions of the object that they are reflecting".

Both perspectives are premised on the idea that individuals' perceptions of international institutions depend considerably on social identity and how this identity is mobilized by political actors (Wendt, 1994: 423; Hooghe and Marks, 2005; Dellmuth and Tallberg, 2015). Defined as the "part of the individual's self-concept which derives from his knowledge of his membership of a social group (or groups) together with the value and emotional significance attached to that membership" (Tajfel, 1981: 255), social identity and the role of mobilizing actors are in both perspectives considered to condition the perception of international institutions and, thus, their politicization. Because group attachments lead to specific loyalties, they constitute a resource for mobilization, collective action, and support for or opposition to political institutions (Risse, 2010: 22). The stronger these collective beliefs about common purpose and vision are, the more they shape citizens' views on international institutions and mobilize more active forms of political engagement.[2]

However, as Diez Medrano (2003: 6) argues with regard to the formation and mobilization of attitudes towards the EU, people approach and evaluate international institutions equipped with cultural repertoires that vary along socio-demographic, political, and national lines. This points to the question of what types of social identity facilitate the politicization of international institutions and provide mobilizing agents with political opportunities. Here, the post-functionalist explanation claims that international institutions become politicized because they threaten nationalist identities (Kriesi et al., 2008: 19) and because this emotion of fear can be mobilized by right-wing and populist parties. In contrast, modernization theory highlights cosmopolitan identities as potentially catalyzing politicization. Both explanations help to identify segments of a given population and agents of mobilization that should drive the politicization of international institutions (Inglehart, 1970b: 768). Cosmopolitans and globophobes constitute the mobilization potential that conditions the politicizing effect of international institutions' authority on the national level and over time (Kriesi et al., 2008: 8). To develop this argument more fully, the following sections first unpack both explanations separately before the final section presents my theory of politicization.

Modernization theory: cosmopolitan agents of politicization

Modernization theory argues that citizens are more likely to politicize international institutions if their sense of belonging transcends national borders and encompasses mankind (Inglehart, 1970a; Inglehart and Welzel, 2005; Ecker-Ehrhardt, 2012). More specifically, the theory suggests that the politicization of international institutions is driven by individuals who are equipped with a set of transnational cognitive skills and cosmopolitan values (Favell, 2008; Favell, 2009).

Modernization theory proposes a twofold explanation of politicization: first, although not explicitly stated, it builds on the institutionalist explanation by suggesting that international interdependence, political denationalization, and the growing authority of international institutions are becoming increasingly relevant for the everyday lives of individuals. Only under this condition is there something that can be recognized and in turn politicized (Zürn et al., 2012: 82). But contrary to the institutionalist explanation, modernization theory does not deem the structural transformation of the international system to be sufficient. Rather, the growing authority of international institutions is seen as a political potential that is only mobilized by specific actors, under specific conditions, and in a particular way. Although the visibility of international institutions is growing due to their mounting authority, citizens still need a specifically curved mirror that exaggerates international institutions so that they can actually see, understand, and debate them in detail. The curve of this mirror is defined by two intertwined processes: a skill revolution and the emergence of cosmopolitan identities since the end of the 1970s.

First, citizens require a specific set of skills to understand what international institutions are doing and why (Dellmuth, 2016). Research on the so-called skill revolution shows that a growing share of citizens has acquired these skills over the past decades (Rosenau, 1992, Rosenau and Fagen, 1997, Koehn and Rosenau, 2002, Rosenau, 2003). Because citizens all over the globe become transnationally connected (Jung, 2008; Kuhn, 2011) and receive university-level education, they acquire a set of skills that make them more likely to engage critically with international institutions. These new skills encompass transnational analytical and behavioral skills, such as language and intercultural and organizational competencies (Koehn and Rosenau, 2002: 109 ff). Transnational analytical skills provide the necessary cognitive abilities to recognize global interdependencies and to grasp the complexity of international politics (Mansfield and Mutz, 2009: 430; Norris and Inglehart, 2009: Ch. 6). New behavioral skills enable citizens to act transnationally and to engage with international institutions (Kuhn, 2011: 814).

Second, this skill revolution results in a stronger identification with cosmopolitan values and models of appropriate behavior that are premised on equal respect for out-groups (Inglehart, 1977; Norris and Inglehart, 2009). Due to societal modernization citizens develop a cosmopolitan identity which transcends national borders and encompasses larger regions or even humanity as a whole (Favell, 2008: Ch. 1; Kriesi et al., 2008: 7); they begin to imagine a supranational political community (Deutsch et al., 1957; Deutsch et al., 1967). Based on the universalistic principles of mutual tolerance and responsibility (Woodward et al., 2008; Held, 2010), this value change helps to level the normative barriers of the nation-state (Held, 2000; Mau et al., 2008; Pichler, 2009). As Hainmueller and Hiscox (2006: 473) argue:

> highly educated individuals are less prone than others to nationalist and antiforeigner sentiments that are often linked with protectionism in political debates. [. . .] Education can foster tolerance, not just by increasing students' knowledge of foreign cultures and raising levels of critical thinking, but also by generating more diverse and cosmopolitan social networks, especially at the college level.

Citizens holding such a cosmopolitan identity, focusing on the global community of world citizens rather than the nation-state, are "characterized by the capacity to mediate between different cultures, the recognition of the increasing interconnectedness of political communities and the approval of political responsibilities at the supranational and global level" (Mau et al., 2008: 2).[3] Consequently, international institutions are predominantly seen as a solution to global and regional interdependence (Koehn and Rosenau, 2002: 113) and are thus politicized in a positive manner. To be sure, this argument does not imply a "love, peace, and harmony" scenario in which everybody is happy with global governance and politicization is characterized by outright support based on the outstanding cosmopolitan achievements of international institutions. Rather, it refers to the idea that cosmopolitan values constitute a distinct set of normative standards against which actors assess the quality of international institutions (Diez Medrano, 2003: 104).

In essence, modernization theory widens the institutionalist explanation by adding the share of cosmopolitans in a given society to the explanatory framework. The specific timing and level of the politicization of international institutions' authority are conditioned by the extent to which citizens hold cosmopolitan skills and identity. Well-educated, better-off citizens who frequently travel abroad are likely to have a cosmopolitan mindset (Fligstein, 2008: Ch. 5; Risse, 2010: Ch. 4; Kuhn, 2011) and to engage with international institutions (Inglehart and Welzel, 2005: 15–47; Tarrow, 2011: Ch. 12; Ecker-Ehrhardt, 2014: 6) because national societal barriers are eroding and the individual awareness and understanding of international institutions increases.

How do these arguments modify the empirical implications of the institutionalist explanation? To what extent should the level and pattern of politicization vary across institutions, over time, and across countries under these conditions? Table 2.2 summarizes how societal modernization conditions the politicizing effect of international institutions' authority. First, similar to the institutionalist

Table 2.2 Observable implications of modernization theory

Level of variance	*Level of politicization*	*Pattern of politicization*
Across institutions	–	–
Over time	In addition to the growing level and scope of authority, levels of politicization are likely to grow with societal modernization (linear trend).	Societal modernization should shift the focus of both problem-solving and legitimacy debates toward the global/supranational common good.
Across countries	The higher the share of cosmopolitans in a given country, the higher the level of politicization.	The higher the share of cosmopolitans in a given country, the stronger the focus on the global/supranational common good.

explanation, the level of politicization can be expected to vary with the scope and level of international institutions' authority. Since the modernization approach also acknowledges the authority of international institutions as a driver of politicization, I expect that more powerful institutions are likely to be accompanied by higher levels of politicization independent of the conditioning effect of societal modernization.

Second, modernization theory points to variance over time. Levels of politicization should follow a linear trend.[4] As Inglehart and Welzel (2005: 17–48) show, societal modernization and the respective emergence of cosmopolitan values began during the 1980s. Hence levels of politicization should be higher during the 1990s and 2000s than during the 1980s. This implies that growing levels of politicization can even be expected for institutions with a stable level and scope of authority. As societal modernization widens the vision of individuals towards global governance, politicization processes should even result for international institutions that are not empowered over time. Although the objects do not grow, they become visible because the specifically curved mirror of cosmopolitanism increases citizens' range of vision to spheres that were previously hidden by a "veil of national ignorance".

Third, under modernization conditions, politicization also varies across countries. In addition to the varying degree of international authority over a given country, cross-country variance is conditioned by the share of cosmopolitans. The higher the share of individuals holding a cosmopolitan identity mobilizing public debate about international institutions, the higher should be the level of politicization.

Finally, modernization shifts the focus of public controversy to a different set of objects and criteria of politicization. A cosmopolitan pattern of politicization should emphasize a specific set of criteria of politicization: I expect a pattern of politicization that emphasizes input and output criteria built on cosmopolitan values (Ecker-Ehrhardt, 2014: 9). Not only will cosmopolitans press for political results that advance the global common good instead of national preferences, but they are also likely to demand the expansion of citizen input as well as democratic reforms in global governance (Dalton, 1984: 282; Scholte, 2011).

Post-functionalist theory: nationalist agents of politicization

While globalization may push some individuals towards cosmopolitanism, other individuals will develop resistance identities (Diamond et al., 2016; Mudde, 2016). This specific type of identity lies at the core of Hooghe and Marks' (2009) post-functionalist theory of European integration and their explanation for the growing constraining dissensus that might hinder further steps toward integration. They argue that citizens holding an exclusive nationalist identity are predisposed to oppose and thus to politicize the EU in particular and international institutions more broadly. More specifically, the post-functionalist explanation expects populist right-wing parties to utilize the tension between exclusive nationalist identity and the transfer of political authority to international institutions for mobilizing nationalist backlash against international institutions' authority (Checkel and Katzenstein, 2009: Ch. 1; Hoeglinger, 2016; Börzel and Risse, 2018).

The post-functionalist explanation also departs from the observation that the authority of international institutions is growing and that this process generates a political potential that can give rise to politicization (Hooghe and Marks, 2009: 12–14). This political potential is not as much magnified by societal modernization as by the absence of a shift in expectations and loyalty towards the international level (Schmitter, 1969: 166). As social identities remain fixed to the nation-state, the shift of political authority to international institutions constitutes a significant loss to citizens "who possess a strong sense of identification with their national community, and who are attached to its exclusionary norms and/or its political institutions" (Kriesi et al., 2012: 15). The post-functionalist explanation describes a curved mirror that exaggerates international institutions not so much because citizens know more about these institutions and are normatively more attached to them, but because they are fearful about their potential effects on individual economic well-being, national cultural and ethnic homogeneity, and political decision-making (Teney et al., 2014). This perspective proposes that politicization is likely to result from an exclusive nationalist backlash led by globophobes and mobilized by populist parties (Burgoon, 2009; Hooghe and Marks, 2018).

At the core of the argument lies a divergence between the structure of jurisdiction and political decision-making on the one hand and social identity on the other. While political authority migrates to international institutions, it is not accompanied by social identity because many citizens and political parties are still bound to the nation-state (Kriesi et al., 2012: 3). As fundamental lines of political conflict, alliance, opposition, and respective social identities emerged at critical historical junctures that were characterized by the formation of the external boundaries and internal structures of the nation-state (Lipset and Rokkan, 1967; Rokkan, 1999), today the social identity of many citizens is still tied to these national boundaries. As a result, the post-functionalist explanation does not highlight the role of cosmopolitans as agents of politicization. Rather, it highlights that those citizens who feel strongly attached to the nation-state are likely to be discontented with the weakening of their cultural, economic, and political anchor points (De Vreese and Boomgaarden, 2005: 63) and thus tend to politicize international institutions.

However, respective research on political attitudes towards national political regimes and international institutions has shown that the concept of national identity – defined as a bond of belonging that arises from the sharing of homeland, cultural myths, symbols and historical memories, economic resources, and legal-political rights and duties (Norris and Inglehart, 2009: 180) – is too broad to understand effects of identity on politicization. European integration scholars have, for instance, demonstrated that different formations of national identity either mobilize support for European integration or opposition against it. While some studies show that individuals who identify with their national community tend to mobilize opposition to the European integration project (Taggart, 1998; McLaren, 2002; De Vreese and Boomgaarden, 2005), others have demonstrated that national identity can reinforce European identity and thus mobilize support for European integration (Herrmann et al., 2004; Fligstein, 2008: 144; Risse, 2010: Ch. 8).

Consequently, Hooghe and Marks (2004, 2005) distinguish between exclusive and inclusive national identity. They show that individuals who conceive of their national identity as exclusive of other senses of territorial belonging – for instance, to regions, continents, or the globe – feel more threatened by European integration than those who conceive of their national identity in more inclusive terms (see also McLaren, 2004; McLaren, 2006; Garry and Tilley, 2009: 364). This specific feeling of threat and dissatisfaction of exclusive nationalists is hypothesized to trigger a politicization process that differs from those predicted by the institutional and the modernization explanation.

More specifically, the sharp in-group/out-group distinction of exclusive nationalists has been shown to be a characteristic of citizens who essentialize the properties of their in-group and thus hold a strong appreciation of national superiority (Blank, 2003: 262; Huddy and Khatib, 2007). Shmuel Eisenstadt and Bernhard Giesen (1995: 77) have called this type of national identity a "primordial identity" because it builds on primordial features such as race or ethnic properties. They distinguish this exclusive nationalism from other forms of national identity that put less emphasis on the differences between in-group and out-group, and are more inclusive, including patriotism characterized by a critical loyalty to the nation-state and its leaders and at the same time an appreciation of democratic principles and other cultures (Wagner et al., 2012: 320). While both exclusive nationalists and patriots hold comparable feelings of national identification, patriots feel less threatened by out-groups due to their appreciation of other cultures and democratic principles (Davidov, 2009: 66). Patriots are less likely to politicize the authority of international institutions because they do not feel particularly threatened by international institutions and their activities. This group can be considered to be of less relevance to the present study because it neither belongs to the cosmopolitan nor to the exclusive nationalist camp.

But can exclusive nationalists actually be expected to mobilize against international institutions and contribute to their politicization? Are they likely to engage actively with global governance when they not only lack the cognitive skills to fully comprehend this sphere of political decision-making but also the organizational skills and the internal motivation that characterize their cosmopolitan counterparts? Two answers have been given to this question: first, research on American national identity has demonstrated that civic participation is central to a strong national identity and that those who think of themselves as being strongly attached to the national community also have a strong political interest and are politically involved (Huddy and Khatib, 2007). However, this finding could be restricted to national politics. While it seems plausible that nationalists engage with domestic politics, it is less clear why the same effect should be observable as regards the international sphere (Bartolini, 2005: Ch. 6). Second, European integration scholars have argued that national identity lays dormant as a catalyzer of politicization as long as it is not mobilized by political elites (Hooghe and Marks, 2004: 417; Risse, 2010: Ch. 3). Catherine De Vries and Erica Edwards (2009) demonstrate that the engagement of radical right and populist parties is necessary to mobilize nationalist opposition to international institutions. Only if these radical right parties tap into the feeling of threat to national sovereignty stimulated by the activities of international institutions are exclusive nationalists mobilized to politicize them (Kriesi et al., 2008, see also Kriesi et al., 2012).

In sum, the post-functionalist explanation widens the institutionalist approach by adding the share of exclusive nationalists in a given society and the role of mobilizing political parties to the explanatory framework. The specific timing and level of the politicization of international institutions' authority are conditioned by the extent to which citizens hold an exclusive national identity and are mobilized by radical right parties. As Thomas Risse (2010: 49) argues in the context of party competition on European integration, such nationalists are considered "the social basis and potential for the sleeping giant of anti-EU political mobilization by mostly right-wing populist parties across Europe".

How do these arguments modify the institutionalist explanation? To what extent should levels and patterns of politicization vary across institutions, over time, and across countries, if the post-functionalist approach is valid? Table 2.3

Table 2.3 Observable implications of post-functionalist theory

Level of variance	*Level of politicization*	*Pattern of politicization*
Across institutions	–	–
Over time	The stronger exclusive nationalism, the higher the levels of politicization. Due to the importance of party mobilization, politicization is likely to be more episodic.	The stronger exclusive nationalism and party mobilization, the higher the focus on nationalistic legitimacy debates.
Across countries	The stronger exclusive nationalism and party mobilization in a given country, the higher the level of politicization.	The stronger exclusive nationalism and party mobilization in a given country, the higher the focus on nationalistic legitimacy debates.

summarizes the observable implications of the post-functionalist modifications of the institutionalist perspective.

First, similar to the institutionalist explanation, the level of politicization should vary according to the scope and level of international institutions' authority. Since post functionalism also departs from the growing authority of international institutions as a necessary condition for politicization, I hypothesize that stronger and more influential institutions are likely to be accompanied by higher levels of politicization independent of the conditioning effect of exclusive nationalism.

Second, the post-functionalist explanation points to variance over time. In general, exclusive nationalists should condition the politicizing effect of international institutions' authority to the extent that the share of this group in a given population is likely to change over time. While I have argued above that social identities are sticky and do not vary strongly on a short-term basis, long-term developments may alter the course of politicization.

In addition, the post-functionalist emphasis on party politics and the mobilization of exclusive nationalist identity by radical right and populist parties for the politicization of international institutions alludes to more episodic developments that are marked by issue-attention cycles. While both the institutionalist and modernization explanation predict stable and linear trends of politicization that parallel the long-term structural transformations highlighted by both approaches, post-functionalism introduces an element of volatility. Since party competition is marked by the ongoing search for vote shares, political parties will mobilize exclusive nationalist identity whenever it suits their political strategy (Steenbergen and Marks, 2004: 321–322; Bartolini, 2005). As a result, public debates on international institutions should not be marked by constant contestation but by cyclical ebbs and flows: for instance, during election years or during political referenda on international institutions (Farrell and Newman, 2017; Meijers, 2017). The temporal trajectory of politicization – as it is contingent on the mobilization of radical right parties – is likely to be characterized by a mounting number of short-term peaks in the level of politicization.

Finally, post-functionalism points to a distinct pattern of politicization that is likely to proceed in terms of a legitimacy rather than a problem-solving debate. As regards objects of politicization, the post-functionalist perspective points to a focus on the polity aspect of international institutions. Due to the conflict between exclusive nationalist identity and the transfer of political authority to international institutions, I expect exclusive nationalists to contest precisely this transfer of authority to the international level and the legitimacy of international institutions in general. Because exclusive nationalists are determined to defend national self-determination against external interventions, problem-solving debates – focusing on the question of whether a given international institution does a good job in a specific policy area – should be less relevant. Rather, a nationalist pattern of politicization should focus on the fundamental question of the adherence to or the opting out from international integration as a whole and/or on the magnitude of integration – that is, the scope and level of competencies and powers transferred to the international level (Bartolini, 2000).

In terms of the criteria of politicization, nationalists are likely to emphasize demarcation and concerns about the critical loss of national autonomy or sovereignty. While modernization theory points to a set of politicization criteria concerned with the integrative effects of both the input and output of international institutions, exclusive nationalists are likely to frame international institutions negatively and in terms of national closure (Scheepers et al., 2002) due to their potential infringement with national decision-making, legislation, and jurisdiction. Consequently, I expect criteria of nationalist politicization to concentrate on the preservation of national sovereignty, the national public good, and national differences.

Conclusion

This chapter has demonstrated that both institutionalist and society-based theories tend to highlight the growing political authority of international institutions as the main driving force of politicization. However, the society-based explanation of modernization theory and post-functionalism stress that the political potential of these institutional transformations is only mobilized under specific socio-cultural conditions and by specific agents of politicization. While most of the present literature conceptualizes these perspectives on domestic context as distinct and competing explanations, I claim that their full explanatory potential is best utilized by combining them into one integrated theory of politicization.

Exclusive nationalist and cosmopolitan identities constitute the endpoints of a continuous scale. On the nationalist endpoint of this scale, citizens are convinced that the nation-state is *the* constituency to which they belong and with which they identify. On the cosmopolitan endpoint of the scale, by contrast, citizens conceive humankind and the globe as the most relevant constituency (Norris and Inglehart, 2009: 181; Pichler, 2009: 708). Individuals can position themselves at only one point on this scale. These two positions are, in other words, mutually exclusive (Roudometof, 2005: 124). This is not to imply that citizens cannot and do not identify with several territorial communities simultaneously. It is not at all unusual for citizens to hold multiple identities and to feel, for instance, Bavarian, German, and European (Diez Medrano, 2003; Furia, 2005; Fligstein, 2008: Ch. 5). This mixing of various identities can be conceptualized with the help of the marble-cake model of social identities (Risse, 2010: 45). According to this model, multiple identities blend into each other to different degrees. What is relevant for my argument here is that citizens at the extreme points of this distribution do hold identities and respective sets of values on political objects that tend to be more exclusively focused on one particular identity. Accordingly, those who have strongly integrated a supranational sense of belonging into their identity hold cosmopolitan values and are more likely to politicize international institutions. On the other side of the distribution, those who have not integrated these values into their national identities – that is, exclusive nationalists – are also likely to politicize international institutions because of the threat to their national in-group posed by the authority of these institutions. On aggregate, individual

Table 2.4 Conditioning effects of country profiles

		Share exclusive nationalists	
		High	*Low*
Share of cosmopolitans	High	Level: high Timing: frequent peaks Pattern: strong clash of perspectives on the legitimacy of international institutions	Level: medium Timing: mild linear growth Pattern: Mix of problem-solving and legitimacy debates with a focus on the global public good
	Low	Level: medium Timing: mild episodic growth Pattern: legitimacy debate with a focus on national sovereignty	Level: low Timing: weak growth Pattern: mix of problem-solving and legitimacy

countries should be characterized by different distributions of citizen's attitudes and mobilizing political parties adding up to specific country profiles, that is, country-specific mobilization potentials that condition the politicizing effect of international institutions' authority. The share of both groups and their distribution in a given country at a specific point in time condition the politicization of international institutions. Mobilization potentials shape the specific timing, level, and pattern of politicization. Table 2.4 summarizes these effects on the politicization of a given international institution.

First, as regards the level of politicization, I hypothesize that polarized countries hosting a substantial share of nationalist and cosmopolitan citizens and parties are most likely to be characterized by a strong politicization of international institutions for two reasons: (a) the sum of both groups is likely to make up a substantial share of the entire population, and (b) the interaction between both groups should result in political conflict that intensifies the politicization process (De Wilde, 2011: 567; De Wilde and Zürn, 2012: 148). If the demarcation/integration cleavage between globophobes and cosmopolitans is strongly mobilized, the level of politicization should be higher than in other domestic contexts because the political conflict between both fractions constitutes a reoccurring issue of public debate and party competition (Kriesi et al., 2012: 15). Countries hosting only one strong group of either cosmopolitans or globophobes are still likely, albeit to a lesser extent, to be cases of strong politicization. In these cases, I expect politicization to be substantially lower than in polarized cases. Countries in which neither globophobes nor cosmopolitans play an important role should politicize international institutions even less.

Second, in terms of variance over time, different national mobilization potentials at a given point in time yield different levels of politicization and different temporal trajectories. I expect politicization to increase over time with the level of polarization between globophobes and cosmopolitans. The more this cleavage is mobilized over time, the higher should be the level of politicization. Furthermore, time periods during which a country is characterized by polarization should be marked by frequently reoccurring episodes of politicization. Because the growing authority of international institutions provides a broad array of issues on which cosmopolitans and globophobes can clash, episodes of politicization should be frequent. By contrast, countries characterized by a growing cosmopolitan and weak nationalist outlook should display less growth of politicization levels and a more stable and less-episodic temporal trajectory. Structural societal transformations highlighted by modernization theory point to the idea that politicization should grow constantly over time. In addition, modernization theory indicates that politicization should even increase if the political authority of a given international institution is constant. Increasingly cosmopolitan societies should moderately politicize international institutions, even if their scope and level of authority remain more or less constant because citizens' "field of vision" widens and unveils international institutions.

Countries characterized by a growing nationalist and a weak cosmopolitan mobilization potential are likely to display different temporal trajectories. Growing levels of politicization can only be expected if rising exclusive nationalism and right-wing mobilization are accompanied by the mounting authority of international institutions. The reason for this difference to cosmopolitan societies is that the post-functionalist perspective conceptualizes politicization as a result of the conflict between growing political internationalization and exclusive nationalist identity. Furthermore, given that the authority of international institutions increases, exclusive nationalism should result in less constant and more episodic temporal trajectories. Due to the important role of right-wing party mobilization of exclusive nationalist identity, politicization is less likely to proceed constantly but rather by a mounting number of short issue-attention cycles.

Finally, these country-specific mobilization potentials shape distinguishable patterns of politicization. In countries characterized by the polarization between globophobes and cosmopolitans, a twofold pattern of politicization can be expected. Due to the substantial cleavage between both groups, the bulk of public debate should focus on the most general aspects, that is, the legitimacy of international institutions. While cosmopolitans are likely to argue in favor of more and better international institutions as a solution to global problems, globophobes should reject these arguments on the basis of their defense of national sovereignty and self-determination. A smaller portion of public debate should focus on problem-solving. Here, cosmopolitans discuss the performance of international institutions quite critically, while globophobes reject the idea of supranational institutions as a solution to global problems altogether. Rather, they will ask to what extent international institutions' specific policies can help to protect national interests.

In countries either dominated by cosmopolitans or globophobes, the pattern of politicization can be expected to be skewed accordingly. More cosmopolitan societies should shape a mix of legitimacy and problem-solving debates emphasizing questions of how international institutions can contribute to the global public good and how these solutions can accommodate democratic principles on a global scale. More nationalist societies, by contrast, should shape narrower discussions on the general legitimacy of international institutions and their interventions into national spheres of self-determination.

In the following three chapters, I proceed to test the individual and combined explanatory power of these causal and conditioning factors through descriptive statistical analysis and comparative case studies.

Notes

1 For a conceptual discussion of authority delegation and pooling see, for instance, David Lake (2007). For more specific research on delegation see Darren Hawkins and colleagues (2006) and on pooling see Moravcsik (1998).

2 This explanation resembles what Jon Hurwitz and Mark Peffley (1987: 1103) have called "an information processing perspective" on the formation of foreign-policy attitudes and preferences. Grounded in cognitive psychology, this perspective argues that because humans have severe cognitive limitations, they rely on their general store of knowledge to guide the processing of more specific and complex information. As the international sphere is exceptionally complex, individuals depend even more on their general stock of knowledge when interpreting this aspect of the political environment.

3 Scholars interested in the connections between trust and world politics (Herrmann et al., 1999; Hetherington and Husser, 2011) have noted that international trust – that is, a general belief about whether foreign countries behave in accordance with normative expectations regarding the conduct of nations – is a crucial determinant of how citizens see the realm of world affairs. Citizens who see international politics as a "friendly environment where trust and cooperation among nations are the norms [and] who give other nations the benefit of the doubt" (Brewer et al., 2004: 96) are more likely to support international cooperation and in turn international institutions.

4 One might argue that international institutions' growing authority and societal modernization are not entirely independent of each other because both phenomena are to some extent rooted in processes of globalization. However, research on cosmopolitan identity has shown that education, occupation, and transnational communication are much stronger predictors for cosmopolitanism than is, for instance, a country's integration into the global economy (Jung, 2008; Norris and Inglehart, 2009: Ch. 6).

References

Abbott, K. and Snidal, D. 2010. International Regulation Without International Government: Improving IO Performance Through Orchestration. *Review of International Organizations*, 5, 315–344.

Alter, K. J. 2014. *The New Terrain of International Law*, Princeton: Princeton University Press.

Barnett, M. and Finnemore, M. 2004. *Rules for the World: International Organizations in Global Politics*, Ithaca: Cornell University Press.

Bartolini, S. 2000. National Cleavage Structures and the Integration Issue Dimension. *In: Colloque Science Po, L'intégration Européene: Entre Emergence Institutionellee et Recompositionen de L'Etat*, Paris: Science Po.

Bartolini, S. 2005. *Restructuring Europe: Centre Formation, System Formation, System Building, and Political Structuring Between the Nation State and the European Union*, Oxford: Oxford University Press.

Beck, U. and Grande, E. 2007. *Das kosmopolitische Europa*, Frankfurt a.M.: Suhrkamp.

Blake, D. J. and Payton, A. L. 2015. Balancing Design Objectives: Analyzing New Data on Voting Rules in Intergovernmental Organizations. *Review of International Organizations*, 10, 377–402.

Blank, T. 2003. Determinants of National Identity in East and West Germany: An Empirical Comparison of Theories on the Significance of Authoritarism, Anomie, and General Self-Esteem. *Political Psychology*, 24, 259–288.

Börzel, T. A. and Risse, T. 2018. From the Euro to the Schengen Crises: European Integration Theories, Politicization, and Identity Politics. *Journal of European Public Policy*, 25, 83–108.

Brewer, P. R., Kimberly, G., Aday, S. and Willnat, L. 2004. International Trust and Public Opinion About World Affairs. *American Journal of Political Science*, 48, 93–109.

Burgoon, B. 2009. Globalization and Backlash: Polanyi's Revenge. *Review of International Political Economy*, 16, 145–177.

Castanho Silva, B. 2018. Populist Radical Right Parties and Mass Polarization in the Netherlands. *European Political Science Review*, 10, 219–244.

Checkel, J. T. and Katzenstein, P. (eds.) 2009. *The Politicization of European Identity*, Cambridge: Cambridge University Press.

Coleman, W. D. and Wayland, S. 2006. The Origins of Global Civil Society and Nonterritorial Governance: Some Empirical Findings. *Global Governance*, 12, 241–261.

Cooper, S., Hawkins, D., Jacoby, W. and Nielsen, D. 2008. Yielding Sovereignty to International Institutions: Bringing System Structure Back In. *International Studies Review*, 10, 501–524.

Dalton, R. J. 1984. Cognitive Mobilization and Partisan Dealignment in Advanced Industrial Democracies. *Journal of Politics*, 46, 264–284.

Davidov, E. 2009. Measurement Equivalent of Nationalism and Constructive Patriotism in the ISSP: 34 Countries in a Comparative Perspective. *Political Analysis*, 17, 64–82.

Dellmuth, L. M. 2016. The Knowledge Gap in World Politics: Assessing the Sources of Citizen Awareness of the United Nations Security Council. *Review of International Studies*, 42, 673–700.

Dellmuth, L. M. and Tallberg, J. 2015. The Social Legitimacy of International Organizations: Interest Representation, Institutional Performance, and Confidence Extrapolation in the United Nations. *Review of International Studies*, 41, 451–475.

Deutsch, K. W., Burrell, S. A., Kann, R. A., Lee, M., Lichterman, M., Lindgren, R. E., Loewenheim, F. L. and Van Wagenen, R. W. 1957. *Political Community and the North Atlantic Area*, New York: Greenwood Press.

Deutsch, K. W., Edinger, L. J., Macridis, R. C. and Merritt, R. L. 1967. *France, Germany and the Western Alliance: A Study of Elite Attitudes on European Integration and World Politics*, New York: Charles Scribner's Sons.

De Vreese, C. H. and Boomgaarden, H. G. 2005. Projecting EU Referendums: Fear of Immigration and Support for European Integration. *European Union Politics*, 6, 59–82.

De Vries, C. and Edwards, E. E. 2009. Taking Europe to Its Extremes: Extremist Parties and Public Euroscepticism. *Party Politics*, 15, 5–28.

De Wilde, P. 2011. No Polity for Old Politics? A Framework for Analyzing the Politicization of Europen Integration. *Journal of European Integration*, 33, 559–575.

De Wilde, P., Leupold, A. and Schmidtke, H. 2016. Introduction: The Differentiated Politicisation of European Governance. *West European Politics*, 39, 3–22.

De Wilde, P. and Zürn, M. 2012. Can the Politicization of European Integration Be Reversed? *Journal of Common Market Studies*, 50, 137–153.

Diamond, L., Plattner, M. F. and Walker, C. (eds.) 2016. *Authoritarianism Goes Global: The Challenge to Democracy*, Baltimore: Johns Hokins University Press.

Diez Medrano, J. 2003. *Framing Europe: Attitudes Towards European Integration in Germany, Spain, and the United Kingdom*, Princeton: Princeton University Press.

Dobson, H. 2007. *The Group of 7/8*, London: Routledge.

Down, I. and Wilson, C. 2008. From "Permissive Consensus" to "Constraining Dissensus": A Polarizing Union? *Acta Politica*, 43, 26–49.

Ecker-Ehrhardt, M. 2012. Cosmopolitan Politicization: How Perceptions of Interdependence Foster Citizens' Expectations in International Institutions. *European Journal of International Relations*, 18, 481–508.

Ecker-Ehrhardt, M. 2014. Why Parties Politicise International Institutions: On Globalization Backlash and Authority Contestation. *Review of International Political Economy*, 21, 1275–1312.

Ecker-Ehrhardt, M. and Wessels, B. 2013. Input- oder Output-Politisierung internationaler Organisation? Der kritische Blick der Bürger auf Demokratie und Leistung. *In:* Zürn, M. and Ecker-Ehrhardt, M. (eds.) *Die Politisierung der Weltpolitik*, Berlin: Suhrkamp.

Eisenstadt, S. N. and Giesen, B. 1995. The Construction of Collective Identity. *European Journal of Sociology*, 36, 72–102.

Farrell, H. and Newman, A. L. 2014. Domestic Institutions Beyond the Nation-State: Charting the New Interdependence Approach. *World Politics*, 66, 331–363.

Farrell, H. and Newman, A. L. 2017. Brexit, Voice and Loyalty: Rethinking Electoral Politics in an Age of Interdependence. *Review of International Political Economy*, 24, 232–247.

Favell, A. 2008. *Eurostars and Eurocities: Free Movement in the Making of Europe*, Oxford: Blackwell.

Favell, A. 2009. Immigration, Migration, and Free Movement in the Making of Europe. *In:* Jeffrey, T. C. and Katzenstein, P. (eds.) *European Identity*, Cambridge: Cambridge University Press.

Fligstein, N. 2008. *Euroclash: The EU, European Identity, and the Future of Europe*, Oxford: Oxford University Press.

Furia, P. A. 2005. Global Citizenship, Anyone? Cosmopolitanism, Privilege and Public Opinion. *Global Society*, 19, 331–359.

Garry, J. and Tilley, J. 2009. The Macroeconomic Factors Conditioning the Impact of Identity on Attitudes Towards the EU. *European Union Politics*, 10, 361–379.

Genschel, P. and Jachtenfuchs, M. (eds.) 2014. *Beyond the Regulatory Polity? The Integration of Core State Powers*, Oxford: Oxford University Press.

Genschel, P. and Zangl, B. 2014. State Transformations in OECD Countries. *Annual Review of Political Science*, 17, 1–18.

Grande, E. and Hutter, S. 2016. Beyond Authority Transfer: Explaining the Politicisation of Europe. *West European Politics*, 39, 23–43.

Green-Pedersen, C. 2012. A Giant Fast Asleep? Party Incentives and Politicisation of European Integration. *Political Studies*, 60, 115–130.

Gstöhl, S. 2007. Governance Through Government Networks: The G8 and International Organizations. *Review of International Organizations*, 2, 1–37.

Hainmueller, J. and Hiscox, M. J. 2006. Learning to Love Globalization: Education and Individual Attitudes Towards International Trade. *International Organization*, 60, 469–498.

Hale, T., Held, D. and Young, K. (eds.) 2013. *Gridlock: Why Global Cooperation Is Failing When We Need It Most*, Cambridge, MA: Polity Press.

Hawkins, D. G., Lake, D. A., Nielson, D. L. and Tierney, M. J. (eds.) 2006. *Delegation and Agency in International Organizations*, Cambridge: Cambridge University Press.

Held, D. 2000. Regulating Globalization? The Reinvention of Politics. *International Sociology*, 15, 394–408.

Held, D. 2010. *Cosmopolitanism: Ideals, Realities & Deficits*, Cambridge, MA: Polity Press.

Herrmann, R. K., Risse, T. and Brewer, M. B. (eds.) 2004. *Transnational Identities: Becoming European in the EU*, Lanham: Rowman & Littlefield.

Herrmann, R. K., Tetlock, P. E. and Visser, P. S. 1999. Mass Public Decisions to Go to War: A Cognitive-Interactionist Framework. *American Political Science Review*, 93, 553–573.

Hetherington, M. J. and Husser, J. A. 2011. How Trust Matters: The Changing Political Relevance of Political Trust. *American Journal of Political Science*, 56, 312–325.

Hoegliner, D. 2016. *Politicizing European Integration – Struggling With the Awakening Giant*, Basingstoke: Palgrave Macmillan.

Hooghe, L. and Marks, G. 2004. Does Identity or Economic Rationality Drive Opinion on European Integration? *PS: Political Science and Politics*, 37, 415–420.

Hooghe, L. and Marks, G. 2005. Calculation, Community and Cues. *European Union Politics*, 6, 419–443.

Hooghe, L. and Marks, G. 2009. A Postfunctionalist Theory of European Integration: From Permissive Consensus to Constraining Dissensus. *British Journal of Political Science*, 39, 1–23.

Hooghe, L. and Marks, G. 2012. Politicization. *In:* Jones, E., Menon, A. and Weatherill, S. (eds.) *Oxford Handbook on the European Union*, Oxford: Oxford University Press.

Hooghe, L. and Marks, G. 2018. Cleavage Theory Meets Europe's Crises: Lipset, Rokkan, and the Transnational Cleavage. *Journal of European Public Policy*, 25, 109–135.

Hooghe, L., Marks, G., Lenz, T., Bezuijen, J., Ceka, B. and Derderyan, S. 2017. *Measuring International Authority: A Postfunctionalist Theory of Governance*, Vol. IV, Oxford: Oxford University Press.

Huddy, L. and Khatib, N. 2007. American Patriotism, National Identity, and Political Involvement. *American Journal of Political Science*, 51, 63–77.

Hurrelmann, A., Gora, A. and Wagner, A. 2012. The Politicization of European Integration: More than an Elite Affair? *IPSA XXII World Congress of Political Science*, Madrid, Spain.

Hurwitz, J. and Peffley, M. 1987. How Are Foreign Policy Attitudes Structured? A Hierarchical Model. *American Political Science Review*, 81, 1099–1120.

Hutter, S. and Grande, E. 2014. Politicizing Europe in the National Electoral Arena: A Comparative Analysis of Five West European Countries: 1970–2010. *Journal of Common Market Studies*, 52, 1002–1018.

Hutter, S., Grande, E. and Kriesi, H. (eds.) 2016. *Politicising Europe: Integration and Mass Politics*, Cambridge: Cambridge University Press.

Inglehart, R. 1970a. Cognitive Mobilization and European Identity. *Comparative Politics*, 3, 45–70.

Inglehart, R. 1970b. Public Opinion and Regional Integration. *International Organization*, 24, 764–795.

Inglehart, R. 1977. *The Silent Revolution: Changing Values and Political Styles Among Western Publics*, Princeton: Princeton University Press.

Inglehart, R. and Welzel, C. 2005. *Modernization, Cultural Change and Democracy: The Human Development Sequence*, Cambridge: Cambridge University Press.

Jung, K. J. 2008. Growing Supranational Identities in a Globalising World? A Multilevel Analysis of the World Value Survey. *European Journal of Political Research*, 47, 578–609.

Keohane, R. O. 2011. Global Governance and Legitimacy. *Review of International Political Economy*, 18, 99–109.

Keohane, R. O., Macedo, S. and Moravcsik, A. 2009. Democracy-Enhancing Multilateralism. *International Organization*, 63, 1–31.

Koch, M. 2009. Autonomization of IGOs. *International Political Sociology*, 3, 431–448.

Koehn, P. and Rosenau, J. 2002. Transnational Competence in an Emergent Epoch. *International Studies Perspectives*, 3, 105–127.

Koremenos, B. 2016. *The Continent of International Law: Explaining Agreement Design*, Cambridge: Cambridge University Press.

Kriesi, H., Grande, E., Dolezal, M., Helbling, M., Höglinger, D., Hutter, S. and Wüest, B. 2012. *Political Conflict in Western Europe*, Cambridge: Cambridge University Press.

Kriesi, H., Grande, E., Lachat, R., Dolezal, M., Bornschier, S. and Frey, T. 2008. *West European Politics in the Age of Globalization*, Cambridge: Cambridge University Press.

Kuhn, T. 2011. Individual Transnationalism, Globalization and Euroscepticism: An Empirical Test of Deutsch's Transnationalist Theory. *European Journal of Political Research*, 50, 811–837.

Kux, S. and Sverdrup, U. 2000. Fuzzy Borders and Adaptive Outsiders: Norway, Switzerland and the EU. *Journal of European Integration*, 22, 237–270.

Lake, D. A. 2007. Delegating Divisible Sovereignty: Sweeping a Conceptual Minefield. *Review of International Organizations*, 2, 219–237.

Lenz, T., Bezuijen, J., Hooghe, L. and Marks, G. 2015. Patterns of International Organization: Task Specific vs. General Purpose. *Politische Vierteljahesschrift*, 49, 131–156.

Leuffen, D., Rittberger, B. and Schimmelfennig, F. 2013. *Differentiated Integration: Explaining Variation in the European Union*, Basingstoke: Palgrave Macmillan.

Lipset, S. and Rokkan, S. (eds.) 1967. *Cleavage Structures, Party Systems, and Voter Alignments*, New York: The Free Press.

Lowi, T. 1964. American Business, Public Policy, Case Studies, and Political Theory. *World Politics*, 16, 677–715.

Mair, P. 2007. Political Opposition and the European Union. *Government and Opposition*, 42, 1–17.

Mansfield, E. D. and Mutz, D. C. 2009. Support for Free Trade: Self-Interest, Sociotropic Politics, and Out-Group Anxiety. *International Organization*, 63, 425–257.

Mau, S., Mewes, J. and Zimmermann, A. 2008. Cosmopolitan Attitudes Through Transnational Practices. *Global Networks*, 8, 1–24.

McLaren, L. M. 2002. Public Support for the European Union: Cost/Benefit Analysis or Perceived Cultural Threat? *Journal of Politics*, 64, 551–566.

McLaren, L. M. 2004. Opposition to European Integration and Fear of Loss of National Identity: Debunking a Basic Assumption Regarding Hostility to the Integration Project. *European Journal of Political Research*, 43, 895–911.

McLaren, L. M. 2006. *Identity, Interests and Attitudes to European Integration*, Basingstoke: Palgrave Macmillan.

Meijers, M. 2017. Contagious Euroscepticism: The Impact of Eurosceptic Support on Mainstream Party Positions on European Integration. *Party Politics*, 23, 413–423.

Moravcsik, A. 1998. *The Choice for Europe: Social Purpose and State Power From Messina to Maastricht*, Ithaca: Cornell University Press.

Mudde, C. 2016. *On Extremism and Democracy in Europe*, London: Routledge.

Norris, P. and Inglehart, R. 2009. *Cosmopolitan Communications: Cultural Diversity in a Globalized World*, Cambridge: Cambridge University Press.

Nullmeier, F., Biegoń, D., Gronau, J., Nonhoff, M., Schmidtke, H. and Schneider, S. 2010. *Prekäre Legitimitäten: Rechtfertigung von Herrschaft in der postnationalen Konstellation*, Frankfurt a.M.: Campus.
Oppermann, K. and Vierig, H. 2009. The Public Salience of Foreign and Security Policy in Britain, Germany and France. *West European Politics*, 32, 925–942.
Oppermann, K. and Vierig, H. (eds.) 2011. *Issue Salience in International Politics*, Oxon: Routledge.
Peters, G. B. and Pierre, J. 2004. *Politicization of the Civil Service in Comparative Perspective: The Quest for Control*, London: Routledge.
Pichler, F. 2009. Down-to-Earth Cosmopolitanism: Subjective and Objective Measurements of Cosmopolitanism in Survey Research. *Current Sociology*, 57, 704–732.
Pollack, M. A. 1994. Creeping Competence: The Expanding Agenda of the European Community. *Journal of Public Policy*, 14, 95–145.
Risse, T. 2010. *A Community of Europeans? Transnational Identities and Public Spheres*, Ithaca: Cornell University Press.
Rittberger, B., Leuffen, D. and Schimmelfennig, F. 2014. Differentiated Integration of Core State Powers. *In:* Genschel, P. and Jachtenfuchs, M. (eds.) *Beyond the Regulatory Polity? The Integration of Core State Powers*, Oxford: Oxford University Press.
Rixen, T. and Zangl, B. 2013. The Politicization of International Economic Institutions in US Public Debates. *Review of International Organizations*, 8, 363–387.
Rocabert, J., Schimmelfennig, F., Winzen, T. and Crasnic, L. 2018. *The Rise of International Parliamentary Institutions: Purpose and Legitimation*, Online First, https://doi.org/10.1007/s11558-018-9326-3.
Rokkan, S. 1999. *State Formation, Nation-building, and Mass Politics in Europe: The Theory of Stein Rokkan*, Oxford: Oxford University Press.
Rosenau, J. N. 1992. Citizenship in Changing Global Order. *In:* Rosenau, J. N. and Czempiel, E.-O. (eds.) *Governance Without Government: Order and Change in World Politics*, Cambridge: Cambridge University Press.
Rosenau, J. N. 2003. *Distant Proximities: Dynamics Beyond Globalization*, Princeton: Princeton University Press.
Rosenau, J. N. and Fagen, M. W. 1997. A New Dynamism in World Politics: Increasingly Skillful Individuals? *International Studies Quarterly*, 41, 655–686.
Roudometof, V. 2005. Transnationalism, Cosmopolitanism and Glocalization. *Current Sociology*, 53, 113–135.
Ruggie, J. G. 1992. Multilateralism: Anatomy of an Institution. *International Organization*, 46, 561–598.
Scharpf, F. W. 1999. *Governing in Europe: Effective and Democratic*, Oxford: Oxford University Press.
Scheepers, P., Gijsberts, M. and Coenders, M. 2002. Ethnic Exclusionism in European Countries: Public Opposition to Civil Rights for Legal Migrants as a Response to Perceived Ethnic Threat. *European Sociological Review*, 18, 17–34.
Schimmelfennig, F., Leuffen, D. and Rittberger, B. 2015. The European Union as a System of Differentiated Integration: Interdependence, Politicization and Differentiation. *Journal of European Public Policy*, 22, 764–782.
Schmitter, P. 1969. Three Neo-Functional Hypotheses About International Integration *International Organization*, 23, 161–66.
Scholte, J. A. (ed.) 2011. *Building Global Democracy? Civil Society and Accountable Global Governance*, Cambridge: Cambridge University Press.

Statham, P. and Trenz, H.-J. 2013. *The Politicization of Europe: Contesting the Constitution in the Mass Media*, London: Routledge.

Steenbergen, M. R. and Marks, G. 2004. European Integration and Political Conflict. *In:* Marks, G. and Steenbergen, M. R. (eds.) *European Integration and Political Conflict*, Cambridge: Cambridge University Press.

Taggart, P. 1998. A Touchstone of Dissent: Euroscepticism in Contemporary Western European Party Systems. *European Journal of Political Research*, 33, 363–388.

Tajfel, H. 1981. *Human Groups and Social Categories: Studies in Social Psychology*, Cambridge: Cambridge University Press.

Tallberg, J. and McCall Smith, J. 2014. Dispute Settlement in World Politics: States, Supranational Prosecutors, and Compliance. *European Journal of International Relations*, 20, 118–144.

Tarrow, S. G. 2001. Transnational Politics: Contention and Institutions in International Politics. *Annual Review of Political Science*, 4, 1–20.

Tarrow, S. G. 2011. *Power in Movement: Social Movements and Contentious Politics Revised and Updated*, 3rd ed., Cambridge: Cambridge University Press.

Teney, C., Lacewell, O. P. and De Wilde, P. 2014. Winners and Losers of Globalization in Europe: Attitudes and Ideologies. *European Political Science Review*, 6, 575–595.

Wagner, U., Becker, J. C., Christ, O., Pettigrew, T. F. and Schmidt, P. 2012. A Longitudinal Test of the Relation Between German Nationalism, Patriotism, and Outgroup Derogation. *European Sociological Review*, 28, 319–332.

Wendler, F. 2014. Justification and Political Polarization in National Parliamentary Debates on EU Treaty Reform. *Journal of European Public Policy*, 21, 549–567.

Wendt, A. 1994. Collective Identity Formation and the International State. *American Political Science Review*, 88, 384–396.

Woodward, I., Skrbis, Z. and Bean, C. 2008. Attitudes Towards Globalization and Cosmopolitanism: Cultural Diversity, Personal Consumption and the National Economy. *The British Journal of Sociology*, 59, 207–224.

Zürn, M. 2004. Global Governance and Legitimacy Problems. *Government and Opposition*, 39, 260–287.

Zürn, M. 2013. Politisierung als Konzept der Internationalen Beziehungen. *In:* Zürn, M. and Ecker-Ehrhardt, M. (eds.) *Die Politisierung der Weltpolitik*, Berlin: Suhrkamp.

Zürn, M. 2018. *A Theory of Global Governance: Authority, Legitimacy, and Contestation*, Oxford: Oxford University Press.

Zürn, M., Binder, M. and Ecker-Erhardt, M. 2012. International Authority and Its Politicization. *International Theory*, 4, 69–106.

Zürn, M. and Ecker-Ehrhardt, M. (eds.) 2013. *Die Politisierung der Weltpolitik*, Berlin: Suhrkamp.

3 The politicization of global tax governance

Descriptive findings

This chapter introduces the dataset on the politicization of global tax governance in the quality press of Germany, Ireland, and Switzerland. It addresses the first core question of the inquiry: can we observe a politicization of global tax governance? The chapter lays the descriptive foundation for the subsequent examination of the explanatory framework presented in Chapter 2. To this end, I introduce the indicators of the three operationalizing components of politicization (salience, controversy, and plurality) and examine their development over time. More specifically, I first present the operationalization and measurement of politicization. Second, I address the questions of whether the issue of global tax governance passes the minimum threshold of being present in mass media communication at all, and how this presence of the topic develops over the period of analysis (1981–2011). Third, I analyze the controversy over global tax governance. I ask whether global tax governance is at all controversial in the mass media and how this public controversy develops over time. Finally, I examine the plurality of the public debate on global tax governances. Here, I probe whether and to what extent actors other than national executives voice their positions, evaluations, and demands. I present the information in the most aggregated form and leave disaggregation and comparison across the EU and the OECD and across national publics for the subsequent explanatory chapters. The three operationalizing components of politicization are unpacked and disaggregated into the individual dimensions, which help to operationalize the concept as a whole. In the final section, I examine a politicization index – aggregating all three components into one politicization measure. Both individual components and the politicization index indicate a growing politicization of global tax governance over time. The data show that global tax governance is an increasingly salient, controversial, and plural issue in the mass media of Germany, Ireland, and Switzerland.

Measuring politicization: a public sphere perspective

This section describes the dataset that underpins my measurement of politicization on which this chapter and the comparative case studies presented in chapter 4 and chapter 5. I present the procedure used to collect and code the corpus of politicization-related newspaper articles that is the empirical basis of this book.

The basic methodological choice was to explore the politicization of global tax governance based on quality newspaper articles. I focus on the mass media because it constitutes a society-wide public arena in which a broad variety of actors can voice their positions (Norris, 2000: Ch. 1). Quality newspapers reflect public controversy over issues on the public agenda, including international institutions and potentially increasingly politicized global tax governance (De Wilde, 2012; Hutter and Grande, 2014; Hutter and Kerscher, 2014). The quality press provides a unique and information-rich data source from which the levels and patterns of politicization as well as actors' positions can be mapped because mass media communication and more specifically the quality press function as a transmission belt and gatekeeper between political institutions and citizens (Hallin and Mancini, 2004: Ch. 1; Gerhards et al., 2007: 3; Habermas, 2008; Wessler et al., 2008: Ch. 1). My dataset comes from quality newspapers rather than tabloids and television because newspapers report political topics more extensively and in a more nuanced fashion (Druckman, 2005).

My research strategy therefore differs from two dominant approaches in the literature on the politicization of international institutions: opinion research based on survey data (Dellmuth and Tallberg, 2015; Schlipphak, 2015) and the analysis of political behavior, including protest events and voter turnout (Tarrow, 2005; Hobolt and Spoon, 2012; Hutter and Grande, 2014). There is no doubt that each of these approaches has comparative advantages in the study of politicization (Baglioni and Hurrelmann, 2016). Yet, the media data used here have the important advantage of revealing how the salience of global tax governance and respective political conflict among a broad variety of actors has changed over time. Furthermore, media data indicate more clearly the specific focus of politicization processes on how actors justify their demands and evaluations. This allows me to specify concrete patterns of politicization and thus a more thorough analysis of my hypotheses on the drivers and conditions of politicization.

For each country, I chose two widely read opinion-leading quality newspapers (see Table 3.1). Quality newspapers are particularly suited for studying the politicization of global governance because they reflect broad public debates in a nuanced fashion and because they influence the content published by a wide range of other media outlets (Walgrave et al., 2008; Sevenans, 2018). I chose one center-right and center-left newspaper per country. These newspapers are major voices, covering the political mainstream in each selected country (Schneider et al., 2010: 51). Finally, the selection of newspapers was also based on pragmatic considerations of data availability in electronic newspaper archives and my limited language skills.[1]

Comparative content analysis of newspapers involves enormous time and effort. Appropriate sampling and coding strategies are thus crucial. My dataset covers the politicization of global tax governance in three countries and six newspapers over a period of 30 years. The content analysis was, however, not conducted for the complete calendar years between 1981 and 2011, but on the basis of four randomly "constructed" weeks per newspaper and year. This sampling strategy ensures a representative sample from an extensive population of newspaper

Table 3.1 Newspaper characteristics and data availability

Newspaper (Country)	*Political orientation*	*Circulation size*[a]	*Daily news hole*[b]	*Data availability*[c]
Irish Independent (II, Ireland)	Center-left	134,836	91	2003–2011
Irish Times (IT, Ireland)	Center-right	99,347	116	1982–2011
Süddeutsche Zeitung (SZ, Germany)	Center-left	429,476	192	1995–2011
Frankfurter Allgemeine Zeitung (FAZ, Germany)	Center-right	384,895	192	1981–2011
Tagesanzeiger (TA, Switzerland)	Center-left	210,665	127	1999–2011
Neue Zürcher Zeitung (NZZ, Switzerland)	Center-right	154,707	120	1994–2011

a "Circulation size" refers to average circulation for 1981 to 2011, as reported by the newspaper.
b "News hole" describes the average number of news articles per day for 1981 to 2011.
c "Data availability" indicates the time period for which newspaper articles are provided by online databases.

articles, without limiting my searches to the front pages or politics sections of the newspapers examined. I am thus able to make plausible inferences for entire countries and years on the basis of the sample (Lacy et al., 2001). For each year in the study period, one constructed week per newspaper and quarter of a year – one Monday, one Tuesday, one Wednesday, one Thursday, one Friday, and one Saturday – was selected by means of a random number generator. This procedure ensured that all weekdays and quarters of a year (with the exception of Sundays) are equally represented in the sample, without bias due to the preponderance of particular weekdays or periods of the year, which may differ in terms of volume or content (for more details on sampling, data retrieval, and coding procedures see Appendix 4).

As indicated in Table 3.1, data availability is restricted for some of the selected newspapers and the time series is incomplete for some of the selected countries. While the dataset provides complete time series for the *FAZ* and an almost complete time series for the *IT* (beginning in 1982), time series are more limited for the *Neue Züricher Zeitung* (beginning in 1994) and the *SZ* (beginning in 1995), and are quite restricted for the *TA* (beginning in 2000) and the *II* (beginning in 2003). Consequently, the dataset provides reliable information on the politicization of global tax governance for the complete time period in Germany and Ireland. For Switzerland, the dataset provides information for a 17-year period between 1994 and 2011. In almost all cases, the missing years are the result of a lack of digitized newspaper articles in electronic newspaper archives.

Public controversy over global tax governance is at the core of this study. While this controversy may manifest itself in different forms, including public protest or individual attitude formation, I conceptualize politicization as an essentially communicative phenomenon in which language plays a significant role and that is most directly observed by analyzing public debates and arguments used by different actors. Following this public-sphere perspective (Koopmans and Statham, 2010a; Statham and Trenz, 2013b), I chose a method of data retrieval suitable for collecting systematic, detailed, and reliable data on the content of public debates.

More specifically, I apply a combination of political valuation analysis (Schneider et al., 2007; Schmidtke and Nullmeier, 2011) and political claims analysis (Koopmans and Statham, 1999; Koopmans and Statham, 2010b) because both approaches are analytic descriptive tools tailored to describe who and what is present in the public sphere (Statham and Trenz, 2013a: 970). In combination, both approaches target those elements of public debate that form the core of politicization. They identify and describe public speech acts that problematize and contest a given issue by either looking at diagnostic assessments of a given issue (political valuation analysis) or by analyzing prescriptive statements – that is, articulations of demand, calls to action, or proposals – that follow from valuation. Taken together, public speech acts taking the form of valuations, demands, and proposals constitute the public controversy of a given issue. These affective statements form the empirical basis of the analysis of the politicization of global tax governance because they indicate which actors take what positions and for what reason (for a similar approach see Kriesi et al., 2008; Kriesi et al., 2012).

Both claims analysis and political valuation analysis take individual statements as the coding unit. They are thus particularly valuable to analyze the relations between actors and their positions on global tax governance. I identify and describe these statements by means of a stylized grammar which consists of four core elements (Table 3.2): A *speaker* uttering the valuation or claim, the *object* of

Table 3.2 Grammar of valuation and claims analysis

Example 1 (Claim): "Tax Commissioner Laszlo Kovacs wants a 'common base' which would see companies sharing their corporation tax among different member states in which they operated" (*II*, 27 September 2007).

Speaker	Object of claim (object of politicization)	Addressee of the claim	Justification (criteria of politicization)
EU Commissioner Laszlo Kovacs	Demands a common consolidated corporate tax base (EU tax regulation)	Who is expected to implement the claim remains unclear	A reason is also not given

Example 2 (Valuation): "Ireland is leading opposition to the tax strategy being developed by the commission and has warned that harmonising the base would inevitably lead to the harmonisation of corporate tax rates, the rock upon which Ireland's economic success is founded" (*IT*, 14 December 2006).

Speaker	Object of valuation (Object of politicization)	Tone	Justification (criteria of politicization)
The Irish government	The European Commission's proposal for a common consolidated corporate tax base	Negative	Because it would affect Ireland's economic success

a valuation or claim, the *addressee* of the valuation or claim, and the *justification* given, when a speaker takes a position. Furthermore, valuation statements are marked by a clearly identifiable positive or negative *tone*.

The object of a claim or valuation is predetermined by the study's focus on EU and OECD tax governance. To be pertinent to the present analysis, a statement is required to deal with the issue area of global tax governance, including international cooperation on taxation, international tax harmonization, international tax competition, and other issues of international taxation, in which the EU, the OECD, or both are involved. The identification of affective statements on EU or OECD tax governance, the measurement of their volume, and the analysis of the four core variables of the grammar help me to map the levels and patterns of politicization of global tax governance over time, and to make inferences on its causal drivers. I introduced the specific operationalization of these variables, that is, groups of speakers, objects and criteria of politicization, evaluative tone, and a number of additional attributes of affective statements, including the name, origin and affiliation of speakers, the more specific activities of OECD and EU tax governance discussed in statements, and the specific tax areas targeted by these activities in more detail over the course of the following empirical chapters (for a comprehensive codebook detailing all variables and coding rules see Appendix 4).

The salience of global tax governance

The first operationalizing component of politicization denotes the increasing salience of an issue. This concept of salience refers to the relative importance that actors ascribe to a given issue on the political agenda and the resulting political mobilization (Wlezien, 2005: 556–561). The higher the salience of an issue is to an actor, the more motivated the actor is to make his or her views heard and the more influential the actor's preferences are likely to become (Oppermann and Vierig, 2011: 6). To become politicized an issue has to be increasingly present in public discussions and thus more important on the agenda of politicians and their constituencies. In the present case, this implies that global tax governance should become relatively more important in quality newspapers over the course of the period of investigation.

The concept of media salience is well-established in political science and communication studies (Kiousis, 2006: 74). It is most prominently applied in research on political and media agenda-setting (Baumgarnter and Jones, 1993; McCombs, 2004). In this literature, salience is often portrayed as a multi-dimensional construct. On the one hand, the salience of an issue is determined by its position within a given media environment. On the other hand, the qualities and properties of respective news coverage (valence) are also seen as important indicators (Kiousis, 2006: 77). As the dimension of valence denotes the contentiousness of a text or its evaluative tone – concepts that are at the core of the controversy component of politicization – I focus exclusively on the attention quality newspapers devote to global tax policy. This attention is generally gauged by the sheer volume of newspaper articles or space dedicated to a topic in the media (Norris,

2000: 185; Oppermann and Vierig, 2011: 14; Hutter and Grande, 2014). As James Dearing and Everett Rogers (1996: 18, italics as in the original) note: "the *number* of news stories measures the relative salience of an issue on the media agenda". Following this approach, I measure salience as the total number of newspaper articles per year that mention global tax governance.

Determining theoretical thresholds and rating scales that indicate at what point a debate shall be labeled as politicized are artificial and prone to researcher bias (Down and Wilson, 2008: 30) – a problem that applies to most empirical research on the politicization of international institutions. Hence, I focus on comparison over time. However, from a public sphere perspective (Koopmans and Statham, 2010a; Risse, 2010; Statham and Trenz, 2013b) media presence is an absolute threshold that has to be reached for an issue to become politicized because the press "may not be successful much of the time in telling people *what to think*, but it is stunningly successful in telling its readers *what to think about*" (Cohen, 1963: 13, my italics). The regular presence of an issue on the agenda of widely read quality newspapers puts this issue on citizens' agendas (Soroka, 2006) and is thus an important threshold. Without regular newspaper coverage, there can be no meaningful politicization in the public arena. This implies that only if global tax governance reaches the critical threshold of regular news coverage is politicization likely to take place (Hallin and Mancini, 2004: 33–34; Statham and Trenz, 2013b: 10).

The bars in Figure 3.1 plot the salience of global tax governance over the past 30 years. The curve describes the overall trend in the data.[2] More specifically, Figure 3.1 displays the number of articles per year that mention global tax governance issues as the percentage of the "news hole", that is, the average number of

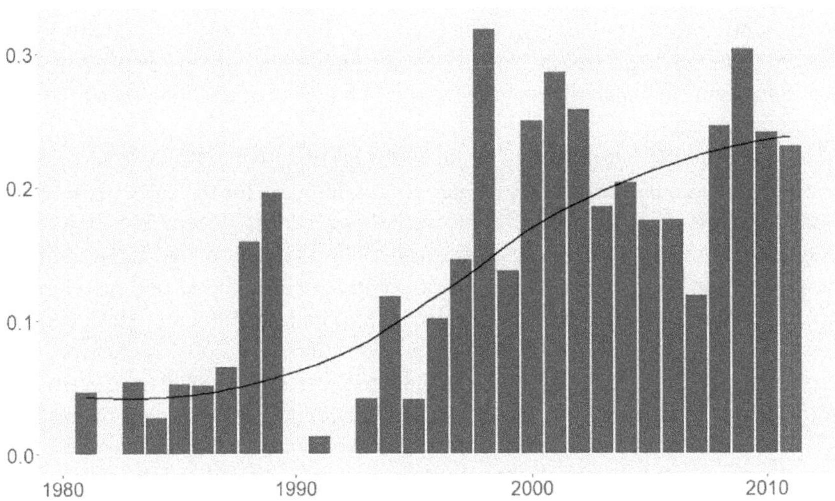

Figure 3.1 Salience of global tax governance, 1981–2011

all articles published in a newspaper per year.[3] This format helps to exclude the potential biases of both varying numbers of newspapers in the sample (due to the previously discussed data restrictions) and the varying size of the news hole per newspaper (Riffe et al., 2018).

Three core observations stand out. First, global tax governance reaches the minimum threshold criterion of being present in the news media. With the exception of 1982, 1990, and 1992, the media cover the issue over the entire observation period. Second, salience increases. Over time, the salience of global tax governance increases fivefold. Finally, the curve depicting the overall trend in the data points to the early and mid-1990s as a crucial period for the politicization process. During this time period, salience grows strongly. The slope of both curves is steeper than during the 1980s and 2000s.

More specifically, the 1980s are characterized by a lack of salience. The percentage of pertinent articles fluctuates around a value of 0.05 and exceeds 0.1 only in 1988 and 1989. This picture starts to change during the late 1990s and continues to do so during the following years. After a prolonged period of media disinterest, salience accelerates rapidly to much higher levels during a comparably short period of three years (1996–1998). During this period the percentage of articles reaches the level of 0.3 percent in 1998, which is almost 10 times as much as during the 1980s. Subsequently, salience does not fall below the threshold of 0.1 percent for the rest of the analyzed time period. Instead, newspaper coverage continues to grow. It reaches absolute peaks close to 0.3 percent in 1998 and 2009. This third period between 1999 and 2011, during which the dataset covers all selected newspapers, is not marked by a significant increase of newspaper articles on global tax governance. Rather, the first decade of the new millennium is characterized by a stabilization or even slight decrease of salience. This trajectory shifts again with the beginning of the Great Recession. During this final period, salience grows again to the second peak in 2009 before it returns to lower levels similar to the beginning of the decade in 2010 and 2011. While the 1990s are characterized by a strong growth of salience, the first decade of the new millennium seems to experience a stabilization of the level of attention paid to global tax governance.

My salience indicator corrects for the changing number of articles in newspaper issues, which could bias the results due to missing data for the early observation period and potential changes of the news hole over time. Nonetheless, one could argue that the steep increase during the mid-1990s is driven by the higher number newspapers in the dataset. The 1980s are represented by the *IT* and the German *FAZ*. The Swiss *NZZ* and German *SZ* enter the picture in 1994 and 1995, respectively. The Swiss *TA* and the *II* are present since 2000 and 2003, respectively. To probe this objection, I calculate the percentage of articles on global tax governance for the two newspapers for which I have data for the entire period of analysis (*FAZ*, *IT*). The highly significant correlation between the results for both sets of newspapers ($r = 0.93$, $n = 31$, $p < 0.0001$) demonstrates that the observed changes over time are not driven by the addition of further newspapers. Rather, we observe a genuine trend of increasing salience of global tax governance in the news media.

These developments over time suggest that public debate on global tax governance is subject to non-linear causal effects. The trajectory of salience seems to point to a ratchet-like effect, in which a long period of low salience is followed by a crucial period of sharply increasing salience to much higher levels, which subsequently are not or only rarely undercut.[4] Similar to a ratchet, the politicization of global tax governance seems to permit higher levels of salience but inhibits the relapse to the low salience of the 1980s. Once on the media agenda, global tax governance seems to be there to stay and does not go away again easily. This suggests that the late 1990s are of special interest for the subsequent causal analysis. This period seems to form a critical juncture for the politicization of global tax governance (on the importance of critical junctures for the timing and frequency of contentious politics see Imig and Tarrow, 2000: 85; McAdam and Sewell, 2001: 101). During these years, something seems to have changed the salience of global tax governance profoundly. Accordingly, it will be interesting to see whether this ratchet-like trajectory can also be observed for the remaining components of politicization.

Overall, we see that global tax governance has become a relatively salient topic in the analyzed news media. This was clearly not the case during the early 1980s. Today, citizens are more often and more prominently confronted with issues of global tax governance. They are thus more likely to be interested in global tax governance and to be better informed about what is at stake, who is responsible, and who should be held accountable. The question of whether global tax governance is indeed politicized, can however only be answered in the light of the two remaining operationalizing components of the politicization concept – controversy and plurality.

Controversy over global tax governance

This section turns to the second component of politicization: the controversy over global tax governance in public debate. At the core of this component is the question whether media coverage of global tax governance is of a descriptive and factual nature or whether it is borne by prolonged public disagreement, evaluations, the exchange of controversial arguments, and the polarization of public opinion (Kriesi et al., 2012: 57). Such controversy emerges when actors mobilize conflicting views over global tax governance that resonate in the public sphere (Statham and Trenz, 2013b: 12). Similar to salience, the controversy of public debates about global tax governance is a necessary component of politicization. On one hand, only if citizens are or become aware of conflicting positions and preferences on how global tax governance should be handled are they likely to become more partisan and more involved in the politics of global tax governance. If, on the other hand, global tax governance is depicted as uncontroversial, apolitical, and without alternative, large-scale public mobilization and fundamental transformations of global tax governance are rather unlikely. In other words, the public must not only perceive a difference in the salience of an issue, but it must also care about this difference. When both conditions are met political conflict grows and is likely to spur potentially fundamental transformations of political processes (Carmines and Stimson, 1986: 903; Norris, 2000: 183).

The literature on news routines claims that media producers use various strategies to sell their products and shape public debate (Bennett, 2016) because news production is first and foremost a business, which seeks to attract customers (Hamilton, 2004). One of the most important of these strategies is to cover issues through a lens of conflict (Norris, 2000: Ch. 1; Soroka, 2014). This implies that, compared to other public arenas, the mass media are a most likely case for the analysis of the controversy of public debate about global tax governance. If controversy does not increase in this arena it is fairly unlikely that other public arenas are characterized by controversial debates.

My controversy indicator builds on public communication research. In this field, a common way to operationalize controversial media coverage – often labeled as the valence or the affective tone of newspaper articles (Norris, 2000: 196; Sheafer, 2007) – is to count and subtract the number of supportive and critical positions (Soroka, 2006; Scheufele et al., 2011; Fowler et al., 2012). The resulting value helps to classify individual newspaper articles or complete debates as being positive, negative, or neutral. In terms of the coding unit, this perspective implies a move from the level of newspaper articles to paragraphs, quasi-sentences (Klingemann et al., 2006), core-sentences (Kriesi et al., 2012: 41), claims (Koopmans and Statham, 1999), or other sequences of text below the level of complete articles. The present analysis follows this approach and analyzes individual statements, that is both claims and evaluations.

My indicator of controversy is, however, not so much interested in the overall positive or negative tone of the debate. Rather, I am interested in the overall level of controversy. Therefore, I deviate from these approaches in two ways: first, I do not look at evaluative statements only, such as Mary Harney's (former Deputy Head of the Irish Government) fundamental critique of an EU tax initiative: "I do not believe that it is appropriate that the EU should tell nations what taxes to have" (*IT*, 17 May 2001). I also take into account political claims or demands that ask for changes in the field of global tax governance. Although the evaluative tone of these claims, like Tony Blair's plea that "strong rules to govern tax and spending in the EU will have to be created" (*II*, 14 November 2011), is difficult to classify, these statements constitute an important aspect of controversy which is often overlooked in communication studies. Political decisions and public controversy are not solely based on conflicting evaluations of the status quo but are also shaped by the competition between different policy solutions and demands (Kingdon, 1984). Therefore, the controversy over different demands for specific global tax policies or institutional changes is an integral aspect of controversy. Second, I count the number of evaluative statements with both positive and negative tone. While other approaches consider debates which contain similar numbers of positive and negative propositions as neutral, I claim that such debates are not neutral at all but marked by significant controversy.

Overall, my measure of the controversy over global tax governance in public debates measures the percentage share of articles, which are characterized by controversial communication. Articles are classified as controversial if a minimum threshold of two affective statements on global tax governance is reached. This threshold builds on the argument that there can only be a controversy if there is a minimum of two conflicting arguments (De Wilde, 2011: 567).

In total, the dataset contains 793 affective statements (361 claims and 432 evaluations) spread over 697 newspaper articles. While some of these articles are completely descriptive, others yield a high number of affective statements. Figure 3.2 depicts the controversy over global tax governance over time and a smoothed curve, describing the overall trend in the data.

Two observations are particularly important. First, similar to salience, controversy increases over time. The share of controversial articles increases from very low levels in the 1980s to around one-fourth or even one-third of all articles during the 2000s. With the exception of 1985, 1988, and 1989, public debate on global tax governance is characterized by neutrality and descriptive news coverage during the first decade of the observation period.

Second, similar to salience, the level of controversy begins to grow substantively during the late 1990s. As the curve in Figure 3.2 indicates, this growth is stronger than during the 1980s and 2000s. After a period of low controversy, controversy grows strongly during the late 1990s. This critical juncture is followed by a period of stabilization during the 2000s. Although controversy still fluctuated during this third period, its level does not longer drop to the considerably lower numbers of the 1980s and early 1990s. However, the ratchet-like effect is less pronounced than for the salience of global tax governance. Although controversy intensifies most strongly during the 1990s, the difference between this period and the remainder of the sample is less strong compared to salience. The smoothed

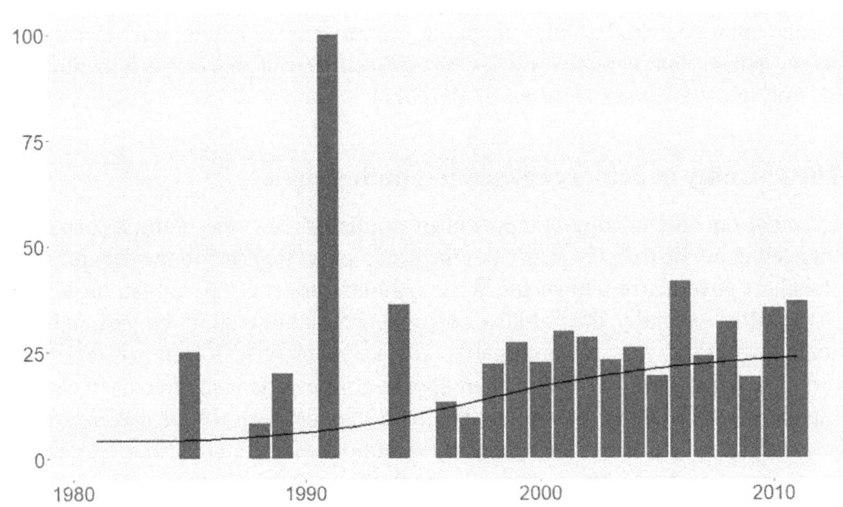

Figure 3.2 Controversy over global tax governance, 1981–2011

curve rather resembles a straight line. This points to a more linear growth of controversy.

This diagnosis is underlined by a view to the absolute numbers of newspaper articles that underpin this analysis. In particular, the high peak for 1991 should not be overestimated because it results from a single – though controversial – article. In 1991, the German *FAZ* featured one article with three affective statements that discuss a proposal by the European Commission to increase the tax on mineral oil.

Overall, the data show that global tax governance has become a relatively more controversial topic in the analyzed news media. After a period of low controversy during the 1980s, the debates of the 1990s are marked by increasing controversy. Subsequently, the debate stabilizes and does not fall back to the earlier low levels of controversy. Hence the politicization criterion of increasing controversy over time is satisfied. As regards the conjecture that the period of the mid-1990s is a critical juncture for the politicization of global tax governance, it can be noted that the results on controversy are less conclusive than for salience. Although the 1990s again seem to be different from the other years, this difference is less pronounced and controversy seems to increase in a more linear way.

Substantially, this increase in controversy does not only point to the politicization of global tax governance. It also indicates a higher democratic quality of the debate. The emergence of public dissent over global tax governance transforms public debate "into the stuff of normal politics" – that is, contestation, criticism, and competition (Statham and Trenz, 2013b: 80) – and brings it closer to the population. In this view, advocated, for instance, by Follesdal and Hix in the context of European integration (2006, see also Hix, 2008), public contestation and competition over global governance help to reconnect alienated citizens to the political process. Because citizens often lack detailed information about and first-hand experience with politics (Dellmuth, 2016; Lupia, 2016), providing them with clearly defined alternatives, and giving them the opportunity to scrutinize what is done in international politics via public controversy, is an important element of democratizing international politics (for a discussion of this effect in context of EU voting behavior see De Vries et al., 2011).

The plurality of actors engaged in public debate

The final operationalizing component of politicization – the plurality of actors engaged in public debate – describes the group of participants in the debate about global tax governance (Down and Wilson, 2008; Zürn et al., 2012; Van Ingelgom, 2014). Most generally, the plurality component assumes that, in the past, international institutions were the prerogative of state executives, bureaucrats, and lawyers (De Wilde et al., 2016: 7). International politics was made in closed circles, outside the spotlight of public scrutiny, and the vast majority of non-executive actors did not care about international institutions (for the context of global tax governance see, for instance, Radaelli, 1999; Rixen, 2008). Politicization research thus expects a "*widening of the audience or clientele* interested and active" (Schmitter, 1969: 166, italics as in the original) in the debate about global tax governance. Because the issue becomes more salient and controversial, a growing number of non-executive actors – including individual citizens, civil society organizations, political parties, and lobby groups – should begin to participate in public debates about global tax governance (Rixen and Zangl, 2012; Hutter and Grande, 2014). In other words, we should observe "that a variety of opinions, actors, and expressed positions are publicly visible, relative to those of government and executive actors" (Statham and Trenz, 2013b: 78). As Jürgen Habermas (2004: 28) pointed out in the context of European integration, the formation of public opinion on international politics and thus its politicization depends on this broad input of civil society and other non-executive actors. This group is often assumed to take the role of agents of change, who function as opinion leaders in the early stages of politicization processes (De Vries et al., 2011: 19; Tallberg et al., 2013).

Although plurality is an important component of politicization, I argue that it is subordinate to the first two components as it merely helps to specify the politicization process. If both the salience and the controversy criterion are fulfilled, it does not make a crucial difference for the politicization concept whether a debate is borne by a broad or narrow group of speakers because the issue can still be considered to be controversial and high on the political agenda. As Mancur Olson (1965), Elmer Schattschneider (1960), and others (for a recent application of collective action theory see, for instance, Lehman Schlozman et al., 2012) have argued forcefully, small and highly organized interest groups are often well equipped to advance their interests and to politicize issues. Hence the plurality component mainly contributes to a better understanding of the extent and pertinence of a politicization process. In this vein, the political clout of a politicization process mainly driven by artists, public intellectuals, and other representatives of the cultural sector is clearly weaker than of an encompassing debate mobilized by a broad variety of civil society organizations, interest groups, and political parties. If, by contrast, a debate is borne mainly by interest groups and political parties, its political clout is still likely to be high although it is less encompassing (Korpi, 1985; Kriesi, 2004; Haunss, 2013). All three situations are instances of politicization because they are substantively shaped by non-executive actors. However, their particular configurations have potentially different implications for the political process. The plurality dimension helps to understand who the relevant actors are and how influential the politicization process can become.

I examine the plurality of public debate on global tax governance based on the number of different speaker types expressing affective propositions on the global tax governance. The decision to focus on affective statements is based on the notion of controversy. Additional speakers do contribute to an increasing politicization only if they appear as critical or supportive actors instead of detached commentators or observers. My content analysis data provide detailed information on speakers. First, I categorize speakers with respect to their affiliation to societal groups, that is, journalists, holders of national political offices, national and international non-executive politicians, civil society speakers, economic actors, and other collective non-state actor groups. Second, my data go down to the individual names of every speaker in the dataset. To answer the question of whether the

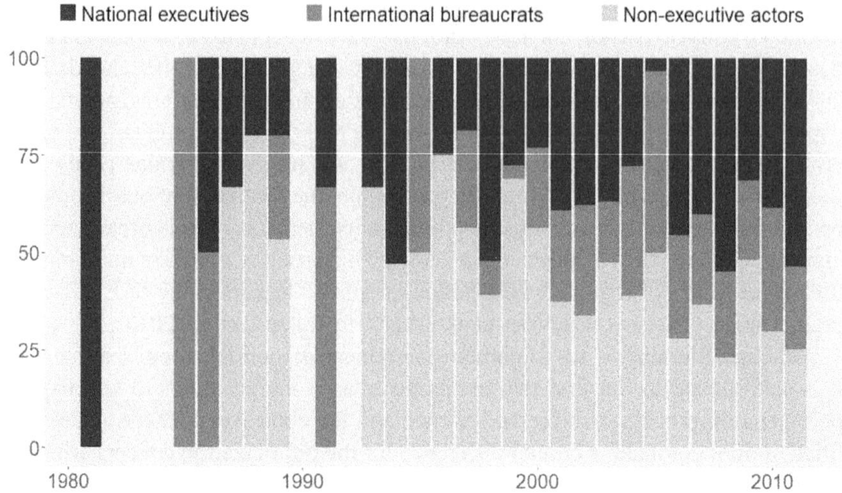

Figure 3.3 Plurality of actors, 1981–2011

share of executive speakers present in the debates over global tax governance has decreased over time, I focus mainly on the categorical information in the dataset and construct an indicator based on the relative share of different speaker groups over time. I differentiate between the three groups of national executives, international bureaucrats, and non-executive actors, including journalists, civil society, economic actors, and national party politicians.

As shown in the previous section, controversy is low during the 1980s. As a result, the number of affective statements underlying Figure 3.3 is low during this period and meaningfully interpretation of the figure is warranted only from the beginning of the 1990s onwards. The figure depicts the distribution of speakers groups over time. The group of national executives denotes speakers that held a national political office when the respective newspaper article was published and that were described as political executives in the article.

I make two core observations. First, there is no clear trend towards an increasing representation of non-executive actors. Rather, the participation of all three groups follows cyclical fluctuations over the entire observation period. Second, the analyzed public debates on global tax governance are dominated by non-executive speakers over the entire period of analysis. Taken together, international bureaucrats and non-executive national speakers account for the clear majority of affective statements. With the exception of 1990, 1992, 1994, 1998, 2008, and 2011, the cumulative share of these two speaker groups is invariably higher than the share of national executives. During the exceptional years, the predominance of national executives is limited and often lower than five percentage points. Overall, non-executive speakers and international bureaucrats contribute 61.5 percent

(488 statements) of all affective statements, whereas national executives account for the remaining 38.1 percent (314 statements).

Given that I compare three groups that differ significantly in size – with national executives representing only a small fraction of potential speakers in comparison to the group of non-executive speakers – it could be expected that non-executive speakers are represented in the debate on global tax governance. However, taking into account the strong dominance of executives in the media due to their high newsworthiness and prominence (Shehata, 2010), these findings have two crucial implications. First, national executives are far from dominating the analyzed debates about global tax governance. Contrary to what Claudio Radaelli (1999) or Thomas Rixen (2008) have argued, public debate on global tax governance is by no means exclusively led by national governments. Hence, the debates are sufficiently plural to be labeled politicized. Second, it is not appropriate to speak of a process of politicization because the share of non-executive speakers does not increase in comparison to governmental executives. Rather, non-executive speakers are dominant in most of the analyzed years; during 1994, 1998, 2008, and 2011, the share of executive speakers is only marginally higher than the share of non-executive speakers. The increasing salience and controversy of public debates about global tax governance are thus borne by a plurality of speakers that come from all spheres of the political landscape.

Furthermore, it is noteworthy that civil society actors account for the largest overall share of affective statements (see Table 3.3). With 38.7 percent (306 statements) of all affective statements, this group has slightly more prominent access to public debates on global tax governance than national executives who contribute a share of 38.5 percent (305 statements). Setting aside the first years of the analysis (which do not yield meaningful data) and focusing on the period after 1989, civil society representatives are the most frequent speakers in 12 out of 22 years, whereas national executives dominate in nine years. International bureaucrats, who contribute an overall share of 22.8 percent of affective propositions, dominate the debate only in 1991.

Given the expectation of a pronounced dominance of national executives due to their favorable institutional and discursive opportunity structure (Tarrow, 1994: 85; Koopmans, 2007: 188), the strong presence of civil society actors is surprising and warrants a more detailed analysis of individual speakers. In total, the dataset counts 334 individual actors that contribute to the debate on global tax governance. In addition, 63.5 percent of them (212) feature with only one statement, while the most prominent speaker of the debate – the "European Commission" – is accountable for 5.3 percent (43 statements) of all affective statements. It is followed by the "German government" with 3.4 percent (27 statements) of all affective statements and "unnamed journalists" of the Swiss *NZZ* (2.5 percent; 20 statements). The number of individual speakers per year varies from zero in the early years of non-salience to 47 in 2008. The most prominent speaker in terms of annual presence is again the "European Commission", which is present in 14 of 31 years. The German and the British governments follow suit, with 11 and 10 years of presence in the debate, respectively.

Table 3.3 Plurality of actors

Speaker Group	*% of group*	*% of total*
National executives		38.5
Germany	8.6	3.4
Great Britain	5.6	2.1
France	4.3	1.6
Hans Eichel	3.6	1.4
Peer Steinbrück	3.6	1.4
International Politicians		22.8
European Commission	23.2	5.3
EU	9.4	2.1
László Kovacs	8.8	2.0
Frits Bolkestein	7.2	1.6
José Manuel Barroso	5.0	1.1
Civil Society, Interest Groups, Parties		38.7
NZZ	6.5	2.5
Andreas Oldag (*SZ*)	2.3	0.9
SZ	2.3	0.9
Günther Strunk (German Academic)	2.0	0.8
Peter Hort (*FAZ*)	2.0	0.8

n = 793

Table 3.3 informs about the share of individual speakers within the three groups of speakers. It displays the five most prominent individual speakers per group. Three observations stand out here: first, civil society speakers are clearly the most diverse group. The top five individual speakers account for merely 15.1 percent of all speakers in this group. This number is considerably higher for national executives (25.6 percent) and international bureaucrats (53.6 percent). Second, both national executives and civil society speakers are clearly dominated by German actors. In the first group, the German government and the two former German Ministers of Finance, Peer Steinbrück and Hans Eichel, dominate. In the group of civil society actors, journalists from the German newspapers *SZ* and *FAZ* are accompanied by the German academic Günther Strunk. While there are also journalists from the Swiss *NZZ* present in the group of civil society speakers, it is quite surprising that national executives from Ireland and Switzerland are not among the most prominent individual contributors to the debate. Finally, the group of international actors is clearly dominated by speakers from the EU. All top five speakers come from this institution.

Table 3.3 reveals that there is a simple reason why civil society actors are the most prominent speakers in the entire debate on global tax governance. Journalists account for 17.1 percent of all affective statements and 38.5 percent of all statements from civil society actors. They utilize their privileged position to place affective statements and to influence the debate. However, other types of speakers are also present in this group. This underlines the basic result of this section. The debate on global tax governance is sufficiently plural to be called politicized. This politicization of global tax governance has the potential to influence the policy-making process because the debate is borne by a variety of actors of which some can be considered to be influential political actors (most notably the European Commission).

Conclusion

This chapter presented my key indicators for the salience, controversy, and plurality of public debate about global tax governance. Building on data on these operationalizing components of the politicization concept, I address the fundamental question whether global tax governance has become politicized over the course of the past three decades. Although all indicators show minor particularities not perfectly in line with the concept, the overall results provide considerable evidence for the politicization of global tax governance (see Table 3.4 for an overview).

Most importantly, the results demonstrate that the public salience of global tax governance has increased significantly over time. This mounting media attention to global tax governance is the basis of the politicization process. If a debate is essentially not visible in the public arena, it cannot become politicized because it does not exist on the public agenda. The second component of politicization looks at the controversy of the debate. Although controversy does not increase as strongly as salience, the growing number of controversial articles shows that global tax governance becomes more contested over time. Finally, the data on the plurality of the debate on global tax governance corroborate the diagnosis of politicization. Non-executive actors dominate the discussions over the entire time period. Instead of becoming more important over time, speakers outside of national governments are important from the start. In association with executive speakers, they push global tax governance on the agenda.

In addition to this main message of the present chapter, the detailed analysis of all three components of politicization reveals a second important finding. The late 1990s seem to be crucial for the process because both the salience and the controversy of the debate grow during this period. During subsequent years, scores

Table 3.4 Politicization components, indicators, and results

Components	*Indicators*	*Results*
Salience	Share of articles on global tax governance relative to news hole	Strong increase Most pronounced during the late-1990s
Controversy	Share of controversial articles relative to all pertinent articles	Medium increase Pronounced during the late-1990s
Plurality	Share of speaker groups	Plural share of speakers No clear trends

appear to stabilize rather than grow to even higher values. Both indicators seem to be shaped by a ratchet-like effect. After a period of low salience and controversy during the 1980s, the debates of the 1990s are marked by accelerating politicization. Subsequently, the debates stabilize and do not fall back to the earlier low levels. This trajectory could indicate that triggers for the politicization of global tax governance can be found during these years.

To illustrate these two core results more clearly, I provide a politicization index that integrates the results for all three components into one combined measure. The index builds on Christian Rauh's (2011: 67) approach, which uses z-score transformations to level the different scales of the three components and computes an additive measure to combine the results into one index. In this index, all three operationalizing components of the concept are (a) equally important for the overall state of politicization and can (b) be considered to be independent of each other at a single point in time (for a slightly different approach see Hutter and Grande, 2014). This implies that a combined index can be created by adding the results of all three components.

Figure 3.4 plots the index over time. It underlines the two main messages of this chapter. First, there is a clear politicization trend of global tax governance. Second, this development is most pronounced during the late 1990s when the index grows to constantly positive values. The peaks during the late 1980s and early 1990s should not be overestimated because they build on very low numbers of articles.

To be sure, this diagnosis is not a statement about the relative importance of global tax governance on the public agenda of the selected countries. I do not claim that global tax governance has become one of the most important issues on

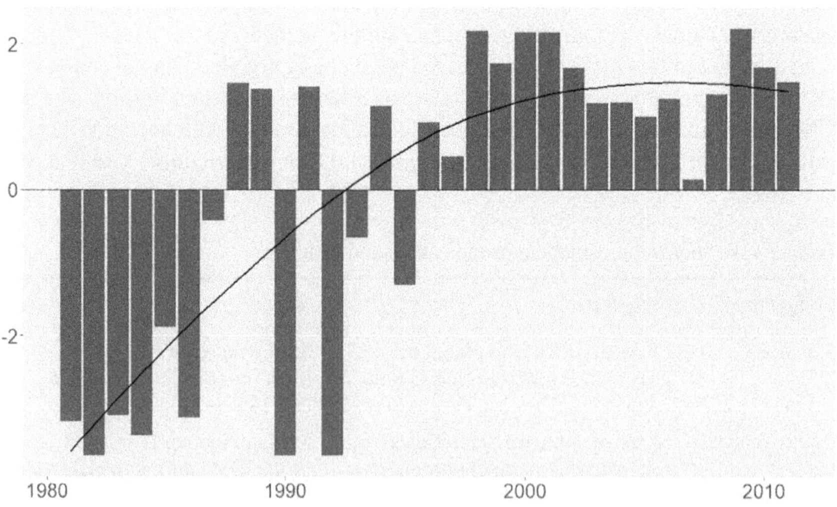

Figure 3.4 Politicization index, 1981–2011

the public agenda. There are obviously other issues that are more salient and more controversial than global tax governance. My argument is simply that there has been a remarkable shift in salience and controversy over the course of the past decades, which suggests that global tax governance is subject to a politicization process. The precise impact of this politicization depends strongly on the question of which international institutions are politicized and whether politicization varies across countries. These questions are addressed in Chapters 4 and 5.

Notes

1 In this context some argue that a focus on German-language newspapers for Switzerland fails to account for political cleavages along the so-called Röstigraben. However, respective research on public opinion and voting behavior shows that differences between language groups are marginal (Dardanelli, 2007: 28).
2 The curve is created with the help of locally weighted scatterplot smoothing (LOESS function), a mathematical way to fit a curve to a dataset (Cleveland and Devlin, 1988).
3 Note that the dataset utilizes constructed weeks instead of a census analysis. The displayed data do therefore not indicate the absolute numbers of all articles of a year but an approximation of the ratio of pertinent articles to all published articles.
4 In the context of welfare state research, the concept of the policy-ratchet effect describes the impact of early policy initiatives on long-term political processes (Pierson, 1996; Huber and Stephens, 2001).

References

Baglioni, S. and Hurrelmann, A. 2016. The Eurozone Crisis and Citizen Engagement in EU Affairs. *West European Politics*, 39, 104–124.
Baumgarnter, F. and Jones, B. 1993. *Agendas and Instability in American Politics*, Chicago: Chicago University Press.
Bennett, L. W. 2016. *News: The Politics of Illusion*, 10th ed., Chicago: University of Chicago Press.
Carmines, E. G. and Stimson, J. A. 1986. On the Structure and Sequence of Issue Evolution. *American Political Science Review*, 80, 901–920.
Cleveland, W. S. and Devlin, S. J. 1988. Locally Weighted Regression: An Approach to Regression Analysis by Local Fitting. *Journal of the American Statistical Association*, 83, 596–610.
Cohen, B. C. 1963. *The Press and Foreign Policy*, Princeton: Princeton University Press.
Dardanelli, P. 2007. Federalism: Institutional Adaptation and Symbolic Constraints. *In:* Church, C. (ed.) *Switzerland and the European Union*, Oxon: Routledge.
Dearing, J. W. and Rogers, E. M. 1996. *Agenda-Setting: Communication Concepts 6*, London: Sage.
Dellmuth, L. M. 2016. The Knowledge Gap in World Politics: Assessing the Sources of Citizen Awareness of the United Nations Security Council. *Review of International Studies*, 42, 673–700.
Dellmuth, L. M. and Tallberg, J. 2015. The Social Legitimacy of International Organizations: Interest Representation, Institutional Performance, and Confidence Extrapolation in the United Nations. *Review of International Studies*, 41, 451–475.
De Vries, C., Van Der Burg, W., Van Egmond, M. H. and Van Der Eijk, C. 2011. Individual and Contextual Variation in EU Issue Voting: The Role of Political Communication. *Electoral Studies*, 30, 16–28.

De Wilde, P. 2011. No Polity for Old Politics? A Framework for Analyzing the Politicization of Europen Integration. *Journal of European Integration*, 33, 559–575.

De Wilde, P. 2012. Politicisation of the EU Budget: Concflict and the Constraining Dissensus. *West European Politics*, 35, 1075–1094.

De Wilde, P., Leupold, A. and Schmidtke, H. 2016. Introduction: The Differentiated Politicisation of European Governance. *West European Politics*, 39, 3–22.

Down, I. and Wilson, C. 2008. From "Permissive Consensus" to "Constraining Dissensus": A Polarizing Union? *Acta Politica*, 43, 26–49.

Druckman, J. N. 2005. Media Matter: How Newspapers and Television News Cover Campaigns and Influence Voters. *Political Communication*, 22, 463–481.

Follesdal, A. and Hix, S. 2006. Why There Is a Democratic Deficit in the EU: A Response to Majone and Moravcsik. *Journal of Common Market Studies*, 44, 533–562.

Fowler, E. F., Gollust, S. E., Dempsey, A. F., Lantz, P. M. and Ubel, P. A. 2012. Issue Emergence, Evolution of Controversy, and Implications for Competitive Framing: The Case of the HPV Vaccine. *International Journal of Press/Politics*, 17, 169–189.

Gerhards, J., Offerhaus, A. and Roose, J. 2007. Die öffentliche Zuschreibung von Verantwortung. *Kölner Zeitschrift für Soziologie und Sozialpsychologie*, 59, 105–124.

Habermas, J. 2004. Why Europe Needs a Constitution. *In:* Eriksen, E. O., Fossum, J. E. and Menedez, A. J. (eds.) *Developing a Constitution for Europe*, London: Routledge.

Habermas, J. 2008. *Ach Europa: Kleine Politische Schriften XI*, Frankfurt a.M.: Suhrkamp.

Hallin, D. and Mancini, P. 2004. *Comparing Media Systems: Three Models of Media and Politics*, Cambridge: Cambridge University Press.

Hamilton, J. 2004. *All the News That's Fit to Sell: How the Market Transforms Information Into News*, Princeton: Princeton University Press.

Haunss, S. 2013. *Conflicts in the Knowledge Society: The Contentious Politics of Intellectual Property*, Cambridge: Cambridge University Press.

Hix, S. 2008. *What's Wrong with the European Union and How to Fix It*, Cambridge, MA: Polity Press.

Hobolt, S. B. and Spoon, J.-J. 2012. Motivating the European Voter: Parties, Issues, and Campaigns in European Parliament Elections. *European Journal of Political Research*, 51, 701–727.

Huber, E. and Stephens, J. D. 2001. *Development and Crisis of the Welfare State*, Chicago: Chicago University Press.

Hutter, S. and Grande, E. 2014. Politicizing Europe in the National Electoral Arena: A Comparative Analysis of Five West European Countries: 1970–2010. *Journal of Common Market Studies*, 52, 1002–1018.

Hutter, S. and Kerscher, A. 2014. Politicizing Europe in Hard Times: Conflicts Over Europe in France in a Long-Term Perspective: 1974–2012. *Journal of European Integration*, 36, 267–282.

Imig, D. and Tarrow, S. 2000. Political Contention in a Europeanising Polity. *West European Politics*, 23, 73–93.

Kingdon, J. 1984. *Agendas, Alternatives, and Public Policies*, Boston: Little, Brown.

Kiousis, S. 2006. Explicating Media Salience: A Factor Analysis of New York Times Issue Coverage During the 2000 U.S. Presidential Election. *Journal of Communication*, 54, 71–87.

Klingemann, H.-D., Volkens, A., Budge, I. and McDonald, M. D. 2006. *Mapping Policy Preferences II: Estimates for Parties, Electors, and Governments in Eastern Europe, European Union, and OECD 1990–2003*, Oxford: Oxford University Press.

Koopmans, R. 2007. Who Inhabits the European Public Sphere? Winners and Losers, Supporters and Opponents in Europeanised Political Debates. *European Journal of Political Research*, 46, 183–210.

Koopmans, R. and Statham, P. 1999. Political Claims Analysis: Integrating Protest Event and Political Discourse Approaches. *Mobilization: An International Quarterly*, 4, 203–221.

Koopmans, R. and Statham, P. (eds.) 2010a. *The Making of a European Public Sphere*, Cambridge: Cambridge University Press.

Koopmans, R. and Statham, P. 2010b. Theoretical Framework, Research Design, and Methods. *In:* Koopmans, R. and Statham, P. (eds.) *The Making of a European Public Sphere*, Cambridge: Cambridge University Press.

Korpi, W. 1985. Power Resources Approach vs. Action and Conflict: On Causal and Intentional Explanations in the Study of Power. *Sociological Theory*, 3, 31–45.

Kriesi, H. 2004. Political Context and Opportunity. *In:* Snow, D. A., Soule, S. A. and Kriesi, H. (eds.) *The Blackwell Companion to Social Movements*, Malden: Blackwell.

Kriesi, H., Grande, E., Dolezal, M., Helbling, M., Höglinger, D., Hutter, S. and Wüest, B. 2012. *Political Conflict in Western Europe*, Cambridge: Cambridge University Press.

Kriesi, H., Grande, E., Lachat, R., Dolezal, M., Bornschier, S. and Frey, T. 2008. *West European Politics in the Age of Globalization*, Cambridge: Cambridge University Press.

Lacy, S., Riffe, D., Stoddard, S., Martin, H. and Chang, K.-K. 2001. Sample Size for Newspaper Analysis in Multi-Year Studies. *Journalism and Mass Communication Quarterly*, 78, 836–845.

Lehman Schlozman, K., Verba, S. and Brady, H. E. 2012. *The Unheavenly Chorus: Unequal Political Voice and the Broken Promise of American Democracy*, Princeton: Princeton University Press.

Lupia, A. 2016. *Uniformed: Why People Know So Little About Politics and What We Can Do About It*, Oxford: Oxford University Press.

McAdam, D. and Sewell, W. H. 2001. Temporality in the Study of Social Movements and Revolutions. *In:* Aminzade, R. R., Goldstone, J. A., McAdam, D., Perry, E., Sewell, W. H., Tarrow, S. and Tilley, J. (eds.) *Silence and Voice in the Study of Contentious Politics*, Cambridge: Cambridge University Press.

McCombs, M. 2004. *Setting the Agenda: The Mass Media and Public Opinion*, Cambridge, MA: Polity Press.

Norris, P. 2000. *A Virtuous Circle: Political Communications in Postindustrial Societies*, Cambridge: Cambridge University Press.

Olson, M. 1965. *The Logic of Collective Action: Public Goods and the Theory of Groups*, Cambridge, MA: Harvard University Press.

Oppermann, K. and Vierig, H. (eds.) 2011. *Issue Salience in International Politics*, Oxon: Routledge.

Pierson, P. 1996. The New Politics of the Welfare State. *World Politics*, 48, 143–179.

Radaelli, C. M. 1999. Harmful Tax Competition in the EU: Policy Narratives and Advocacy Coalitions. *Journal of Common Market Studies*, 37, 661–682.

Rauh, C. 2011. *Politicisation, Issue Salience, and Consumer Policies of the European Commission: Does Public Awareness and Contestation of Supranational Matters Increase the Responsiveness of Europe's Central Agenda-Setter*? Berlin: Departement of Political Sciences, Freie Universität Berlin.

Riffe, D., Kim, S. and Sobel, M. R. 2018. News Borrowing Revisited: A 50-Year Perspective. *Journalism and Mass Communication Quarterly*, 95, 909–929.

Risse, T. 2010. *A Community of Europeans? Transnational Identities and Public Spheres*, Ithaca: Cornell University Press.

Rixen, T. 2008. *The Political Economy of International Tax Governance*, Basingstoke: Palgrave Macmillan.

Rixen, T. and Zangl, B. 2012. Legitimation durch Konstitutionalisierung oder durch Souveränität. *Leviathan*, 40, 118–134.

Schattschneider, E. 1960. *The Semisovereign People: A Realist's View of Democracy in America*, New York: Harcourt College Publications.

Scheufele, B., Haas, A. and Brosius, H.-B. 2011. Mirror or Molder? A Study of Media Coverage, Stock Prices, and Trading Volumes in Germany. *Journal of Communication*, 61, 48–70.

Schlipphak, B. 2015. Measuring Attitudes Towards Regional Organizations Outside Europe. *Review of International Organizations*, 10, 351–375.

Schmidtke, H. and Nullmeier, F. 2011. Political Valuation Analysis and the Legitimacy of International Organizations. *German Policy Studies*, 7, 117–153.

Schmitter, P. 1969. Three Neo-Functional Hypotheses about International Integration. *International Organization*, 23, 161–66.

Schneider, S., Hurrelmann, A., Krell-Laluhová, Z., Nullmeier, F. and Wiesner, A. 2010. *Democracy's Deep Roots*, Basingstoke: Palgrave Macmillan.

Schneider, S., Nullmeier, F. and Hurrelmann, A. 2007. Exploring the Communicative Dimension of Legitimacy: Text Analytical Approaches. *In:* Hurrelmann, A., Schneider, S. and Steffek, J. (eds.) *Legitimacy in an Age of Global Politics*, Basingstoke: Palgrave Macmillan.

Sevenans, J. 2018. One Concept, Many Interpretations: The Media's Causal Roles in Political Agenda-setting Processes. *European Political Science Review*, 10, 245–265.

Sheafer, T. 2007. How to Evaluate It: The Role of Story-Evaluative Tone in Agenda Setting and Priming. *Journal of Communication*, 57, 21–39.

Shehata, A. 2010. Marking Journalistic Independence: Official Dominance and the Rule of Product Substitution in Swedish Press Coverage. *European Journal of Communication*, 25, 123–137.

Soroka, S. N. 2006. Good News and Bad News: Asymmetric Responses to Economic Information. *Journal of Politics*, 68, 372–385.

Soroka, S. N. 2014. *Negativity Bias in Democratic Politics: Causes and Consequences*, Cambridge: Cambridge University Press.

Statham, P. and Trenz, H.-J. 2013a. How European Union Politicization Can Emerge Through Contestation: The Constitution Case. *Journal of Common Market Studies*, 51, 965–980.

Statham, P. and Trenz, H.-J. 2013b. *The Politicization of Europe: Contesting the Constitution in the Mass Media*, London: Routledge.

Tallberg, J., Sommerer, T., Squatrito, T. and Jönsson, C. 2013. *The Opening Up of International Organizations*, Cambridge: Cambridge University Press.

Tarrow, S. G. 1994. *Power in Movement: Collective Action, Social Movements and Politics*, Cambridge: Cambridge University Press.

Tarrow, S. G. 2005. *The New Transnational Activism*, Cambridge: Cambridge University Press.

Van Ingelgom, V. 2014. *Integrating Indifference: A Comparative, Qualitative and Quantitative Approach to the Legitimacy of European Integration*, Colchester: ECPR Press.

Walgrave, S., Soroka, S. and Nuytemans, M. 2008. The Mass Media's Political Agenda-Setting Power. *Comparative Political Studies*, 41, 814–836.

Wessler, H., Peters, B., Brüggemann, M., Kleinen-Von-Königslöw, K. and Sifft, S. 2008. *Transnationalization of Public Spheres*, Basingstoke: Palgrave Macmillan.

Wlezien, C. 2005. On the Salience of Political Issues: The Problem With the Most Important Problem. *Electoral Studies*, 24, 555–579.

Zürn, M., Binder, M. and Ecker-Erhardt, M. 2012. International Authority and Its Politicization. *International Theory*, 4, 69–106.

4 How international authority and policy output drive politicization

This chapter turns to the question of why global tax governance has become politicized in Western societies. I probe the explanatory value of the institutionalist perspective, which postulates that growing international authority drives the politicization of international institutions.

The institutionalist perspective highlights three main observable implications to be examined in this chapter (see Chapter 2 for details): first, the level of politicization should vary across institutions. The higher the political authority of an international institution, the stronger is its politicization.

Second, levels of politicization should vary with time. As international authority has been growing over the past decades, I expect the politicization of individual institutions to increase over time, or more precisely, to vary with the authority of the international institutions under scrutiny. Levels of politicization should grow in times of institutional change, increasing the political authority of the EU or the OECD. This expectation is not to be confused with a mechanistic understanding of the institutionalist perspective, which claims that politicization follows increasing authority. Rather, I expect different temporal sequences in which politicization, for instance, precedes authority growth or only occurs with a certain time lag.

Third, if growing international authority drives the politicization of international institutions, this should be reflected in particular patterns of politicization, that is, specific combinations of objects and criteria discussed in public debate. Here, the institutionalist approach proposes that increasing *levels* of political authority should spur public debates that focus mainly on institutional design, decision-making procedures, and their input qualities (legitimacy debates). In contrast, the growing *issue scope* of political authority and policy output should create a public debate that is mainly interested in the global tax policy output and the quality of these policies (problem-solving debates).

The chapter proceeds in four steps. First, the next section introduces the research design and the comparative historical focus of the case studies. Second, I discuss the concept of international authority. I argue that the formal political authority of international institutions has two principal components, the *level* of authority pooled in and delegated to international institutions and the *scope of issue* areas in which this authority is exercised. Furthermore, I propose that politicization is not only driven by this formal international authority but that the concrete policies that follow from it are also crucial to explain politicization. The section concludes by presenting the operationalization of these variables for the EU and the OECD. Third, I present the two in-depth comparative historical case studies that examine the causal link between the politicization of EU and OECD tax governance and their authority. Both case studies are presented separately. They focus specifically on disentangling the complex interaction between the overall level and issue scope of both institutions' authority, their formal tax authority, and their tax policy output. As much of the literature is either silent on this complex interplay of different aspects of political authority or refers to formal authority and policy output in an interchangeable manner (see, for instance, Zürn et al., 2012: 94; Rixen and Zangl, 2013: 6), this focus helps to develop more precise explanations of politicization. The chapter specifies how different aspects of authority feed into the politicization of international institutions. To this end, the case studies integrate quantitative indicators with a qualitative reading of the public debates. The final section concludes by comparing politicization processes across both institutions.

The case study design

Starting from the integrated theory of politicization laid out in Chapter 2, the empirical analysis explores how exactly these factors play out in the politicization of global tax governance. More precisely, I first probe the plausibility of the theory and, second, aim to theorize the interaction effects between different aspects of international authority. Consequently, the empirical analysis is not limited to a purely deductive logic of theory-testing but provides room for inductive theory development. This nature of the endeavor and the need for systematic quantitative and qualitative data make a comparative historical case study design a suitable compromise between an individual case study and the quantitative analysis of a wide array of international institutions (Mahoney and Rueschemeyer, 2003; Mahoney and Thelen, 2015).

The two case studies on the politicization of EU and OECD tax governance utilize cross- and within-case variance of the key variables highlighted by institutionalist explanations. In the first step, I hold organizational context constant to investigate how growing formal authority and tax policy output *within* the two institutions have shaped levels and patterns of politicization. To this end, I trace the historical processes that link growing international authority and levels and patterns of politicization over the time period 1981 to 2011. This in-depth analysis focuses on the micro-dynamics of politicization processes and is particularly well-suited for studying causal mechanisms.

My analysis of the politicization of 31 years of EU and OECD tax governance covers a large part of the institutional developments of both institutions. Although both the EU and the OECD were created almost two decades earlier, all major transformations of their scope and level of authority in general and in the area of taxation more specifically took place during the selected time period. Furthermore, growing demand for global tax governance emerged only during the

1980s. Although the League of Nations had already considered the implications of international trade for taxation during the 1920s, global tax governance became salient only with the onset of deep economic integration during the 1980s. Due to the erosion of barriers to the mobility of individuals, goods, and capital, issues of double taxation, tax competition, and tax arbitrage started to rise on the political agenda (Edwards and Keen, 1996; Swank, 2006; Genschel and Schwarz, 2011). Consequently, the case studies cover the complete time period relevant to the institutionalist explanation. This long-term historical analysis complements the existing literature, which focuses mainly on short periods of time (see, for instance, Ecker-Ehrhardt, 2012; Statham and Trenz, 2013).

In the second step, I compare the results of the individual case studies to gain additional analytical leverage. This final section focuses on differences and commonalities across the two cases. It helps to verify the results of the individual cases studies and to increase the generalizability of my findings. Since the EU and the OECD constitute different organizational contexts, comparison across these cases helps to separate organization-specific processes and the more general effects of growing international authority.

Measuring global tax authority and tax policy output

I refer to global tax authority as the "power to make collective decisions based on a recognized obligation to obey" (Hooghe et al., 2017: 3) in the issue area of global taxation. The literature on global governance has developed a broad array of concepts to describe the idea that the authority in global governance varies from complete anarchy to some form of order in which international institutions exercise authority. These concepts include legalization (Abbott et al., 2000), autonomy (Barnett and Finnemore, 2004), independence (Haftel and Thompson, 2006), institutionalization (Boehmer et al., 2004), centralization (Abbott and Snidal, 1998), control (Koremenos et al., 2001), delegation (Hawkins et al., 2006), and pooling (Moravcsik, 1998). Each of these concepts deals with the extent to which the behavior of states and private actors is constrained by international institutions. This chapter is rooted in this common understanding.

More specifically, I suggest that the formal legal authority of international institutions is a key driver of politicization. This type of authority is (a) institutionalized, that is, codified in recognized rules; and (b) circumscribed because the rules define who has authority over whom (Hooghe et al., 2017: 14). For international institutions, such rules are found in the constitutions, conventions, protocols, and rules of procedure. These formal treaties specify (a) the issue *scope* in which international institutions are granted authority and (b) the *level* of political authority delegated to international bureaucracies, parliaments, and judicial bodies, and the level of national decision-making authority pooled in joint international bodies.

The scope of authority captures the issue areas in which international institutions are supposed to operate. Are the respective institutions designed for policy specific tasks, do they operate more generally around an entire issue area, or are they even multi-purpose or general purpose institutions that address a variety of issue areas (Jacobson et al., 1986; Volgy et al., 2008; Hooghe and Marks, 2015)? As I have argued in Chapter 2, institutionalist explanations expect growing issue scope to trigger politicization processes and to shape public debates that focus on the performance of international institutions' policies (problem-solving debate).

The level of international authority describes how strongly international institutions constrain the sovereignty of nation-states to make binding decisions. Who sets the agenda, what are the decision-making rules, how and by whom are policies implemented, and is there a judicial review or dispute settlement mechanism (Boehmer et al., 2004; Lake, 2007; Blake and Payton, 2015; Hooghe et al., 2017)? Institutionalist explanations suggest that politicization grows with the level of formal authority states that have granted to international institutions, and their individual bodies (delegation) and the level of authority that states have transferred to collective member state bodies (pooling). A growth in the level of international authority should be accompanied by intensifying public debates about the procedures of this international decision-making (legitimacy debate).

These perspectives on scope and levels of international authority are fruitfully combined by European integration scholars (Donahue and Pollack, 2001; Börzel, 2005; Leuffen et al., 2013: Ch. 1). Their work shows that a more fine-grained picture can be produced by analyzing institutional procedures separately for different issue areas. I follow this design and operationalize the formal authority of the EU and the OECD on the basis of two indicators: first, politicization could be driven by overall formal authority, that is, the sum of the scope and level of authority in all policy areas in which an institution is engaged. Second, the specific formal authority in the field of taxation of both institutions is an equally plausible cause for their politicization.

I measure both the general and tax specific authority of the EU and the OECD with the help of Tanja Börzel's (2005: 221) "scope of authority" indicator, which ranks the level of authority pooled and delegated to international institutions in a given issue area according to the decision-making procedures codified in international treaties. The indicator distinguishes six levels that vary in terms of the participation of international bodies in the decision-making process (agenda-setting and decision-making), the decision-making rules among member states (unanimity or majority voting), and the application of judicial review (see Table 4.1).[1]

An issue area scores 0 if there is no international coordination at all. An issue area scores 1 if common decisions are taken by unanimity vote, while international bodies, such as the European Commission, are not involved. A score of 2 is given to issue areas if international bodies are involved to a limited extent. Scores of 3 and 4 capture procedures of joint decision-making in which international bodies can exercise legislative influence. A score of 3 is given in cases where these procedures result in a unanimity vote of the main decision-making body. A score of 4 describes joint decision-making with majority voting. The highest score of 5 describes fully internationalized issue areas. This mode of decision-making delegates full political authority in terms of agenda-setting, legislation, and judicial review to the international institution and excludes member states.

Table 4.1 Measuring the formal political authority of international institutions

Degree of centralization	*Score*
No international coordination	0
Intergovernmental coordination (main body decision by unanimity vote, no involvement of supranational bodies)	1
Intergovernmental cooperation (main body decision by unanimity vote, shared right of initiative of supranational bodies, consultation of supranational bodies during legislation, restricted judicial review)	2
Joint decision making I (main body decision by unanimity and consultation of supranational bodies, exclusive right of initiative of supranational body, full judicial review)	3
Joint decision making II (co-legislation of main body and other supranational bodies, decisions taken by majority, exclusive right of initiative of supranational bodies, full judicial review)	4
Supranational centralization (unilateral decision by supranational bodies, no involvement of state representatives, full judicial review)	5

Source: (Börzel, 2005: 221)

Scores on the overall authority of the EU result from adding up individual issue area scores provided by Dirk Leuffen and colleagues (2013: 20). As 18 issue areas are rated, the overall political authority score ranges from 0 for no political coordination to 90 for complete international authority. The score for EU tax authority focuses on the specific type of decision-making laid down in treaty provisions and ranges from 0 to 5 (for details on both indicators see Appendices 1 and 2).

The scores on OECD overall authority and tax authority build on my own analysis of the scope and level of formal authority enshrined in the individual mandates of the OECD's 41 main substantive committees and the attached 264 subsidiary bodies that were in place during the period of analysis. This slightly different approach results from the specific organizational structure of the OECD.

An exclusive focus on formal authority has two drawbacks. First, international institutions are often governed by informal practices and relationships (Stone, 2011; Kleine, 2013; Nelson, 2017). This could lead to a misinterpretation of the actual effect that international institutions have on policy output. On the one hand, international institutions might enjoy a high level and scope of formal authority without producing substantial policy output and thus leave almost all authority exclusively in the hands of nation-states. On the other hand, international institutions' formal authority might be rather limited, whereas their output of binding policies and therefore their constraints on national policy choices is considerable.

Second, as Fritz Scharpf (1988, 2006) has shown in the context of European integration, even limited formal authority and consensus decision-making can have strong constraining effects on national sovereignty. Because little political authority is pooled states are locked into earlier decisions. As decisions are taken by unanimity, earlier decisions persist because modifying them later takes considerable effort. Consequently, even low levels of formal authority may result in national sovereignty being lost in the "joint decision trap" (for a similar argument on EU tax policy-making see Genschel and Jachtenfuchs, 2011: 308).

I account for these issues by introducing a third indicator of global tax authority, the *tax policy output* of the EU and the OECD (Page and Dimitrakopoulos, 1997). This variable does not so much emphasize authority codified in formal rules but focuses on international institutions manifest policy output (Tallberg et al., 2016), that is, secondary law issued by international institutions. I expect growing tax policy output to increase levels of politicization and to create a pattern that is mainly interested in this policy output and the quality of policies (problem-solving debates).

I measure the tax policy output of the EU with the help of the dataset compiled by Philipp Genschel and Markus Jachtenfuchs (2011). These data provide time series information on the number of legally binding legislative acts issued by the EU for the time period of 1958 to 2007, including decisions, regulations, and directives (for similar approaches see Pollack, 1994; Franklin and Wlezien, 1997; Wessels, 1997; Pollack, 2000). Furthermore, the data detail which areas of taxation are targeted by this legislation (private income, corporate income, value-added tax, excise). I have extended this dataset to include all tax legislation up until 2011.[2]

The scope and frequency of OECD tax legislation are limited, and a large share of policies take the form of ongoing processes rather than the conventional format of legislation (Rixen, 2008). This specificity makes it difficult to quantify OECD tax policy output. Hence a more qualitative analysis of OECD tax governance is provided in the case study.

The politicization of EU tax governance

This section discusses the causal nexus of the political authority between the EU and the politicization of its tax governance. The structure of the case study follows the changing institutional design of the EU over time. The most relevant treaty revisions of European integration, the Treaty of Rome (1958), the Single European Act (SEA 1987), the Treaty of Maastricht (1993), the Treaty of Amsterdam (1999), the Treaty of Nice (2003), and the Treaty of Lisbon (2010) mark important watersheds in the history of the institution and thereby provide a clear way to divide the period of observation into comparable periods (Moravcsik, 1998: 2). These treaties are critical events that accentuate tensions induced by integration and are likely to draw public attention to European affairs (Wessels, 2004; Hutter and Grande, 2014: 4).[3]

The case study examines the quantitative indicators on the EU's formal authority, tax authority, and tax policy output. I trace how changes in these three types of EU authority have shaped levels and patterns of politicization. Before I delve into the in-depth process tracing, I present these quantitative data on EU authority and the operationalizing components of politicization.

Figure 4.1 plots the development of my three authority indicators over time. It shows how the EU's overall authority, tax authority, and tax policy output have

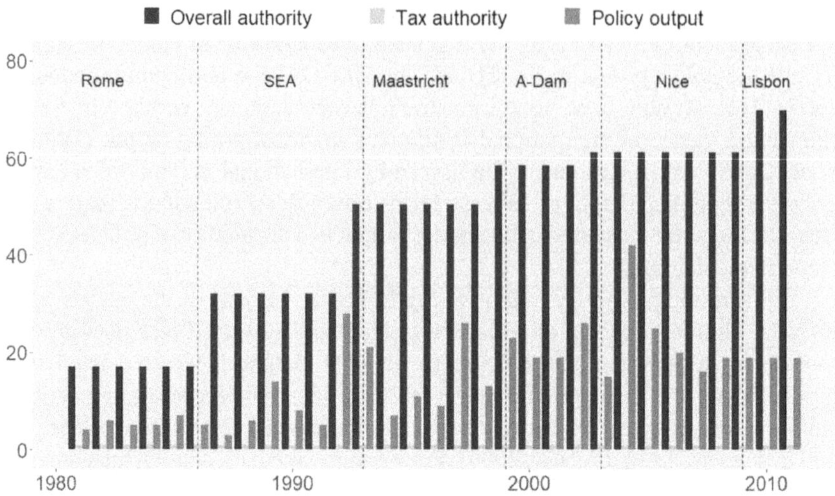

Figure 4.1 EU authority, 1981–2011

changed with time. The figure suggests that formal tax authority is unlikely to have a substantive causal effect. As I have shown in Chapter 3, the level of politicization of global tax governance has grown over time. Yet, the EU's formal tax authority remains on a constantly low level over the entire period of analysis (see also Genschel, 2002; Genschel and Jachtenfuchs, 2011).

A detailed reading of the respective paragraphs in EU treaties underlines this conclusion. The initial chapter on taxation in the Treaty of Rome (Art. 95–99) is exclusively concerned with guaranteeing the free movement of goods. The main purpose of the provisions is to prevent member states from contradicting the elimination of customs duties by discriminating against foreign products by means of taxation (Genschel, 2002: 45). The European Commission's competencies are limited to the narrow task of proposing ways to harmonize turnover taxes, excise duties, and other forms of indirect taxation which could potentially interfere with the functioning of the common market (Radaelli, 2008: 316). Decision-making in the European Council requires unanimity. The SEA leaves these statutes essentially untouched. Of the five articles on taxation in the Treaty of Rome, the SEA only introduces minor changes to one, namely Art. 99. These changes establish consultative rights for the EP in the European Commission's agenda-setting process. Furthermore, the SEA introduces some time pressure because it demands the harmonization of taxes, necessary to ensure the establishment and functioning of the internal market, to be accomplished by the end of 1992.

Similarly, the Treaty of Maastricht contains only minor changes. It alters Art. 99 and adds another consultation procedure to the legislative process by giving consultative rights not only to the EP but also to the European Economic and

Social Committee (EESC). The inclusion of this body, which aims to enable civil society organizations to express their views on EU legislation (EESC, 2011), does not, however, substantially increase the level of formal tax authority because it only gives a very limited say to civil society actors chosen by member states (Fitzgibbon, 2013: 6). The subsequent Treaties of Amsterdam, Nice, and Lisbon do not contain any substantial changes to the provisions on taxation. Hence formal tax authority appears to be inconsequential for the politicization of EU tax governance.

The data on the three dimensions of the politicization of EU tax governance substantiate this presumption. Figure 4.2 plots the three individual operationalizing components of politicization for EU tax governance (see Table 4.2 for descriptive statistics). The plots result from the dataset presented in Chapter 3. The data include 707 statements on EU tax governance published in 578 newspaper articles.

The top-left plot shows the salience of EU tax governance, that is, the percentage of newspaper articles discussing issues of EU tax governance relative to the overall number of newspaper articles published per year. The top-right plot displays the controversy dimension of politicization, which measures the share of newspaper articles that feature a minimum of two affective statements. The bottom-left plot shows the final component of politicization. The plurality of the debate measure considers the share of affective statements contributed by non-executive actors. Finally, the bottom-right plot integrates these data into the politicization index which adds up the z-scores for salience, controversy, and plurality.

I make use of the graphical information provided by figures 4.1 and 4.2 to analyze the causal link between politicization and authority. In addition, I turn to the descriptive statistics (see Table 4.2) for key periods of European integration

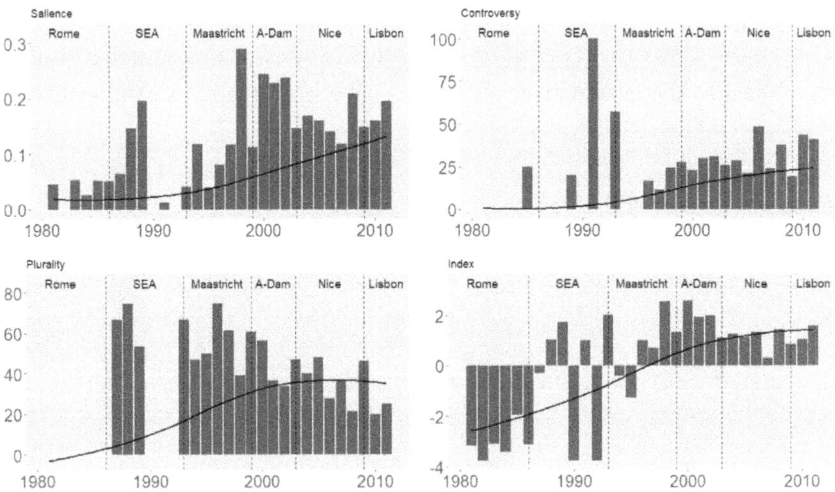

Figure 4.2 EU politicization indicators, 1981–2011

Table 4.2 Descriptive statistics for periods of EU tax governance, 1981–2011

Descriptive statistics	*Politicization indicators*			*Formal authority*			*Tax policy output*	
	Attention	*Controversy*	*Plurality*	*Scope*	*Level*	*Overall*	*Frequency*	*Scope*
1981–1986 (Treaty of Rome)[a]								
Min	0	0	0	9	1.9	17	4	0
Max	0.05	25	0	9	1.9	17	7	3
Mean	0.03	4.2	0	9	1.9	17	5	2
SD	0.01	9.3	0	0	0	0	0.94	0.69
1987–1992 (SEA)								
Min	0	0	0	14	2.3	32	3	2
Max	0.2	100	75	14	2.3	32	28	3
Mean	0.07	20	32.5	14	2.3	32	11	3
SD	0.08	36.5	33.1	0	0	0	8.48	0.5
1993–1998 (Treaty of Maastricht)								
Min	0.04	0	39.1	18	2.8	50.5	7	2
Max	0.29	57.1	75	18	2.8	50.5	26	3
Mean	0.11	18.3	56.6	18	2.8	50.5	15	3
SD	0.08	19.4	12.3	0	0	0	6.78	0.47
1999–2011 (Treaties of Amsterdam, Nice, Lisbon)								
Min	0.11	19.4	20	18	3.25	58.5	15	2
Max	0.24	48.3	60.9	18	3.9	69.8	42	5
Mean	0.17	30.9	38.3	18	3.4	61.3	22	4
SD	0.04	8.75	12.4	0	0.2	3.6	6.6	0.84

a While the Treaty of Rome was signed in 1957, my time series data on politicization only starts with the year 1981

to achieve a better understanding of periodical levels of politicization indicators. Subsequently, the quantitative results are qualified on the basis of a qualitative reading of public debates on EU tax governance.

Founding years (1957–1986)

In 1957, the Treaty of Rome established the EU.[4] At that time, the European integration project started in the area of "high politics" (Börzel, 2005: 219) to create peace and security among its six founding members.[5] The European Communities on Atomic Energy (EURATOM), Coal and Steel (ECSC), and Economic Cooperation (EEC) constituted the nucleus of today's most advanced regional integration arrangement. The initial authority of these institutions was marginal (see Figure 4.1). Although the Treaty of Rome spelled out a broad scope of issue areas in which the EU was supposed to work, there were only four issue areas in which the level of EU authority exceeded Börzel's (2005: 221) category of intergovernmental coordination: economic freedoms, competition and industry, energy and transport, and agriculture). The early European institutions were little more than forums for intergovernmental coordination (Pollack, 2000: 521); during the first 30 years of their existence, these institutions were mainly engaged in economic market making and did not exercise strong authority over member state governments, let alone their citizens (Moravcsik, 1998: Ch. 2). In sum, the EU's overall authority was low during its founding years. Although the Treaty of Rome subjected quite a few issue areas to the authority of European institutions, the level of this authority was marginal.

Similarly, tax policy output was low since the EU issued its first two tax directives on value-added taxes (VATs) in 1967. Figure 4.1 shows that the EU produced a relatively low but constant number of legislative acts from 1981 to 1986. With a minimum output of four legislative acts in 1981 and maximum of seven policies in 1985, the mean value of regulations for this period amounts to no more than five per year. In total, I note 32 legislative acts for this period.

The scope of EU tax legislation closely follows the formal mandate written down in the Treaty of Rome (Art. 95–99). With the exception of two directives on capital duty, legislation focuses exclusively on the regulation of VAT. In sum, both formal authority and tax policy output are relatively weak during this first period.

For this situation of weak formal authority and low policy output, the institutionalist perspective predicts low levels of politicization. In terms of politicization patterns, a relatively broad scope but low level of formal authority in combination with low policy output should be accompanied by a weak problem-solving debate. Newspaper articles and affective statements should be characterized by a focus on individual EU tax legislation instead of the EU as a polity. Legitimacy debates induced by the level of formal authority should be scarce and only add some scattered discussions that stretch beyond specific policies.

The inspection of politicization indicators (Figure 4.2) reveals that the level of politicization during the early years was indeed low (for descriptive statistics, see Table 4.2). From 1981 to 1986 issue attention experienced little variance and remained on a low level (mean value 0.02). These observations of little variance (SD 0.01) and a low level of attention are consistent with the institutionalist perspective.

This is also the case for controversy. Except for a minor peak in 1985, there was no controversial discussion of EU tax governance. Newspaper articles remained mostly on a descriptive level. There was just one article in 1985 that exceeded the minimum threshold of two affective statements to qualify as a controversial article. Furthermore, the small number of affective statements was mainly voiced by national executives or representatives of international institutions. As the plurality indicator indicates, non-executive speakers were silent during the early 1980s.

The comparably high level of controversy in 1985 (25 percent) is to some extent a statistical artifact. Since the number of articles found during the first few years is low, some scattered statements have a strong effect on the indicator. For 1985, the dataset includes just four articles on EU tax governance – all published in the German *FAZ*. Hence the 25 percent share of controversial articles is the result of one article, which featured one claim and one evaluation brought forward by a member of the EP – Dieter Rogalla – discussing the harmonization of VAT in European countries. The former member of the German Social Democrats (SPD) criticized the slow progress of harmonization and demanded swifter action (*FAZ*, 12 April 1985). Without neglecting this article, its impact on the controversy indicator should not be overestimated due to the low level of attention during the early 1980s.

That being said, it should be noted that the institutionalist predictions on politicization patterns (objects and criteria) can hardly be addressed on the basis of the low amount of affective statements (see Figure 4.3). As both objects and criteria are coded on the statement level, only three affective statements provide pertinent information for the period between 1981 and 1986. In 1981, one statement mentioned the Dutch government's demand for harmonized taxation of liquid petroleum gas (LPG) in the EU (*FAZ*, 1 April 1981). This claim was indeed on the policy level but it was not backed by an explicit justification. Rogalla's statements from 1985 also referred to policy issues, but in addition, Rogalla was also concerned with the politics dimension. This is demonstrated when he criticized

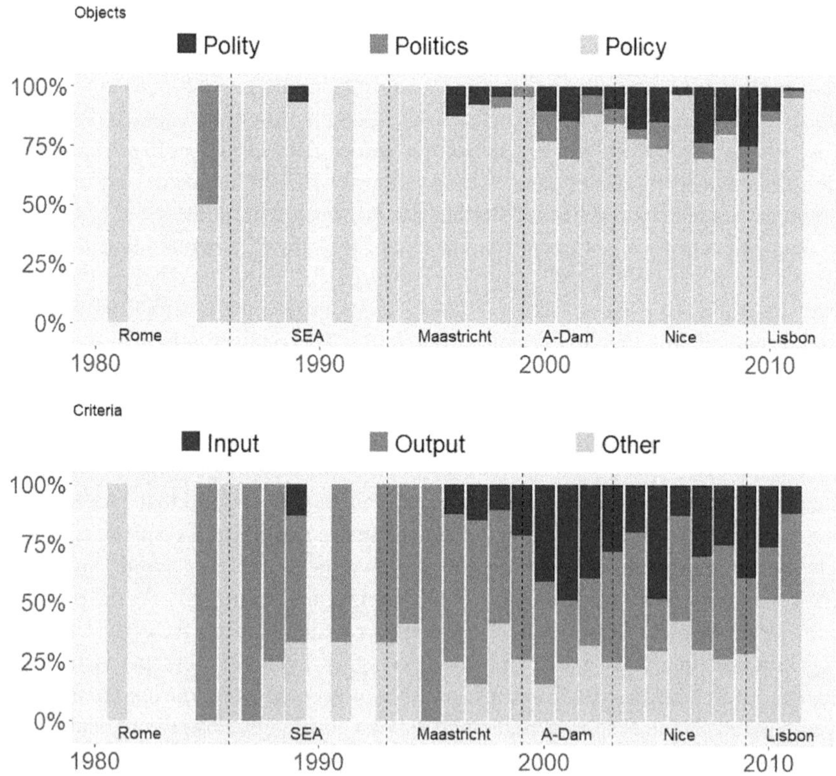

Figure 4.3 EU politicization patterns, 1981–2011

the slow mode of EU decision-making in VAT harmonization. Because he claimed that European institutions' reluctance to harmonize VAT does not contribute to the public good, both statements were backed by output criteria.

A qualitative reading of the textual material shows that both formal authority and tax policy output shaped these public debates. On the one hand, the debate focused mostly on VAT and excises – that is, the tax areas in which the EU was active during the period. On the other hand, most of the news coverage did not refer to specific legislation but to more general issues. Some of the topics, like the earlier mentioned discussion of the harmonization of LPG taxation or the demand for a harmonized taxation of corporate income voiced by the former Prime Minister of the German state Baden-Württemberg, Lothar Späth, (*FAZ*, 15 February 1986), were not at all related to specific policies but addressed completely different areas of taxation. Consequently, I suspect that both tax policy output and formal authority intertwined to trigger the fledgling debate on EU tax governance. Despite the limitations of the data, it can be noted that the results for the levels and changes of politicization indicators corroborate the institutionalist approach.

Strongly increasing authority with the SEA (1987–1992)

The SEA increased the EU's formal authority substantially. While European institutions held some, albeit limited, authority for policies aimed at dismantling national barriers to the free movements of goods and services and securing undistorted competition, in 1987 the SEA increased both the scope and level of EU's formal authority (see Appendix 1). In terms of scope, the first major revision of the Treaty of Rome marked an important watershed (Moravcsik, 1998: Ch. 2). The number of policies in which the EU was formally supposed to exercise authority increased from 10 to 14 under the SEA. The treaty extended EU authority to the issues of social and market-correcting regulation. Since national regulations in these fields often worked as non-tariff barriers to trade, the EU acquired authority in various relevant issue areas (Pollack, 1994) and started to develop into what Giandomenico Majone (1996) has called a "regulatory polity".

This trend was further intensified by an increase in the level of formal authority. Most importantly, the SEA introduced the cooperation procedure – that is, joint decision-making in Börzel's terms (2005: 221) – strengthening the role of the EP by giving it consultative rights in the decision-making process. These and other changes are reflected in the mounting overall score on formal authority (see Figure 4.1), which resulted mainly from high levels of authority over the newly communitarized issue areas. With the exception of the issue areas of security and defense, in which member states only began to coordinate their policies, the SEA equipped European institutions with significantly more formal authority in the other three new issue areas. In the fields of environment and consumer protection, occupational health and safety standards, and research and development, the SEA increased formal authority to the level of joint decision-making I or II (roman numerals refer to two levels of centralization presented in Table 4.1). By contrast, the level of authority remained constant in almost all areas that were part of the EU's original issue scope. Overall, average formal authority grew beyond the threshold of intergovernmental coordination and moved towards intergovernmental cooperation (see Appendix 1).

Although the SEA did not change the EU's formal tax authority, tax policy output increased considerably during this period. With a minimum output of three legislative acts in 1987 and a maximum of 28 in 1992, the EU more than doubled its average tax policy output after the enactment of the SEA. Yet, as Figure 4.1 shows, this increase was not the result of constantly growing output but of two periods of exceptional activity. In four out of six years the frequency of legislative acts was quite similar to the pre-SEA period. But in 1989 and 1992 the EU generated an exceptionally high amount of tax policies. During these years, the EU the slightly broadened the scope of its tax legislation. Similar to the previous period, the main focus was still on the harmonization of VAT. But in 1990, the EU issued its very first legislative act on corporate income (Radaelli, 1997: 79). With one policy on excises in 1988 and 1989 and nine in 1992, this tax type became a regular component of EU tax governance. In sum, the SEA period was characterized by two episodes of substantially higher policy output.

Compared to the strong growth of the EU's formal authority under the SEA, tax policy output grew modestly. Hence, the interaction effect of formal authority and tax policy output on levels and patterns of politicization should be dominated by the former. The growing scope and level of formal authority should result in substantial changes in the level and pattern of politicization. Salience, controversy, and plurality of EU tax governance should grow during the period, whereas public debate is less likely to react directly to tax policy output. This suggests a temporal pattern that is marked by strong growth in politicization immediately before and after the enactment of the SEA and a period of stabilization during the subsequent years. Furthermore, politicization is likely to grow during the years surrounding the peaks of tax legislation, that is, around 1987 and 1992. The politicization pattern resulting from this interaction of mildly growing policy output and strongly increased formal authority should be characterized by a balancing distribution of problem-solving and legitimacy debates.

Overall, Figure 4.2 supports these expectations. During the SEA period, politicization did indeed grow more strongly than over the previous years. The temporal pattern of this growth in politicization was complex and did not follow a mechanistic scheme. A qualitative reading of the textual material reveals that the interaction effect between formal authority and policy output was dominated by the former.

The descriptive statistics show that salience grew substantially after the first revision of European institutions since the Treaty of Rome. A higher maximum (0.2) and the two times higher mean value (0.07) for the SEA period underline this result. These observations corroborate institutionalist expectation. Yet, a more detailed analysis of annual changes shows that the interaction between formal authority and policy output is complex. On the one hand, salience grew only marginally in 1987, when the SEA came into effect. Salience peaked only later during the subsequent years, up until 1989. This observation suggests that policy output dominated public debate because salience and policy output developed very much in parallel during these years. Salience peaked strongly in 1989 when output was exceptionally high and decreased to almost no press coverage when tax policy output was low subsequently. On the other hand, the second and even stronger peak of tax legislation was not accompanied by a similarly strong growth of salience. Rather, public debate in 1992 was marked by limited salience and its next peak evolved only in 1994. This development shows that even growing formal authority and policy output do not necessarily lead to a growing politicization of EU tax governance.

Controversy, by contrast, appears to be dominated by the effect of policy output both with a view to periodical levels and to annual changes. Relative to the previous period, the mean value of controversy grew by a factor of seven from 4.2 percent of controversial articles to 29.2 percent. Although three years of the SEA period were marked by high levels of controversy, there was no constant increase. Rather the period was characterized by strong ebbs and flows. These fluctuations seem to have followed EU tax policy output.[6] Both increases in tax legislation were accompanied by higher controversy. The remaining years of the SEA period were not marked by any controversy.

Results for plurality were similar to salience as plurality was also marked by a complex interaction of formal authority and policy output. The periodical level of plurality grew substantially from 0 to 29.2 percent. This growth also fluctuated. While non-executive speakers did not contribute to the debate before 1986, they became dominant during the three years of higher attention after the SEA entered into force. Subsequently, this speaker group disappeared completely in 1990 and 1991 only to experience a strong comeback in 1992, when tax policy output reached its highest level during the SEA period. These ebbs and flows of plurality appear to indicate that the SEA period was indeed different from the previous period and annual changes show that both policy output and higher formal authority contributed to this transformation of the debate. Immediately after the enactment of the SEA, a clear and direct effect of increasing formal authority is indicated by the high plurality of the debate and the period of no civil society participation from 1990 to 1991. The subsequent return of non-executive speakers in 1992 seems to reflect higher tax policy output.

At first glance, politicization patterns (Figure 4.3) seem to reflect the effect of policy output. The years between 1987 and 1989, for which the data are more robustly interpretable, were clearly characterized by problem-solving debates. Legitimacy debates were largely missing.

A more detailed comparison of public debate and tax legislation reveals, however, a quite strong misfit between tax policies and what was discussed in the newspaper articles. Most of the discussion focused on tax policy areas that were not subject to EU tax legislation. A noteworthy exception was the debate in 1988 when both EU tax policy and public debate were mainly concerned with VAT and excises. In contrast to the narrow focus of EU tax policy output, public debate covered all main areas of taxation, including private and corporate income.

Frequently affective statements did not even refer to a specific tax area but to the general field of taxation. This rather general nature of the debate provides further evidence for the complex interaction between policy output and formal authority as a combined driver of politicization. During the SEA period, this complex interaction appears to be dominated by formal authority. Especially during the years immediately after the enactment of the SEA, when issue attention was high, most of the articles in the sample dealt with the policy implications of the European single market for taxation.

In sum, periodical levels, annual changes, and politicization patterns can be interpreted as follows: although the salience of EU tax governance was still comparably low for the entire period, there was some politicization during the years directly following the enactment of the SEA. Between 1987 and 1989, salience, controversy, and plurality increased and formed the first episode of EU tax governance politicization. The development was, however, not stable during the subsequent years. Higher levels of politicization from 1987 to 1989 were followed by a period of little salience and barely interpretable values for controversy and plurality. This result supports the institutionalist perspective and shows that both policy output and formal authority interact to spur politicization. On the one hand, the mean values of politicization indicators were much higher after the enactment of the SEA, and public debate changed immediately after the treaty revision. On the other hand, this politicization was short lived and did to lead to a sustained transformation of public debate. Between 1990 and 1992 discussions were marginal and hardly politicized.

A qualitative reading of the textual material further illuminates these results. The debates reveal that although the SEA did not create a stronger focus on the polity dimension and input criteria, the enactment of the treaty raised high expectations with regard to EU tax policy. Individual policies played – with some minor expectations – only a marginal role in the debate. Especially during the years immediately after the enactment of the SEA, the core of the debate was that the European market would function properly only if the EU took the lead in a broad range of policy areas in order to reduce tax-related barriers to free trade.

This leaves me with the conjecture that major treaty revisions that increase the formal authority of an international institution have the potential to trigger politicization processes that even affect issue areas that are not directly targeted by the treaty. Similar to policy spillover effects (Haas, 1968; Johnson and Urpelainen, 2012), growing formal authority spurs politicization that is not necessarily limited to targeted issue areas. Rather, the reaction of public debate to this stimulus may be more diffuse, resulting in a broader politicization that even affects non-targeted issue areas, such as taxation. Furthermore, the SEA period suggests that diffuse politicization processes trigger salience and controversial debates for limited time periods. The SEA effect flattened out quite quickly after the enactment of the treaty. The remaining debate was barely politicized. As Anthony Downs (1972) suggested, public attention is short-lived, leading to recurring ebbs and flows of politicization.

The EU after Maastricht: a critical juncture for politicization? (1993–1999)

The enactment of the Treaty of Maastricht (1993) intensified the trend of increasing EU authority because both the scope and level of formal authority grew strongly (Moravcsik, 1998: Ch. 6). The Treaty of Maastricht ushered in a second big wave of EU scope expansion (Wessels, 1997: 278). It established the Economic and Monetary Union (EMU) and the second and third pillar of integration (common foreign and security policy and justice and home affairs). Thus substantial issue areas became subject to EU authority. Since the enactment of Maastricht, European policy-making has embraced almost every area of political, economic, and social life (Pollack, 2000). Overall, the Treaty of Maastricht transformed the European project from an economic union into a more political one (Marks and Steenbergen, 2004: 258; Garry and Tilley, 2009: 375).

Similarly, levels of authority continued to grow with the Treaty of Maastricht. One of the major changes introduced by the treaty was the legislative co-decision procedure, that is, joint decision-making II. This legislative process gave further weight to the EP, as it required consensus between the EP and the European Council for legislation to be adopted (Burns et al., 2013). The treaty implemented this procedure in the issue areas of economic freedoms and occupational health and safety standards. In addition to this major deepening of authority in a limited number of issue areas, the level of authority increased in many other issue areas. Out of the 18 issue areas on Börzel's (2005: 223–224) list, there were only five in which the level of authority did not grow (macro-economic policy and employment, taxation, energy and transport, research and development, and agriculture).

On average, EU authority thus approached the level of joint decision-making I. Compared to the SEA, the overall score increased by almost 60 percent – numerically, Maastricht triggered the second largest growth of authority in the history of the EU (SEA increased the score by almost 90 percent). Substantially, the incorporation of the EMU and the creation of the second and third pillars of integration made this reform even more important than the SEA. Maastricht extended EU competencies to core state powers. It transformed the EU from an economic intergovernmental institution into a multi-level polity with strong supranational authority.

Despite the still unchanged tax mandate, the EU did expand its tax policy output. With a minimum output of seven legislative acts in 1994 and a maximum of 26 in 1997, the EU raised tax policy output relative to the SEA period from 11 to 15 policies per year. In two out the six years, the number of legislative acts even exceeded a threshold of 20. In total, 87 tax policies were enacted. In comparison to the SEA period, the EU also produced this legislation more steadily during the Maastricht period. Except for 1994 and 1996, the number of legislative acts did not fall below a threshold of 10. In addition, the scope of EU's tax legislation grew as the still strong focus on VAT was supplemented by more steady legislation in the area of excises. After 1993, the EU produced at least one policy in this area.

Overall, the Maastricht period brought about more frequent, more steady, and more diverse tax policy output.

Similar to the SEA period, formal authority grew in many issue areas, except for taxation. In much of the literature on European integration, the Treaty of Maastricht is interpreted as a giant leap that gave a new quality to the overall authority of the EU – which, in turn, gave rise to Euroscepticism, that is, various forms of opposition towards further European integration (Taggart, 1998: 21; Eichenberg and Dalton, 2007: 129; Hooghe and Marks, 2009: 7).[7] This interpretation of the Treaty of Maastricht as an important turning point corresponds to the conjecture that the mid-1990s were a critical juncture for the politicization of global tax governance (Sternberg, 2013; Barth and Bijsmans, 2018). I expect the interaction between policy output and formal authority to play out in a way similar to the SEA period. The effect of the strongly growing formal authority should dominate the policy output effect in terms of levels, changes, and patterns of politicization. The strong increase in formal authority should lead to higher levels of politicization, immediately following the enactment of the treaty. In addition, the moderate changes in tax legislation should add further nuances to public debate. Annual changes in levels of politicization should follow the mild ebbs and flows of tax legislation and thus shape a complex temporal sequence of the politicization process. In terms of politicization patterns, the mounting scope and level of formal authority suggest a growing importance of legitimacy debates.

Politicization indicators reveal a picture very much in line with these expectations (Figure 4.2). The Maastricht period was more strongly politicized than the previous periods, and the temporal sequences were again characterized by the complex interaction of increasing formal authority and policy output. A qualitative reading of the textual material demonstrates that the interaction effect between formal authority and policy output was indeed dominated by the former.

Salience was almost two times higher than it was during the SEA period (see Table 4.2 for descriptive statistics). The period was thus characterized by a stronger increase than during the SEA period. Yet, salience did neither increase strongly immediately after the enactment of the Treaty of Maastricht (pointing to a formal authority effect) nor did it follow the frequency of tax legislation. Rather, salience experienced rapid and almost uninterrupted growth during the entire period. With the exception of 1995, when salience dropped to levels similar to the 1980s, the number of newspaper articles on EU tax governance grew steadily to the absolute maximum in 1998.

The controversy of these public debates followed a path similar to salience. Subsequent to a moderate peak directly after the enactment of Maastricht, controversy decreased in 1995, before the share of controversial articles started to grow steadily up until the beginning of the new millennium. The first peak has to be interpreted cautiously due to the low number of total articles. But after 1996, scores are built on a sufficiently high number of articles. These numbers are a robust sign of growing controversy. The slightly lower mean value of controversy during the Maastricht period relative to the SEA period is not to be misinterpreted.

Controversy levels after the enactment of the SEA resulted from a low level of salience. In three out of six years of the SEA period, public debate was completely uncontroversial. This volatility disappeared after Maastricht. Except for 1993 and 1995, all years were marked by controversy and the respective levels resulted from considerably higher attention. Hence controversy levels were higher and more stable than they were during the SEA period.

Contrary to salience and controversy, plurality was characterized by a strongly increasing share of non-executive speakers in the year of the enactment of Maastricht and subsequent fluctuation between a minimum of 39 percent in 1998 and a maximum of 77 percent in 1996. This seems to underline the dominance of the formal authority effect because plurality grew directly after the enactment of the treaty. Considerably higher minimum and maximum values and a substantial growth of the mean value from 35.2 percent to 56.6 percent demonstrate that the role of non-executive speakers changed considerably. While representatives of CSOs, business, and other non-executive speakers appeared occasionally on the public stage during the SEA period, the enactment of the Treaty of Maastricht transformed the status of this group into a major voice, shaping the debate. Annual changes confirm this impression. While non-executive speakers were not part of public debates in three out of six years during the SEA period, they were constant contributors during the Maastricht period. The volatility of plurality decreased substantially. Growing formal authority seems to have triggered a direct reaction and a strong increase in plurality. Yet, the stabilization of civil society participation after Maastricht is also driven by the steady increase in EU tax legislation. This underlines that formal authority and policy output interacted in shaping public debates.

The patterns of politicization showed some – albeit weak – signs of the expected change towards legitimacy debates (Figure 4.3). Similar to the SEA period, speakers did still focus strongly on EU tax legislation, with relatively little emphasis on input criteria. However, the share of statements evaluating the politics and polity dimension based on input criteria started to grow after the enactment of Maastricht. During the SEA period, the only legitimacy discussion was voiced by Rogalla, who criticized the lack of transparency of negotiations on tax harmonization in the European Commission and the Council (*FAZ*, 26 October 1989). During the Maastricht period, legitimacy debates played a role in four out of seven years. In 1996, the *NZZ* discussed, for instance, how tax cooperation with the EU impedes Swiss national self-determination (14 May 1996). Similar discussions took also place in the German *SZ* and the *II*. These patterns did not amount to a balanced distribution of problem-solving and legitimacy debates. Yet, they show that the content of public debates began to shift. Politicization no longer focused exclusively on policy, but occasionally featured institutional issues of EU tax governance and its input qualities.

Overall, the levels, changes, and patterns of politicization corroborate the conjecture that the complex interaction between tax policy output and formal authority spurred the politicization of EU tax governance during the Maastricht period. The level of politicization grew substantially and public debates began to focus more on legitimacy questions. The Treaty of Maastricht was indeed a critical juncture for the politicization of European tax governance.

A more qualitative reading of the textual material reveals that both policy output and the formal changes introduced by the Treaty of Maastricht shaped the course of public debate. Immediately after the enactment of Maastricht, the debate was clearly driven by a focus on policies, and most of the discussion dealt prospectively with the potential harmonization of energy taxation and taxes on corporate income and private savings. Both issues – especially the regulation of income taxes – were occasionally topical in EU policy-making but were not subject to concrete European Commission proposals at that time (Radaelli, 1997: Ch. 6). However, the European Commission had launched a renewed initiative to regulate preferential corporate tax regimes in 1992, and more comprehensive proposals to introduce a common minimum corporate tax rate were in the making (Kemmerling and Seils, 2009: 765). These anticipating discussions show that politicization can also be spurred by future developments.

This emphasis on individual policy issues started to decline in 1996 when the consequences of the Treaty of Maastricht and especially of the EMU began to take center stage. Many speakers discussed EU tax governance along the lines of a common narrative not present during the previous years. They argued that, given the agreement on the EMU, the EU had to develop a common social policy, in order to become a stable polity. To this end, the EU needed to coordinate and harmonize taxation. Some participants in these discussions mainly addressed individual tax types, such as VAT, excises, or corporate and private income. Other voices considered the broader picture and proposed, for instance, to change decision-making rules from unanimity to majority voting. After 1996, this narrative became dominant, which indicates that increasing formal authority in addition to EU legislation in other issue areas, most notably in the field of monetary policy, shaped the politicization of EU tax governance. The timing of this effect underlines that politicization processes are marked by short attention cycles that appear to be linked more closely to potential outcomes rather than abstract provisions on formal authority. Only with the approaching introduction of the Euro, the Maastricht Treaty or the increased authority of European institutions more generally became a more important driver of public debates on EU tax governance.

Yet, EU tax legislation also played an important role and stimulated parts of the debate. Parallel to the European Commission's policy initiative to limit harmful tax competition (HTC) among member states (Radaelli, 2008; Kemmerling and Seils, 2009), which began with a meeting of the Taxation Policy Group in 1996 (Sharman, 2008: 1055), some speakers began to critically discuss the individual components of this initiative, including the elimination of withholding taxes applied to royalties paid to associated companies, a non-binding code of conduct to abolish harmful tax practices of member states, and the directive on the taxation of non-resident EU savings (Genschel et al., 2011: 595–598). Although these policies were not implemented during the Maastricht period, they did cast their shadow over public discussions.

Amsterdam, Nice, and Lisbon: the slowdown of European integration (1999–2011)

After Maastricht, European authority kept growing with the subsequent treaties of Amsterdam (1999), Nice (2003), and Lisbon (2009). However, the pace of European integration slowed down considerably with these treaties. Consequently, some argue that the EU has reached the state of a "stable constitutional equilibrium" (Moravcsik, 2005: 349).[8] The Treaty of Amsterdam "neither introduces major new Community competences (symbolic proposals on employment aside) nor significantly deepens co-operation in existing substantive fields" (Moravcsik and Nicolaidis, 1998: 14). Similarly, the Treaty of Nice and the Treaty of Lisbon brought only incremental steps that slightly increased the level of EU authority (on Nice, see Wessels, 2001: 201; on Lisbon, see Verdun, 2013) and reweighted votes in the Council. The overall growth of formal authority was marginal in comparison to previous treaties. Taken together, the institutional changes undertaken since the Treaty of Maastricht have not generated a fundamental growth in the scope and level of EU authority (Moravcsik, 2005: 364). EU authority grew moderately in most of the substantive issue areas (13 out of 18) but the changes in overall authority were small compared to the SEA and Maastricht. Amsterdam produced a growth of 15 percent in overall authority. Nice resulted in a 4 percent increase and Lisbon enlarged overall authority by 13 percent.

In contrast, tax policy output continued to grow despite the still-unchanged mandate over the area of taxation (see Figure 4.1). With a minimum output of 15 legislative acts in 2003 and an absolute maximum for the entire observation period of 42 in 2004, average tax policy output increased from 15 during the Maastricht period to 22 legislative acts during the post-Amsterdam period. In total, the EU enacted 281 tax policies during the final observation period. The trend of a more constant level of tax legislation after the enactment of the Treaty of Maastricht continued. Except for 2004, when tax policy output was two times higher than the period average, the frequency of tax legislation fluctuated within a narrow range between 15 and 26 legislative acts per year.

Furthermore, the scope of EU tax legislation broadened after Amsterdam. Income taxation became a more regular issue. Since the enactment of the Amsterdam treaty, the EU has issued policies on corporate income in seven out of 12 years. In 2001, for the first time in EU history, tax policy output targeted private income. This is particularly noteworthy because income taxation was still not part of the EU's formal mandate (Radaelli, 2008: 316). With the exception of one directive on corporate income in 1990, European initiatives to harmonize income taxation had failed over the past decades (Radaelli, 1997: Ch. 6; Kemmerling and Seils, 2009: 764). Compared to the Maastricht years, the post-Amsterdam period was thus characterized by a stable but higher frequency of tax legislation and a broader scope.

Figure 4.1 illustrates that, contrary to the previous period, the change of formal authority introduced by Amsterdam, Nice, and Lisbon was comparable to the growth of EU tax legislation. Both formal authority and tax legislation grew moderately over the course of this period. Thus I expect the interaction between formal authority and policy output to be less strongly dominated by the former. Politicization should grow less strongly than during the previous two periods. Increases immediately after the enactment of the treaties should be followed by mild fluctuations. I also expect a stronger growth of politicization for the years surrounding 2004, when the frequency of tax legislation was exceptionally high and targeted VAT, excises, and private income. The more balanced interaction of formal authority and policy output also suggests a more equal focus on problem-solving and legitimacy issues in public debates.

The inspection of politicization indicators demonstrates that these expectations are generally met (Figure 4.2). The moderate growth of formal authority and tax policy output appears to have a chilling effect on politicization – although different in timing and degree. While this is in line with the moderate growth of formal authority and policy output, annual changes underline the aforementioned complex relationship between both aspects of political authority. Politicization was neither marked by strong growth immediately after treaties were enacted nor did it clearly follow tax legislation. With respect to the latter, it is especially noteworthy that there was little reaction to the exceptionally high output in 2004.

Salience stabilized on a level approximating the absolute maximum of the Maastricht period. The mean value grew from 0.08 for the Maastricht period (between 1993 and 1999) to 0.14 for the post-Amsterdam period (1987–1993). As this is the strongest growth of salience for the entire period of observation, it could be argued that the salience of EU tax governance grew even stronger than the institutionalist perspective expects. A closer look at the annual changes reveals, however, that the increased mean value resulted mainly from a stabilization of salience levels. While the Maastricht period was marked by volatile salience (Min 0.04; Max 0.29; SD 0.08), the lower spread of annual values and the lower standard deviation for the post-Amsterdam period (Min 0.11; Max 0.24; SD 0.04) indicate that salience did not grow in terms of constantly higher levels. It just became more stable. Figure 4.2 visualizes this ratchet-like effect of the Maastricht period. It also indicates that immediate reactions to the enactment of Amsterdam, Nice, and Lisbon varied widely. In the aftermath of Amsterdam and Lisbon, salience developed similar to early periods. The enactment of both treaties was followed by an immediate growth of salience and, in the case of the Treaty of Amsterdam, salience decreased again at the end of the period as it did during the SEA and the Maastricht period.

While these similarities appear to corroborate the dominance of the formal authority effect over the tax policy output effect, the development of salience after the enactment of Nice is puzzling (2003–2007). Here, salience did not grow with the enactment of the treaty. Instead, this component of politicization even decreased to lower values similar to the SEA period. Although this trend was reversed in 2008, when salience grew again, a period of decreasing salience is not in line with the development of formal authority and policy output. Overall, salience does not follow the changes in formal authority and tax legislation very closely. On one hand, tax legislation did not change strongly after Amsterdam, whereas salience grew strongly. On the other hand, the substantial increase of tax policy output after Nice was accompanied by stable or even slightly decreasing levels of salience.

Controversy provides a clearer picture. It had substantively higher levels than for the Maastricht period, and annual changes followed the frequency of tax legislation. The mean controversy grew from 18.3 percent of controversial articles during the Maastricht period to 30.9 percent during the post-Amsterdam period. Similar to salience this growth was not the result of constantly higher annual scores. Rather, controversy began to stabilize on a higher level. While 1993 and 1995 in the aftermath of Maastricht did not feature controversial news stories at all, the minimum level of controversy during the post-Amsterdam period was at 19.4 percent in 2009. While these differences in controversy levels reflected the moderate growth of formal authority and tax legislation, annual changes suggest a more pronounced effect of tax legislation. There were no immediate reactions to treaty revisions. Neither Amsterdam nor Nice nor Lisbon triggered substantially higher shares of controversial news coverage. Rather, the post-Amsterdam period was characterized by the relatively constant controversy of around 30 percent, reflecting the trajectory of tax policy output.

Yet, the plurality of the debate contradicts institutionalist predictions considerably. Not only was plurality lower than during the Maastricht period but also annual changes rarely took expected directions. The mean value of plurality decreased by almost 20 percentage points from 56.6 percent during the Maastricht period to 38.3 percent during the post-Amsterdam period. Minimum and maximum scores were also lower. Furthermore, neither the enactment of the treaties of Amsterdam, Nice, and Lisbon nor the high policy output in 2004 was followed by increasing shares of non-executive speakers. As a result, this speaker group lost its dominant position in the debate to national executives. This is not to say that the debate transformed into a conventional foreign policy discussion mainly led by national executives. The debate still gave voice to a broad range of different actors. But contrary to salience and controversy the post-Amsterdam debate was not characterized by a stabilization of plurality.

The considerable transformation of politicization patterns corroborates my conjecture that the interaction between formal authority and legislation is more balanced during this period. Albeit gradually, the relevance of legitimacy debates grew steadily. While input criteria did not exceed the share of 25 percent before 2000 (in fact the share is much lower in most of these years), the post-Amsterdam period witnessed only four out of 13 years in which the share of input criteria was below this threshold. On average, the share of input criteria for the time period between 1981 and 1999 did not amount to more than five percent of all affective statements. For the post-Amsterdam period, this value grew more than sixfold to 30 percent. In sum, the levels and changes of politicization indicators seem to have been shaped by a balanced interaction effect of growing formal authority and tax policy output. In some years, public debates were dominated by formal authority growth. In other years, tax legislation was the more decisive driver of politicization.

A qualitative review of the debate helps to clarify this interaction. It shows that the redistributive consequences of EU tax legislation, which already played a role during the Maastricht period, were even more important during the post-Amsterdam period. Debates focused strongly on tax competition and the EU's fight against internal and external tax havens and harmful tax practices. The common question of these discussions was whether the EMU should be accompanied by a common fiscal policy or whether tax competition was a valuable tool to improve the competitiveness of the European economy. In this context, two policy initiatives of the European Commission took center stage. First, the three-pronged strategy against HTC initiated in 1996 was as a central theme. Especially a tax on non-residents' savings shaped these discussions. Second, the European Commission's initiative to implement a common consolidated corporate tax base (CCCTB) added to these controversies. Although the European Commission tried to frame this policy as a new initiative for the common market because the CCCTB would help to lower business costs (Mintz, 2004), public debates strongly emphasized the question of whether the initiative itself would have an effect on corporate tax rates and whether this was only the first step towards harmonized corporate tax rates.

The debates also reveal a more indirect but still important effect of growing formal authority. In 2003, when the Draft Treaty Establishing a European Constitution was published and the Treaty of Nice was enacted, policy discussions acquired an additional institutional dimension. Against the backdrop of the heated debates on income taxation, both treaties were confronted with strong opposition because they were expected to expand the EU's formal tax authority. This is particularly noteworthy because neither the draft constitution nor the Treaty of Nice implied a growth in formal tax authority. This mixing of institutional and policy issues underlines my argument that generally increasing formal authority has spillover effects on the politicization of EU tax governance, although taxation was not affected by the respective treaties. In other words, treaty revisions seem to fuel more issue-specific discussions because they produce a general awareness of these topics even if they do not target them directly.

This interaction effect of formal authority and tax legislation on politicization is further exemplified by the strong politicization of the European Commission's CCCTB initiative. Corporate tax coordination and the harmonization of the tax base have been on the EU's agenda for more than 50 years. Already during the 1960s, the European Commission called for harmonization in these areas of taxation (Birch Sörensen, 2004: 91) but the politicization of these proposals was marginal up until the early 2000s. Most strikingly, in 1992 the Ruding Committee proposed not only a harmonized tax base but also a band for tax rates from 30 to 40 percent and minimum standards for the corporate tax base (Radaelli, 1997: 97–100; Devereux, 2004: 71). This initiative would have constrained national tax policy-making much more strongly than the highly politicized 2001 proposal. However, my data do not reveal public debates on the Ruding Committee. This indicates that the strong politicization of the CCCTB initiative resulted to a considerable extent from a more general visibility of EU tax legislation spurred by growing formal authority of the EU.

Finally, the debates also underline that more redistributive policies have stronger politicizing effects. Public debates show an emerging cleavage between opponents and proponents of tax competition and tax harmonization, respectively. Focusing on redistributive consequences, actors from small countries, such as Switzerland and Ireland, were often strongly opposed to the harmonization of income taxation. By contrast, French and German speakers were largely supportive. While taxation is in general conceived as an issue area with redistributive consequences (Genschel, 2007: 753) and thus potentially conflict-ridden, stakes are especially high in the case of income taxation. This is reflected in the strong politicization of EU initiatives in this area of taxation.

Summary

The EU is still far from state-like tax legislation. It does not control a genuine tax base that generates independent financial means and its formal authority in the area is still marginal (Kemmerling, 2011: 1). Yet, the politicization of EU tax governance has grown substantially over the course of the past 30 years. EU tax policies have become a regular and controversial topic of a broad public debate. National executives, representatives of European institutions, and a wide range of non-executive actors – such as civil society organizations, business representatives, and party politicians – argue about matters of taxation ranging from VAT over excises to income taxation.

The analysis shows that salience, controversy, and plurality grew considerably between 1980 and 1998 and began to stabilize during the 2000s. The Maastricht period constituted a critical juncture for the politicization process. During this period the level of politicization reached unprecedented highs that were rarely undercut subsequently. The politicization of EU tax governance was, thus, indeed characterized by a ratchet-like trajectory (see Chapter 3). After a long period of low politicization, the transformation of the Maastricht period put the issue on the public agenda – and it is not going to be displaced so easily.

The combination of quantitative data on levels and annual changes of politicization, as well as a qualitative interpretation of the textual material, suggests that this politicization process was the result of the growing authority of European institutions. However, neither growing formal authority nor mounting tax legislation was the exclusive driver of this process. Rather, the politicization process was shaped by a complex interaction of both factors. While formal authority helped to put EU tax governance on the public agenda, individual policies often trigged heated controversies.

Furthermore, the analysis shows that politicization should not be understood as constantly growing salience and controversy reacting directly to more formal authority or policy output. Rather, politicization is characterized by issue-attention cycles that follow different temporal sequences. Public debates on EU tax governance were periodical, flared up under specific conditions, and were more diffuse than a close reading of the institutionalist approach would imply. At times, discussions were anticipatory and accompanied early stage policy initiatives. At other times, discussions arose with a substantial time lag. Public debates were by no means limited to specific policies or treaty revisions. Actors raised a variety of issues, ranging from demand for more or less formal tax authority to policy debates linked to actual and potential policies. Here, increasing formal authority triggered politicization mainly in the form of discursive spillover effects. Especially the SEA and the Maastricht period show that increasing formal authority contributed to the politicization of tax governance because successful economic integration was increasingly understood as a function of more integrated European tax governance.

Finally, the distinction between more or less redistributive policies is helpful for explaining the politicization process during the Maastricht and the post-Amsterdam period. Both phases point to the redistributive character of policies as an important condition for politicization. While the bulk of EU tax legislation has at least some redistributive consequences, this was most pronounced in the area of income taxation. Income tax harmonization and the lack thereof generated strong redistributive conflict at the EU level (Ganghof and Genschel, 2008). These policies shape national growth strategies, necessitate substantial regulatory adjustments by governments and private actors, and have the potential to reduce the competitive advantage of small member states and even non-members like Switzerland. Consequently, the introduction of a common corporate tax base or a common tax on non-resident savings was more strongly politicized than other policies.

This finding is in line with utilitarian explanations of public opinion on European integration (Eichenberg and Dalton, 1993; Gabel and Palmer, 1995; Anderson and Reichert, 1998; Eichenberg and Dalton, 2007). This research argues that the economic consequences of EU decision-making affect attitudes towards the EU whenever they are perceived with some accuracy and are large enough to matter for individual citizens (Hooghe and Marks, 2005: 422). It points to the idea that the politicizing effect of authority transfer is conditioned by the socio-economic and socio-cultural implications of this authority – that is, the social and economic consequences of EU tax governance.

The politicization of OECD tax governance

In 1957, the Treaty of Rome not only gave impetus to the creation of the European Communities but it was also the starting signal for the creation of the OECD. Its predecessor, the Organization for European Co-operation (OEEC), which was formed in 1948 to administer US aid under the Marshall Plan, had become obsolete with the emergence of the European Communities. Equipped with a renewed task of fostering economic cooperation and sustainable growth, employment, and financial stability on a global scale (OECD, 1960: Art. 1) the transatlantic OECD and its 20 founding member states took up their work in 1961 (Wolfe, 2008).[9] Today the Paris-based organization is one of the biggest international bureaucracies (Webb and Porter, 2008: 45) commanding a staff of around 2,500 and a budget of around 347 million Euro (in 2012).

At first glance, these personnel and financial capabilities suggest that the OECD is equipped with international authority (Heldt and Schmidtke, 2017). Yet, the institution's formal mandate was rather narrow and gave it only limited authority in a limited number of issue areas, including taxation. The founding treaty has not been changed over the past decades. As a result, the issue scope and level of formal authority of the OECD are almost constant over the observation period.

Formal decision-making power lies with the OECD Council, in which each member state and the EU have a seat. The Council meets once a year. It takes decisions almost exclusively by consensus (Martens and Jakobi, 2010: 5). Compliance mechanisms are equally narrow (Mahone and McBride, 2008: 3). A formal judicial review process does not exist. Instead, the institution relies mainly on soft modes of governance, including its legitimacy and expertise (Martens and Jakobi, 2010: 7). In combination, these decision rules and the limited role of the international bureaucracy imply a low level of formal authority (Sharman, 2012: 22). Formally, OECD authority does not go beyond intergovernmental coordination on Börzel's (2005) scale (see Appendix 1).

By contrast, the scope of formal authority is high. Some even argue that OECD's "tentacles delve into almost every aspect of domestic policy making" (Woodward, 2010: 53). The institution has a broad mandate, giving it the authority to work in many issue areas related to economic development. This work is done by OECD committees, which "are the workhorses of the OECD" (ibid.: 56). They are, for the most part, responsible for substantive policies and decide independently on their scope and working methods. Committees are active in 10 out of the 18 issue areas (for similar results see Woodward, 2008: 85; Ougaard, 2010: 30).[10] This broad scope has not changed over time. Although there is some fluctuation of newly created and closed-down committees, issue scope did not change much during the observation period. As a result of this continuity, the overall formal authority appears to be an implausible driver of politicization.

Similarly, the level and scope of formal tax authority are low and constant (see Appendices 1 and 2). The responsible committee – the Fiscal Committee of the OECD and its successor, the Committee of Fiscal Affairs (CFA, established on 1 May 1971) – was established to promote the development of effective and sound tax policies, helping to shape globalization for the benefit of all (OECD, 1971). It is assisted by a specialized secretariat: the Centre for Tax Policy and Administration (CTPA). The scope and level of this committee's formal authority are limited. It focuses mainly on the avoidance of double taxation of corporate and private income. The committee and its small international secretariat are essentially tasked with providing data and technical assistance to facilitate bilateral tax negotiations among states. This mandate has not changed over time. Thus, formal tax authority is also unlikely to explain politicization. Therefore, this case study focuses mainly on the relationship between tax legislation and politicization.

The OECD's tax policy output is more difficult to quantify than the EU's. A large share of policies takes the form of ongoing processes rather than the conventional format of legislation (Rixen, 2008). Hence, Figure 4.4 does not include an indicator for the frequency of tax legislation.

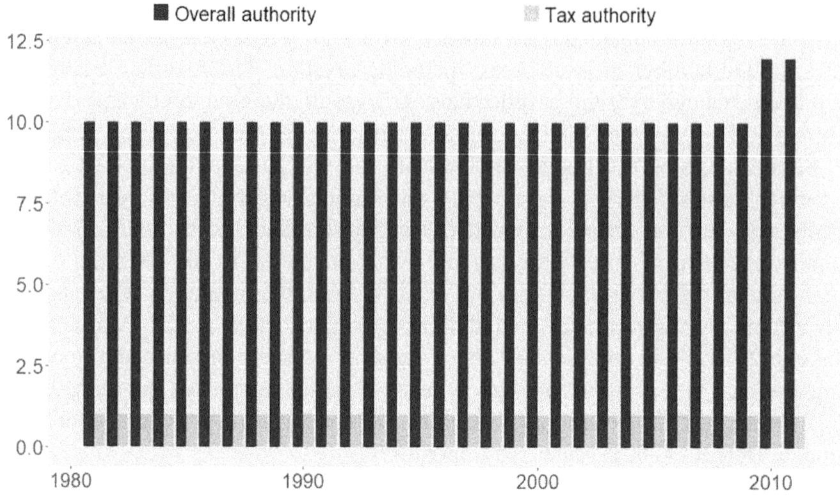

Figure 4.4 OECD authority, 1981–2011

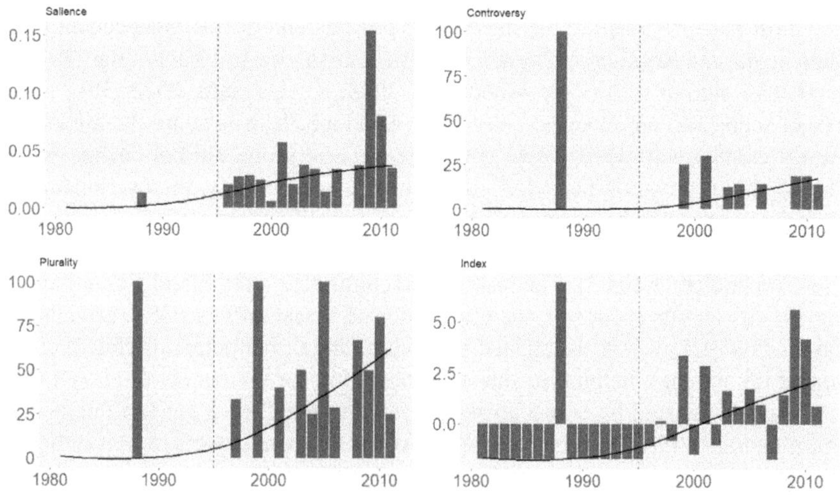

Figure 4.5 OECD politicization indicators, 1981–2011

Figure 4.5 is similar to Figure 4.2 on the politicization of EU tax governance. It plots annual scores for the three dimensions of politicization and the politicization index between 1981 and 2011. Scores for salience and controversy build on 119 newspaper articles, and 86 affective statements form the basis for the plurality score. Table 4.3 presents descriptive statistics for politicization indicators over

Table 4.3 Descriptive statistics for periods of OECD tax governance, 1981–2011

Descriptive statistics	*Politicization indicators*		
	Salience	*Controversy*	*Plurality*
1981–1995			
Min	0	0	0
Max	0.013	100	100
Mean	0.0009	6.67	6.67
SD	0.003	24.94	24.94
1996–2011			
Min	0	0	0
Max	0.15	30	100
Mean	0.04	9.2	37.41
SD	0.04	10.09	33.75

two time periods. While neither formal authority nor tax policy output changed during the first period (1981–1995), the subsequent discussion of the OECD's tax policy output demonstrates that frequency and scope of OECD tax legislation grew over the late 1990s. Hence, I present data for these two distinct periods.

Due to this nature of OECD tax governance, the case study proceeds in the following steps. I first give a general overview of OECD activities in taxation over the course of the past 30 years. Second, I highlight those initiatives that could potentially cause a politicization of OECD tax governance due to their intrusiveness, that is, the limitation of national tax sovereignty. The remainder of the section analyzes politicization indicators and provides a qualitative interpretation of public debates on OECD tax governance to probe the institutionalist perspective's empirical implications.

Many activities of the CFA and its international secretariat, the CTPA, are designed to evaluate and review national tax systems or to provide data on tax issues (Sharman, 2012: 17). These tasks are mostly descriptive and do not have direct constraining effects on national tax sovereignty (Kudrle, 2010: 76). Yet, the OECD also manages a number of regulatory policies that constrain national tax policies more directly. In its self-conception, the OECD even considers itself as playing a "lead role in setting the rules of the game for international taxation" (OECD, 2006: 3). The scope of these activities is for the most part limited to corporate and private income taxation (Kudrle, 2010: 81). More recently the OECD has expanded its activities to the area of VAT.

After World War II, the OECD inherited the work of the League of Nations on the prevention of unnecessary double taxation of transnational income (Paris, 2003: 158). Between the 1960s and 1980s, this work of the CFA focused mainly on principles of international direct taxation. This resulted in the OECD Model Tax Convention (OECD MC). The main purpose of this policy is to attribute slices of global commerce to national tax authorities. The first OECD MC of 1963 and its various subsequent revisions form the basis of a global network of bilateral treaties on double taxation (Rixen, 2008: 108–116). Today, it is often considered to be the OECD's most important contribution to international economic relations (Kudrle, 2010: 81). In the context of double-tax avoidance, a second major OECD policy addressed the taxation of multinational enterprises and the valuation of intra-firm transactions. The Guidelines on Transfer Pricing and Multinational Enterprises (TPG) were first published in 1979 and formally approved by the CFA in 1995. Since then the original provisions have been modified regularly (OECD, 2010).[11]

At the end of the past millennium, the OECD supplemented these two policies with an initiative to counter HTC (Webb, 2004). In 1996, the Group of Seven (G7) requested the institution to work on these issues. Two years later, a CFA task force published a report that defined HTC and identified two broad subcategories: harmful preferential tax regimes (HPTR) and tax havens. The report concluded that HTC is an effort to attract mobile capital to offshore or onshore locations by combining low or zero rates on income taxation (corporate, private or both) with opaque corporate structures or secrecy provisions that prevent other tax authorities from identifying the owners of these assets and taxing them accordingly. Following this definition, the report outlined concrete measures to counter these practices (Kudrle, 2008: 6) and established the Forum on Harmful Tax Practices to address the negative consequences of tax competition (Paris, 2003: 159). This initiative increased the intrusiveness of OECD tax governance because it went beyond the coordination of national tax systems. Both the OECD MC and the Guidelines on Transfer Pricing and Multinational Enterprises have the purpose of providing an interface between national tax systems and helping national tax authorities to coordinate and disentangle their tax claims. The HTC initiative was different. It aimed to establish general rules on income taxation and the design of domestic tax codes (Eccleston, 2012).

In 1998, the OECD also extended the scope of its tax legislation. In reaction to strongly growing electronic commerce, the organization revised the OECD MC and, more importantly, adopted the Ottawa Taxation Framework. For the first time in the history of the CFA, this framework established guidelines for tax collection from cross-border VAT purchases. The respective International VAT/GST Guidelines were first published in 2006 (Cockfield, 2006: 148).

Overall, the OECD has produced three substantial policies in addition to the OECD MC (TPG, VAT/GST, and HTC). All three were introduced during the late 1990s. Following the institutionalist approach, this mildly growing tax policy output should result in mildly growing politicization during the late 1990s.

This expectation also follows the level of authority of OECD tax governance and its development over time. Generally, this level of authority is low (Radaelli and Kraemer, 2005: 7). Most policies rely on multilateral deliberation and consensus-building (Cockfield, 2006: 186), and are essentially non-binding (Paris, 2003: 159). Yet, these policies are not toothless paper tigers. They operate on more a subtle basis. The most direct compliance mechanism is provided by peer pressure among OECD members (Webb and Porter, 2008). Member states and the OECD secretariat assess compliance of other members and publish the results. While this mechanism is clearly weaker than binding policies and judicial reviews, the effects of this social pressure can be substantial (Kelley and Simmons, 2015). Even more indirectly, transnational accounting firms, legal firms that provide tax advice, and transnational corporations supporting the principles codified in OECD standards put pressure on national governments to apply them (Webb, 2004: 811). Finally, the OECD orchestrates tax-related work of other IOs, including the World Bank, the IMF, and the UN. This role also strengthens the impact of OECD tax legislation as it helps to inject this content in the policies of other actors in the field of global tax governance (Sharman, 2012: 23). In line with this argument, Cockfield (2006: 142) claims that the OECD MC has important consequences for national tax systems because many countries base their bilateral treaties on the OECD model and because these provisions are recognized by national courts as secondary sources of authority to assist with treaty interpretation. In 1992, the American Law Institute (1992, cited in Cockfield 2006: 142) came to the conclusion that the OECD MC "has almost acquired the status of a multilateral instrument" due to its dominant role in determining the content of bilateral agreements and influencing their subsequent interpretation by domestic courts. Despite this impact, the intrusiveness of these policies is low compared to the binding tax legislation of the EU. As final decisions are still taken by national governments, the politicization effect of these policies should be mild.

This soft governance approach changed with the HTC initiative (Rixen and Zangl, 2013: 371). Threatening even non-OECD members to put them on a blacklist of uncooperative tax havens and coordinated countermeasures, this policy increased the authority of OECD tax legislation (Radaelli and Kraemer, 2005: 5; Sharman, 2012: 29). Both being blacklisted and potential countermeasures increased the costs of non-compliance significantly. The HTC initiative was thus the most authoritative OECD tax policy.

Although it was watered down over the years (Kudrle, 2008), the OECD remained true to its naming and shaming approach. In the aftermath of the 9/11 terrorist attacks, and more recently in the wake of the financial crisis in 2008, the initiative regained momentum (Eccleston, 2012). In 2001, financial secrecy became linked to terrorism and international security. One year later, the organization published its first list of uncooperative tax havens. This list effectively increased state compliance with standards on transparency and information exchange (Webb, 2004: 817) geared towards preventing private and corporate tax evasion. Since then, OECD members have repeatedly reiterated their will to retaliate against uncooperative tax havens (Cockfield, 2006: 182). As a result of this constant pressure, the OECD's standards of transparency and exchange of information are now the international norm for tax cooperation and have served as a model for more than 3,600 bilateral Tax Information Agreements (TIEAs; Elsayyad and Konrad, 2012: 295; Johannesen and Zucmann, 2012: 7).

The authority of this policy was higher than previous tax legislation. In combination with the higher frequency and scope of OECD tax legislation, I expect this growing authority to trigger growing politicization during the late 1990s.

Especially, the HTC initiative should be a salient issue of public debates because of stronger enforcement mechanisms.

The inspection of politicization indicators corroborates these expectations in terms of changes but not in regards to levels of politicization (Figure 4.5). The first period (1981–1995) was largely characterized by public indifference. Except for a single article published by the *FAZ* (15 March 1988), in which the "Convention on Mutual Administrative Assistance in Tax Matters" developed by the Council of Europe and the OECD in 1988 (OECD, 2013) was criticized for creating legal uncertainty for multinational corporations and national tax authorities, there was no public debate on OECD tax governance.

This began to change slowly with the end of the 1990s. After 1995, average salience grew from 0.0009 percent of news articles on OECD tax governance for the earlier period to 0.04 percent.

Annual changes demonstrate that this growth in salience resulted from a stable but still relatively marginal growth of news coverage. Except for 2007, the dataset contains a very limited number of news articles on OECD tax governance. While the early period was marked by almost invariable public indifference (Min 0; Max 0.013; SD 0.003), the second period shows some signs of emerging salience (Min 0.0; Max 0.15; SD 0.04). Although this indicates a transformation of the public debate on OECD tax governance, the level of salience was still low during most of this period. The number of news articles exceeded a threshold of 10 newspaper articles in only three out of the 16 years. Even a threshold of five articles was reached in only eight years. Hence, OECD tax governance remained largely unpoliticized over the observation period. Consequently, a more detailed analysis of the controversy and plurality does not provide additional insights.

Rather, a qualitative reading helps to probe the institutionalist expectations on the politicizing effect of HTC initiative more closely. The scattered debate on OECD tax governance focused on two main topics. First, from time to time the OECD economic outlook was mentioned and usually utilized to paint a positive picture of the state of the economy. Second, there was indeed a continued and dominant coverage of the HTC initiative, but this debate remained very general. The initiative was rarely discussed in detail. Most of the time, the OECD was portrayed as a tool for powerful countries to bully small tax havens into compliance with their standards of income taxation. Little agency was attributed directly to the OECD as an independent institution. Instead, the organization was mainly described as a forum in which national governments meet and discuss issues of tax competition.

The strong peak of otherwise low salience in 2009 resulted from the financial crisis. Pushed by the G20's promise that "the era of banking secrecy is over" (G20, 2009), public debate became politicized for a short period. However, the content of these discussions did not change much. Actors still focused predominantly on bilateral issues, most notably Switzerland's struggle with Germany and the US over bilateral treaties on information exchange based on the OECD's model convention. The OECD played only a subordinate role in a debate that largely retained the character of a conventional foreign policy debate.

In sum, OECD tax governance was barely politicized during the observation period. The first 15 years were marked by almost invariable public indifference and the second period was characterized by a scattered debate mainly fueled by traditional foreign policy discussions on how to limit HTC bilaterally. Although this discussion did not amount to a fully fledged politicization of OECD tax governance, the HTC initiative supports the institutionalist expectations. The more authoritative mode of this policy and its comparably broad scope gave impetus for a weak and rather short politicization episode. Hence, the OECD case is largely in line with the expectations of the institutionalist perspective. Since formal authority did not grow and because tax policy output was limited, a substantial politicization process did not emerge.

Conclusion: comparison across institutions

The present chapter provides case studies on the causal nexus between the politicization of EU and OECD tax governance and the authority of both institutions. The case studies trace the potentially interlinked causal effect of overall formal authority, formal tax authority, and tax policy output on politicization. As neither the EU nor the OECD has changed their mandate in tax governance, the potential effect of this element of authority is difficult to gauge. Despite this limitation, both cases provide substantial evidence in support of the institutionalist proposition that increasing international authority is a key driver of politicization.

The EU case study shows that overall formal authority and policy output interact in often complex and varying ways to spur the salience, controversy, and plurality of public debates on EU tax governance. This finding is particularly relevant because of its consequences for the EU decision-making processes. Since public debates did not only react to major treaty revisions, as often assumed by EU public opinion research (McLaren, 2006) but did also discuss policy output, the European Commission and Council have to look over their shoulders in their daily work (Rauh, 2016). Prior research (Wlezien, 1995; Wlezien, 2004; Toshkov, 2012) has already alluded to this representative link between citizens and the EU, shedding a more differentiated light on the alleged democratic deficit of the EU (Follesdal and Hix, 2006; Hix, 2008).

Furthermore, the EU case demonstrates that politicization processes do not follow mechanistic cause-effect temporal sequences. Rather, politicization processes emerged (a) during the decision-making process but before the actual result was agreed upon, (b) directly after the implementation of policies or formal treaty revisions, or (c) years after a change in authority had taken place when the consequences of changes became apparent. This also shows that increasing formal authority in other issue areas can have spillover effects. During the SEA and the Maastricht period, changes in formal authority in other issue areas, like monetary policy, spurred the politicization of EU tax governance because these changes gave rise to the argument that the Europeanization of these issue areas would necessitate more cooperation in the field of taxation.

Finally, the post-Amsterdam period points to the conjecture that particular types of policies are more likely to fuel politicization than others. Here, the redistributive character of a policy and comparably high adaptation costs both for national governments and for private actors seem to stand out as two crucial characteristics of politicizing policies.

While the analysis of the EU case has contributed to a better understanding of the interaction of formal authority and policy output, the OECD case study is a test case for the individual effect of policy output. Because the formal authority of the OECD did change over time, the only changes in the authority of the organization resulted from its tax policy output. In this context, the mild politicization of the HTC initiative shows that broader and more authoritative policies have the potential to shape politicization independent of formal authority growth.

The cross-case lends additional support to the institutionalist explanation. First, the institutionalist approach hypothesizes that levels of politicization differ across institutions according to their level and scope of authority. Strong international institutions are likely to be more politicized than weak international institutions. The comparison of the two cases strongly underpins this expectation. The level and scope of authority for both institutions were relatively similar at the beginning of the observation period. As a result, levels of politicization were similarly low for both organizations. This picture changed rapidly as soon as the authority of the EU and OECD started to diverge with the enactment of the SEA in 1987. While the level and scope of OECD authority both in terms of formal mandate and policy output remained constant, both aspects of political authority increased in the EU case. These developments were, in turn, reflected in the increasing politicization of EU tax governance and very low salience of OECD activities. This trend continued over the entire observation period. Today, EU tax governance has become a regular feature of public debates, whereas OECD activities – except for some scattered discussion of the HTC – are still not politicized.

Second, the cross-institutional comparison underpins the important interaction of increasing overall formal authority and policy output. The substantial variance in levels of politicization across the two institutions was mainly the result of the interaction between policy output and formal authority. At the beginning of the observation period, the OECD and the EU had a relatively similar scope and level of formal authority. Both institutions were active in a similar number of issue areas in which their authority barely exceeded intergovernmental coordination. In addition, the tax policy output of both institutions was not too different. While the EU produced legislation in the field of VAT and excises, the similarly limited tax policy output of the OECD focused on coordinating national corporate and private income tax systems. As a result, the politicization of both institutions was marginal and the differences between both debates were small.

Yet, public indifference to global tax governance ended with the enactment of the SEA. The early growth of salience and controversy about EU tax governance highlights the important effect of formal authority on politicization. In the case of the OECD, both tax policy output and formal authority were stable and did not trigger a noteworthy debate. In contrast, the formal authority of the EU grew strongly with the enactment of the SEA, whereas the frequency and scope of policy output remained low. Politicization, however, began to grow and the SEA period experienced the first episode of the politicization of EU tax governance.

Subsequent to this early stage, EU and OECD tax governance diverged strongly. The formal authority of the EU grew steadily over the years, while the OECD's formal mandate did not change. Similarly, the EU broadened the scope of its tax legislation and produced a continuously growing amount of policy output, whereas OECD tax legislation was much more limited in scope and frequency. Overall, the OECD is not only involved in fewer areas of taxation but also its engagement in these areas is – compared to the EU – more restricted. This contrast of low formal authority and limited tax policy output for the OECD, and growing formal authority and tax legislation for the EU, is clearly reflected in levels of politicization. While the EU was confronted with rising salience and controversy, the OECD still flew largely under the radar of public scrutiny.

A more recent episode of global tax governance provides additional evidence for the crucial importance of the interaction between formal authority and policy output for triggering politicization. During the late 1990s, both institutions launched simultaneous initiatives to curb international tax competition. In 1996, the OECD Ministerial Meeting initiated the HTC project. In the same year the informal Verona Council (a high-level Economic and Financial Affairs Council working group) set in motion the EU initiative on direct taxation. This initiative culminated later in a tax package, comprising the code of conduct for business taxation, the directive on taxation of savings income, and the directive on taxation of interest and royalty payments between member state companies (Cattoir, 2007). The EU code of conduct for business taxation and the HTC share quite a few important characteristics (Eggert and Haufler, 2006: 587). They constitute a most-similar set of cases nested within the two cases of EU and OECD tax governance.

By comparing the politicization of both policies, it is possible to disentangle the interaction of formal authority and policy output as the cause of politicization. The only pertinent difference between both cases is the formal authority of the issuing institution. Both policies were initiated and implemented at the same point in time and thus were subject to similar context factors. The EU established the key principles for dismantling harmful tax practices within the code of conduct in 2000. The OECD published its report on HTC in 1998. Both policies addressed the same issue – namely tax measures that provide for a significantly lower effective level of corporate taxation than those generally applied in the country in question. Both also specify similar criteria for assessing these harmful tax measures. Furthermore, the implementation process and compliance mechanisms were similar. Both institutions applied a soft mode of governance. Neither the EU code of conduct nor the OECD HTC were legally binding. Rather, the identification of harmful tax measures and their dismantling were organized in a peer review process, in which member states form working groups to jointly supervise each other. In this situation of very similar policies and the considerably different formal authority of the EU and the OECD, the strong differences between the levels of politicization for this time period (1996–2004) are revealing.

Table 4.4 Descriptive statistics for politicization indicators across institutions, 1996–2004

	Min	*Max*	*Mean*	*SD*
EU				
Salience	0.08	0.29	0.18	0.08
Controversy	11.76	31.11	24.35	6.04
Plurality	33.96	75.0	50.06	13.24
OECD				
Salience	0.006	0.05	0.02	0.01
Controversy	0	30.0	9.09	11.26
Plurality	0	100.0	23.22	34.40

Table 4.4 shows that the mean values for this period were substantially higher for the EU than for the OECD. Most notably, the mean salience of EU tax governance is nine times higher than of OECD tax legislation. Similarly, mean values for controversy and plurality are three times and two times higher, respectively. This quantitative result is underpinned by a qualitative reading of the material, showing that there was a much stronger public debate about the EU code of conduct than about the OECD HTC. This underlines that the combination of formal international authority and policy output is a strong driver of politicization. By contrast, the absence of one of the two components is likely to result in weak and short-lived politicization episodes.

Notes

1 Generally, the typology presupposes that political decisions have some degree of legal bindingness because only legally binding decisions – such as EU regulations, decision, and directives – are considered to limit national autonomy.

2 I thank Hendrik Jacobsen from Jacobs University Bremen for excellent research assistance with the dataset.

3 Clearly, this focus on treaties and legislation neglects more gradual changes introduced by European Court of Justice (ECJ) case law and developments within the Commission and the Parliament (for this supranationalist perspective see Sandholtz and Stone Sweet, 1998) and the widening of the EU. However, I claim that this approach is warranted because more gradual changes over time are barely visible to the public and because widening is beyond the scope of the institutionalist perspective.

4 Although the name "European Union" was established only with the Maastricht Treaty in 1993, I use it to also describe earlier periods.

5 The founding members were Belgium, France, Italy, Luxembourg, the Netherlands, and West Germany.

6 Note that controversy scores for 1991 and 1992 result from a total of one and two articles, respectively.

7 See the *Journal of Common Market Studies* special issue "Confronting Euroscepticism" (Usherwood and Startin, 2013) for a recent review.

8 Note that this statement pertains to the deepening of European Integration. The broadening of the process, that is, the enlargement of the European Union – is subject to a different trajectory and shall not be discussed here.

9 These include Austria, Belgium, Canada, Denmark, France, Germany, Greece, Iceland, Ireland, Italy, Luxembourg, the Netherlands, Norway, Portugal, Spain, Sweden, Switzerland, Turkey, United Kingdom, and United States.
10 For details on issue scope, see Appendix 1 and Appendix 2.
11 Altogether the OECD lists eight changes in 1996, 1997, 1999, 2008, and 2010.

References

Abbott, K., Keohane, R. O., Moravcsik, A., Slaughter, A. M. and Snidal, D. 2000. The Concept of Legalization. *International Organization*, 54, 401–419.

Abbott, K. and Snidal, D. 1998. Why States Act Through Formal International Organizations. *Journal of Conflict Resolution*, 42, 3–32.

American Law Institute. 1992. International Aspects of United States Income. *Taxation II: United States Income Tax Treaties*, 3.

Anderson, C. J. and Reichert, S. M. 1998. Economic Benefits and Support for Membership in the EU: A Cross-National Analysis. *Journal of Public Policy*, 15, 231–249.

Barnett, M. and Finnemore, M. 2004. *Rules for the World: International Organizations in Global Politics*, Ithaca: Cornell University Press.

Barth, C. and Bijsmans, P. 2018. The Maastricht Treaty and Public Debates About European Integration: The Emergence of a European Public Sphere? *Journal of Contemporary European Studies*, 26, 215–231.

Birch Sörensen, P. 2004. Company Tax Reform in the European Union. *International Tax and Public Finance*, 11, 91–115.

Blake, D. J. and Payton, A. L. 2015. Balancing Design Objectives: Analyzing New Data on Voting Rules in Intergovernmental Organizations. *Review of International Organizations*, 10, 377–402.

Boehmer, C., Gratzke, E. and Nordstrom, T. 2004. Do Intergovernmental Organizations Promote Peace? *World Politics*, 57, 1–38.

Börzel, T. A. 2005. Mind the Gap! European Integration Between Level and Scope. *Journal of European Public Policy*, 12, 217–236.

Burns, C., Rasmussen, A. and Reh, C. 2013. Legislative Codecision and Its Impact on the Political System of the European Union. *Journal of European Public Policy*, 20, 941–952.

Cattoir, P. 2007. A History of the "Tax Package": The Principles and Issues Underlying the Community Approach. *European Commission Taxation Papers*, 10, 1–25.

Cockfield, A. J. 2006. The Rise of the OECD as Informal "World Tax Organization" Through National Responses to E-Commerce Tax Challenges. *Yale Journal of Law and Technology*, 8, 136–187.

Devereux, M. P. 2004. Debating Proposed Reforms of the Taxation of Corporate Income in the European Union. *International Tax and Public Finance*, 11, 71–89.

Donahue, J. D. and Pollack, M. A. 2001. Centralization and its Discontents: The Rhythms of Federalism in the United States and the European Union. *In:* Nicolaidis, K. and Howse, R. (eds.) *The Federalist Vision: Legitimacy and Levels of Governance in the United States and the European Union*, Oxford: Oxford University Press.

Downs, A. 1972. Up and Down With Ecology: The Issue Attention Cycle. *Public Interest*, 28, 38–50.

Eccleston, R. 2012. *The Dynamics of Global Economic Governance: The Financial Crisis, the OECD and the Politics of International Tax Cooperation*, Cheltenham: Edward Elgar.

Ecker-Ehrhardt, M. 2012. Cosmopolitan Politicization: How Perceptions of Interdependence Foster Citizens' Expectations in International Institutions. *European Journal of International Relations*, 18, 481–508.

Edwards, J. and Keen, M. 1996. Tax Competition and Leviathan. *European Economic Review*, 40, 113–134.

Eggert, W. and Haufler, A. 2006. Company Tax Coordination Cum Tax Rate Competition in the European Union. *Public Finance Analysis*, 62, 579–601.

Eichenberg, R. C. and Dalton, R. J. 1993. Europeans and the European Community: The Dynamics of Public Support for European Integration. *International Organization*, 47, 507–534.

Eichenberg, R. C. and Dalton, R. J. 2007. Post-Maastricht Blues: The Transformation of Citizen Support for European Integration, 1973–2004. *Acta Politica*, 42, 128–152.

Elsayyad, M. and Konrad, K. A. 2012. Fighting Multiple Tax Havens. *Journal of International Economics*, 86, 295–305.

European Economic Social Committee (EESC). 2011. *The EESC: A Bridge Between Europe and Organised Civil Society*, Brussels: European Union.

Fitzgibbon, J. 2013. Citizens Against Europe? Civil Society and Eurosceptic Protest in Ireland, the United Kingdom and Denmark. *Journal of Common Market Studies*, 51, 105–121.

Follesdal, A. and Hix, S. 2006. Why There Is a Democratic Deficit in the EU: A Response to Majone and Moravcsik. *Journal of Common Market Studies*, 44, 533–562.

Franklin, M. N. and Wlezien, C. 1997. The Responsive Public: Issue Salience, Policy Change, and Preferences for European Unification. *Journal of Theoretical Politics*, 9, 347–363.

G20. 2009. *The Global Plan for Recovery and Reform*, Final Communique of the G20 Summit in London, 2 April 2009.

Gabel, M. and Palmer, H. 1995. Understanding Variation in Public Support for European Integration. *European Journal of Political Research*, 27, 3–19.

Ganghof, S. and Genschel, P. 2008. Taxation and Democracy in the EU. *Journal of Common Market Studies*, 15, 58–77.

Garry, J. and Tilley, J. 2009. The Macroeconomic Factors Conditioning the Impact of Identity on Attitudes Towards the EU. *European Union Politics*, 10, 361–379.

Genschel, P. 2002. *Steuerwettbewerb und Steuerharmonisierung in der Europäischen Union*, Frankfurt a.M.: Campus.

Genschel, P. 2007. Why No Mutual Recognition of VAT? Regulation, Taxation and the Integration of the EU's Internal Market for Goods. *Journal of Common Market Studies*, 14, 743–761.

Genschel, P. and Jachtenfuchs, M. 2011. How the European Union Constrains the State: Multilevel Governance of Taxation. *European Journal of Political Research*, 50, 293–294.

Genschel, P., Kemmerling, A. and Seils, E. 2011. Accelerating Downhill: How the EU Shapes Corporate Tax Competition in the Single Market. *Journal of Common Market Studies*, 49, 585–606.

Genschel, P. and Schwarz, P. 2011. Tax Competition: A Literature Review. *Socio-Economic Review*, 9, 339–370.

Haas, E. B. 1968. *The Uniting of Europe: Political, Social and Economic Forces 1950–1957*, 2nd ed., Stanford: Stanford University Press.

Haftel, Y. Z. and Thompson, A. 2006. The Independence of International Organizations. *Journal of Conflict Resolution*, 50, 253–275.

Hawkins, D. G., Lake, D. A., Nielson, D. L. and Tierney, M. J. (eds.) 2006. *Delegation and Agency in International Organizations*, Cambridge: Cambridge University Press.

Heldt, E. and Schmidtke, H. 2017. Empowering International Organizations: Evolution of Financial and Staff Capabilities. *Global Policy*, 8, 51–61.

Hix, S. 2008. *What's Wrong With the European Union and How to Fix It*, Cambridge, MA: Polity Press.

Hooghe, L. and Marks, G. 2005. Calculation, Community and Cues. *European Union Politics*, 6, 419–443.

Hooghe, L. and Marks, G. 2009. A Postfunctionalist Theory of European Integration: From Permissive Consensus to Constraining Dissensus. *British Journal of Political Science*, 39, 1–23.

Hooghe, L. and Marks, G. 2015. Delegation and Pooling in International Organizations. *Review of International Organizations*, 10, 305–328.

Hooghe, L., Marks, G., Lenz, T., Bezuijen, J., Ceka, B. and Derderyan, S. 2017. *Measuring International Authority: A Postfunctionalist Theory of Governance*, Vol. IV, Oxford: Oxford University Press.

Hutter, S. and Grande, E. 2014. Politicizing Europe in the National Electoral Arena: A Comparative Analysis of Five West European Countries: 1970–2010. *Journal of Common Market Studies*, 52, 1002–1018.

Jacobson, H. K., Reisinger, W. M. and Mathers, T. 1986. National Entanglements in International Governmental Organizations. *American Political Science Review*, 80, 141–159.

Johannesen, N. and Zucmann, G. 2012. The End of Bank Secrecy? An Evaluation of the G20 Tax Haven Crackdown. *Paris School of Economics Working Paper 2012/4*, Paris: Paris School of Economics.

Johnson, T. and Urpelainen, J. 2012. A Strategy of Regime Integration and Separation. *International Organization*, 66, 645–677.

Kelley, J. G. and Simmons, B. A. 2015. Politics by Numbers: Indicators as Social Pressure in International Relations. *American Journal of Political Science*, 59, 55–70.

Kemmerling, A. 2011. From Convergence to Diffusion: The EU's Influence on National Tax Systems. *CEUR Working Paper Series*, 11, 1–21.

Kemmerling, A. and Seils, E. 2009. The Regulation of Redistribution: Managing Conflict in Corporate Tax Competition. *West European Politics*, 32, 756–773.

Kleine, M. 2013. *Informal Governance in the European Union: How Governments Make International Organizations Work*, Ithaca: Cornell University Press.

Koremenos, B., Lipson, C. and Snidal, D. 2001. The Rational Design of International Institutions. *International Organization*, 55, 761–799.

Kudrle, R. T. 2008. The OECD's Harmful Tax Competition Initiative and the Tax Havens: From Bombshell to Damp Squib. *Global Economy Journal*, 8, 1–23.

Kudrle, R. T. 2010. Tax Policy in the OECD: Soft Governance Gets Harder. *In:* Martens, K. and Jakobi, A. P. (eds.) *Mechanisms of OECD Governance: International Incentives for National Policy-Making*? Oxford: Oxford University Press.

Lake, D. A. 2007. Delegating Divisible Sovereignty: Sweeping a Conceptual Minefield. *Review of International Organizations*, 2, 219–237.

Leuffen, D., Rittberger, B. and Schimmelfennig, F. 2013. *Differentiated Integration: Explaining Variation in the European Union*, Basingstoke: Palgrave Macmillan.

Mahone, R. and McBride, S. 2008. Introduction. *In:* Mahone, R. and McBride, S. (eds.) *The OECD and Transnational Governance*, Vancouver: University of British Columbia Press.

Mahoney, J. and Rueschemeyer, D. 2003. Comparative Historical Analysis: Achievements and Agendas. *In:* Mahoney, J. and Rueschemeyer, D. (eds.) *Comparative Historical Analysis in the Social Sciences*, Cambridge: Cambridge University Press.

Mahoney, J. and Thelen, K. (eds.) 2015. *Advances in Comparative-Historical Analysis*, Cambridge: Cambridge University Press.

Majone, G. 1996. *Regulating Europe*, London: Routledge.

Marks, G. and Steenbergen, M. R. (eds.) 2004. *European Integration and Political Conflict*, Cambridge: Cambridge University Press.

Martens, K. and Jakobi, A. P. 2010. Introduction: The OECD as an Actor in International Politics. *In:* Martens, K. and Jakobi, A. P. (eds.) *Mechanisms of OECD Governance: International Incentives for National Policy-Making*? Oxford: Oxford University Press.

McLaren, L. M. 2006. *Identity, Interests and Attitudes to European Integration*, Basingstoke: Palgrave Macmillan.

Mintz, J. 2004. Corporate Tax Harmonization in Europe: It's All About Compliance. *International Tax and Public Finance*, 11.

Moravcsik, A. 1998. *The Choice for Europe: Social Purpose and State Power From Messina to Maastricht*, Ithaca: Cornell University Press.

Moravcsik, A. 2005. The European Constitutional Compromise and the Neofunctionalist Legacy. *Journal of European Public Policy*, 12, 349–386.

Moravcsik, A. and Nicolaidis, K. 1998. Keynote Article: Federal Ideals and Constitutional Realities in the Amsterdam Treaty. *Journal of Common Market Studies*, 36, 13–38.

Nelson, S. C. 2017. *The Currency of Confidence: How Economic Beliefs Shape the IMF's Relationship With Its Borrowers*, Ithaca: Cornell University Press.

OECD. 1960. *Convention on the Organisation for Economic Co-operation and Development*, Paris: OECD.

OECD. 1971. *Resolution of the Council on the Mandate of the Committee on Fiscal Affairs*, Paris: OECD.

OECD. 2006. *OECD Work on Taxation: Tax in a Borderless World*, Paris: OECD.

OECD. 2010. *Taxation of Corporate and Capital Income*, Paris: OECD.

OECD. 2013. *Multilateral Convention on Mutual Administrative Assistance in Tax Matters*, Paris: OECD.

Ougaard, M. 2010. The OECD's Global Role. *In:* Martens, K. and Jakobi, A. P. (eds.) *Mechanisms of OECD Governance: International Incentives for National Policy-Making*? Oxford: Oxford University Press.

Page, E. C. and Dimitrakopoulos, D. 1997. The Dynamics of EU Growth: A Cross-Time Analysis. *Journal of Theoretical Politics*, 9, 365–387.

Paris, R. 2003. The Globalization of Taxation? Electronic Commerce and the Transformation of the State. *International Studies Quarterly*, 47, 153–182.

Pollack, M. A. 1994. Creeping Competence: The Expanding Agenda of the European Community. *Journal of Public Policy*, 14, 95–145.

Pollack, M. A. 2000. The End of Creeping Competence? EU Policy-Making Since Maastricht. *Journal of Common Market Studies*, 38, 519–538.

Radaelli, C. M. 1997. *The Politics of Corporate Taxation in the European Union: Knowledge and International Policy Agendas*, London: Routledge.

Radaelli, C. M. 2008. Governance Areas in the EU Direct Tax Policy. *Journal of Common Market Studies*, 46, 315–336.

Radaelli, C. M. and Kraemer, U. S. 2005. The Rise and Fall of Governance Legitimacy: The Case of International Direct Taxation. *International Conference on "Shifting*

Relations in Governance in the EU: Winners and Losers of Informal Governance", University of Amsterdam.

Rauh, C. 2016. *A Responsive Technocracy? EU Politicisation and the Consumer Policies of the European Commission*, Colchester: ECPR Press.

Rixen, T. 2008. *The Political Economy of International Tax Governance*, Basingstoke: Palgrave Macmillan.

Rixen, T. and Zangl, B. 2013. The Politicization of International Economic Institutions in US Public Debates. *Review of International Organizations*, 8, 363–387.

Sandholtz, W. and Stone Sweet, A. (eds.) 1998. *European Integration and Supranational Governance*, Oxford: Oxford University Press.

Scharpf, F. W. 1988. The Joint Decision-Trap: Lessons from German and European Integration. *Public Administration*, 66, 239–287.

Scharpf, F. W. 2006. The Joint-Decision Trap Revisited. *Journal of Common Market Studies*, 44, 845–864.

Sharman, J. C. 2008. Regional Deals and Global Imperative: The External Dimension of the European Savings Tax Directive. *Journal of Common Market Studies*, 46, 1049–1069.

Sharman, J. C. 2012. Seeing Like the OECD on Tax. *New Political Economy*, 17, 17–33.

Statham, P. and Trenz, H.-J. 2013. *The Politicization of Europe: Contesting the Constitution in the Mass Media*, London: Routledge.

Sternberg, C. 2013. *The Struggle for EU Legitimacy: Public Contestation, 1950–2005*, Basingstoke: Palgrave Macmillan.

Stone, R. W. 2011. *Controlling Institutions: International Organizations and the Global Economy*, Cambridge: Cambridge University Press.

Swank, D. 2006. Tax Policy in an Era of Internationalization: Explaining the Spread of Neoliberalism. *International Organization*, 60, 847–882.

Taggart, P. 1998. A Touchstone of Dissent: Euroscepticism in Contemporary Western European Party Systems. *European Journal of Political Research*, 33, 363–388.

Tallberg, J., Sommerer, T. and Squatrito, T. 2016. The Performance of International Organizations: A Policy Approach. *Journal of European Public Policy*, 23, 1077–1096.

Toshkov, D. 2012. Public Opinion and Policy Output in the European Union: A Lost Relationship. *European Union Politics*, 12, 169–191.

Usherwood, S. and Startin, N. 2013. Euroscepticism as a Persistent Phenomenon. *Journal of Common Market Studies*, 51, 1–16.

Verdun, A. 2013. Decision-Making Before and After Lisbon: The Impact of Changes in Decision-Making Rules. *West European Politics*, 36, 1128–1142.

Volgy, T., Fausett, E., Grant, K. A. and Rodgers, S. 2008. Identifying Formal Intergovernmental Organizations. *Journal of Peace Research*, 45, 837–850.

Webb, M. C. 2004. Defining the Boundaries of Legitimate State Practice: Norms, Transnational Actors and the OECD's Project on Harmful Tax Competition. *Review of International Political Economy*, 11, 787–824.

Webb, M. C. and Porter, T. 2008. Role of the OECD in the Orchestration of Global Knowledge Networks. *In:* Mahone, R. and McBride, S. (eds.) *The OECD and Transnational Governance*, Vancouver: University of British Columbia Press.

Wessels, B. 1997. An Ever Closer Fusion? A Dynamic Macropolitical View on Integration Processes. *Journal of Common Market Studies*, 35, 267–299.

Wessels, B. 2004. Contestation Potential of Interest Groups in the EU: Emergence Structure, and Political Alliances. *In:* Marks, G. and Steenbergen, M. R. (eds.) *European Integration and Political Conflict*, Cambridge: Cambridge University Press.

Wessels, W. 2001. Nice Results: The Millennium IGC in the EU's Evolution. *Journal of Common Market Studies*, 39, 197–219.

Wlezien, C. 1995. The Public as Thermostat: Dynamics of Preferences for Spending. *American Journal of Political Science*, 39, 981–1000.

Wlezien, C. 2004. Patterns of Representation: Dynamics of Public Preferences and Policy. *Journal of Politics*, 66, 1–24.

Wolfe, R. 2008. From Reconstructing Europe to Constructing Globalization: The OECD in Historical Perspective. *In:* Mahone, R. and McBride, S. (eds.) *The OECD in Transnational Governance*, Vancouver: British Columbia University Press.

Woodward, R. 2008. Towards Complex Multilateralism. *In:* Mahone, R. and McBride, S. (eds.) *The OECD and Transnational Governance*, Vancouver: University of British Columbia Press.

Woodward, R. 2010. The OECD and Economic Governance: Invisibility and Impotence? *In:* Martens, K. and Jakobi, A. P. (eds.) *In Mechanisms of OECD Governance: International Incentives for National Policy-Making?* Oxford: Oxford University Press.

Zürn, M., Binder, M. and Ecker-Erhardt, M. 2012. International Authority and Its Politicization. *International Theory*, 4, 69–106.

5 How international authority and domestic context shape differentiated patterns of politicization

The case studies presented in Chapter 4 support the institutionalist proposition that the politicization of international institutions is driven by growing international authority. A complex interaction between formal authority and policy output explains a substantial share of variance across institutions and over time. This chapter turns to the question of whether and why levels, changes, and patterns of politicization not only vary across organizations but also across countries.

My theory of politicization posits that the effect of international authority is conditioned by domestic context. It suggests that politicization is driven by international authority and shaped by domestic socio-cultural conditions. I expect politicization to vary according to the country-specific authority of an international institution and according to the level of cosmopolitans and exclusive nationalists, and the relative distribution of both groups.

To examine the empirical implications of this argument and the explanatory power of domestic context, this chapter disaggregates the dataset on the politicization of EU tax governance to the national level. Individual case studies examine the politicization of EU tax governance in Germany, Ireland, and Switzerland. As the politicization of OECD tax governance is limited to marginal episodes, it is of little analytical value to include OECD tax governance in this analysis. The case studies give a detailed account of the country-specific level and scope of EU formal authority and tax governance and the mobilization potential of cosmopolitans and exclusive nationalists.

The chapter proceeds in three steps. First, I explain the case selection and measurement details. Second, the core of the chapter presents the three country case studies, analyzing quantitative and qualitative data. The final section compares the results and concludes.

Measuring socio-cultural context

Country case selection follows the spirit of the most similar systems design (Gerring, 2007: 131–139). Germany, Ireland, and Switzerland are similar in many important respects and differ in terms of the explanatory factors highlighted in Chapter 3 (see Table 5.1). All four countries are established liberal democracies with consolidated political institutions and party systems. They are among the

Table 5.1 Case selection

Country	*EU integration*	*Economic position*	*Cosmopolitan mobilization*	*Nationalist mobilization*
Germany	Founding member, no opt-outs	• High taxes • Loses from tax competition	Medium	Medium
Ireland	Accession member, limited number of opt-outs	• Low corporate tax • Wins from tax competition	Low	Medium
Switzerland	Customized quasi-membership	• Low corporate and private income tax • Wins from tax competition	High	High

economically most developed and internationally most integrated countries in the world. They are thus strongly affected by the globalization of taxation. Although the selected countries may have varying preferences as regards the specific content and direction of global tax governance due to their different comparative (dis-)advantages in tax competition,[1] their generally high degree of affectedness by the growing supply and demand for global tax governance is an important scope condition for the comparison. Less economically integrated and less democratic countries often have different preferences on global tax governance (Genschel et al., 2016; Genschel and Seelkopf, 2016). They are likely to yield substantially different levels and patterns of politicization. My country selection, thus, helps to increase the internal validity of the study but, in turn, limits external validity. The results presented in this book can be plausibly generalized only to other highly developed and stable democracies.

Within these scope conditions, the selection of countries maximizes the variance of explanatory factors. First, I have selected countries that are subject to different levels of EU authority. The selection of Germany as a founding member of the EU, which has not opted out of any major step of European integration; Ireland as an accession country, which has opted out of a number of integration steps; and Switzerland, which is not a formal member of the EU but is nonetheless considerably integrated with the EU via bilateral treaties, represents a broad spectrum of EU authority.

Second, the economic and cultural contexts also vary across countries. Switzerland has built a strong reputation for its low corporate and individual income tax rates. It is also a country of strong polarization between cosmopolitans and exclusive nationalists. Ireland's economic development is also tied to tax competition and low corporate tax rates. Yet, the mobilization potential of cosmopolitans and nationalists is lower than in Switzerland. The German cultural context is similar to the Irish case, although its economic context is different. Germany represents large, high-tax countries, which potentially lose rather than win in tax competition.

I adapt the measurement of international authority presented in Chapter 4 to account for the varying extent to which EU formal authority and tax governance affect the countries in the sample. The mobilization potential is measured on the basis of survey data on individual feelings of territorial belonging (Norris, 2000; Furia, 2005; Roudometof, 2005). I use a question item on territorial attachment asked in the World Value Survey (WVS) and the European Values Study (EVS) to identify cosmopolitans and exclusive nationalists. In both surveys, respondents are asked the following question:

> To which of these geographical groups would you say you belong first of all? And the next? (1) The locality or town where you live; (2) State or region of country where you live; (3) [The US] as a whole*; (4) [North America]*; (5) The world as a whole.* [substitute your own nation and continent for these].

The WVS and EVS data provide almost complete time series for all three selected countries.[2] Exclusive nationalists are identified by subtracting from the group of respondents, who see themselves as belonging primarily to the nation (Answer 3), those respondents who choose their continent (Answer 4) or the world (Answer 5) as their second territorial identity. The latter may be labeled "inclusive nationalists." Those respondents who see themselves as belonging primarily to their continent or the world are classified as cosmopolitans irrespective of their second choice (for a similar approach, see Jung, 2008: 585).

Finally, the mobilization of radical right parties is measured on the basis of vote shares. I follow the classification of parties provided by Cas Mudde (2007: 21) and Pippa Norris (2005: 54–57). Both authors identify a number of radical right parties in Switzerland and Germany but do not find similar parties in Ireland. Vote share data on national elections are taken from official German (Bundeswahlleiter, 2013) and Swiss (Das Schweizer Parlament, 2013) sources.

Germany: cosmopolitan demand for more European tax governance

Germany is a founding member of the EU and has never opted out of important steps of European integration. Rather, German successive governments have pushed both for the deepening of European integration and the enlargement of the European project to a mounting number of member states (Paterson, 2010). As such, Germany is frequently considered to be one of the main driving forces behind the EU (Katzenstein, 1997; Bulmer and Paterson, 2010). Consequently, the German polity was fully subjected to the growing formal authority of the EU. The scope and level of EU formal authority over German politics grew steadily over the course of the observation time period (for the details of the EU integration process see Chapter 4). The SEA and the Treaty of Maastricht especially transformed the EU from a regional economic institution into a political union that is no longer limited to the elimination of trade barriers but aims to integrate national jurisdictions on a much broader scale. The Treaties of Amsterdam, Nice, and Lisbon continued this trend. Relative to the previous treaties, their impact on the level and scope of EU formal authority was moderate.

Similarly, the EU's tax policy grew steadily over time. The EU started with a limited number of legislative acts, primarily targeting the coordination of VAT systems and excises. Over time, the frequency of tax legislation and its scope increased steadily. Not only did the EU become more active in the regulation of VAT and excises but also it expanded the scope of its legislation to other major fields of taxation. Since the end of the 1990s, private and corporate income taxes have been a regular target of European tax governance.

In sum, the German case is characterized by a strong and direct impact of EU authority. Both formal authority and tax legislation grew over time and limit German tax sovereignty to an ever-increasing extent. The growth of formal authority is marked by strong increases during the first two periods of treaty revision and less tremendous changes during the later revision periods of Amsterdam, Nice, and Lisbon. The development of EU tax legislation followed a more continuous trajectory. The frequency and scope of EU tax legislation grew more slowly but constantly. The interaction effect of both formal authority and tax policy output should contribute to a constant growth of politicization, which should be most pronounced during the Maastricht period.

The German mobilization potential

This effect of formal authority and policy output should be conditioned by domestic context, that is, the share and mobilization of cosmopolitans and nationalists. Figure 5.1 plots the share, distribution, and development of both groups in detail. The figure shows the share of individuals holding a cosmopolitan outlook, the

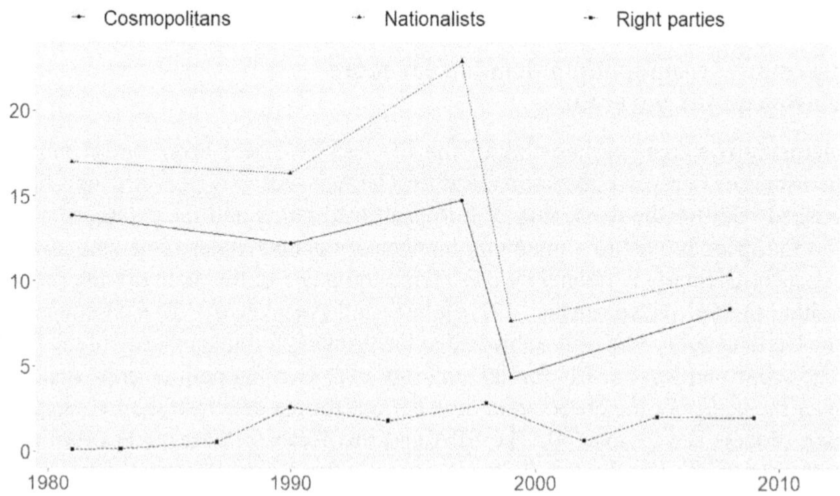

Figure 5.1 German mobilization potential, 1981–2011

share of individuals holding an exclusive nationalist outlook (belonging), and the vote share of radical right parties in national elections.

The data show that the overall mobilization potential of German society results from a strikingly similar share of exclusive nationalists and cosmopolitans. With a share of 17 percent of exclusive nationalists and 14 percent of cosmopolitans, the size of both groups was almost similar in 1981. Together both groups amounted to almost one-third of the German population. Consequently, the 1980s were marked by a considerable polarization between exclusive nationalists and cosmopolitans.

Over the subsequent decade, this constellation remained stable. The share of both groups decreased only marginally in 1990. During the subsequent years, the German mobilization potential grew slightly. In 1997 the share of exclusive nationalists rose by 6 percent to 23 percent and the group of cosmopolitans grew by 3 percent to 15 percent. These changes increased the German mobilization potential by almost 10 percent to 38 percent and contributed to a slightly more unbalanced distribution of both groups in favor of exclusive nationalists. While the difference between the two groups was small during the first two periods of European integration (3 percent in 1981 and 3 percent in 1990), it widened during the Maastricht period to more than 8 percent. Overall, the size of both groups was considerable, which points to a sustained polarization of German society.

A more substantial change took place during the subsequent years. The survey data indicate a substantial decline in both groups by more than two-thirds. The share of nationalists decreased to 8 percent and the size of the cosmopolitan group even fell to an all-time low of 4 percent. Consequently, the mobilization potential declined substantially to an overall share of 12 percent. Although both groups recovered between 1999 and 2008 – the final data point in the survey data – the mobilization potential remained considerably lower than during the first periods of European integration.[3] The share of nationalists recuperated to 10 percent until 2008 and the cosmopolitan group returned to 8 percent. The overall mobilization potential, therefore, came closer to the levels of the previous years. Yet, with a combined share of 19 percent, it was still notably smaller than during the previous periods of European integration. Despite some fluctuation, the polarization between both groups was largely stable.

In sum, the size of both groups and the low mobilization by radical right parties point to an equal mobilization potential of cosmopolitans and nationalists. While the latter group is larger, the constantly low vote share of radical right parties demonstrates that exclusive nationalism has lost social recognition in Germany. In fact, strong nationalistic arguments highlighting German superiority or the uncompromising defense of national sovereignty are difficult to make in German public discourses due to Germany's role during World War II. Even those who feel exclusively attached to the German nation-state are often convinced that Germany should be integrated into international institutions (Diez Medrano, 2003: Ch. 6). The German society is characterized by a polarization between both groups. However, the majority of German citizens see themsleves as inclusive nationalists, resulting in a medium overall politicization potential of the German society.

The politicization of EU tax governance in Germany

How did this mobilization potential condition the politicization of EU tax governance in the German public? An answer to this question is necessarily focused on developments over time. Defining absolute thresholds for the share of cosmopolitans or exclusive nationalists that are necessary to reinforce or hamper the effect of the EU's authority is notoriously difficult. A theoretically convincing answer to the question of whether a share of 30 percent or 50 percent of these groups would be sufficient to reinforce the political authority effect cannot be given. Hence, I follow the route of within-case comparison of periods of European integration to trace the effect of varying shares of exclusive nationalists and cosmopolitans.

The share of both groups was basically constant for the periods 1981–1986 and 1987–1992, and increased slightly during the Maastricht period. The political authority of the EU increased substantially over the course of the three periods. Taking these two observations into account, I expect the politicization of EU tax governance to grow during the early 1980s and the SEA period.[4] Similar expectations apply to the Maastricht period during which EU authority also grew substantially, while the German mobilization potential increased slightly.

With the beginning of the final observation period (1999–2011), expectations change and put post-functionalist and modernization theory to a more demanding test because EU authority and domestic conditions took divergent routes. While political authority in terms of formal treaty revision and tax policy output continued to grow, the share of nationalists and cosmopolitans decreased. If domestic conditions play an important role for politicization, the combination of less strongly growing EU authority and a substantially decreasing mobilization potential should result in a leveling off in politicization, if not a decrease.

Figure 5.2 and Table 5.2 detail the quantitative data on the politicization of EU tax governance in Germany. The plots in Figure 5.2 show the three individual

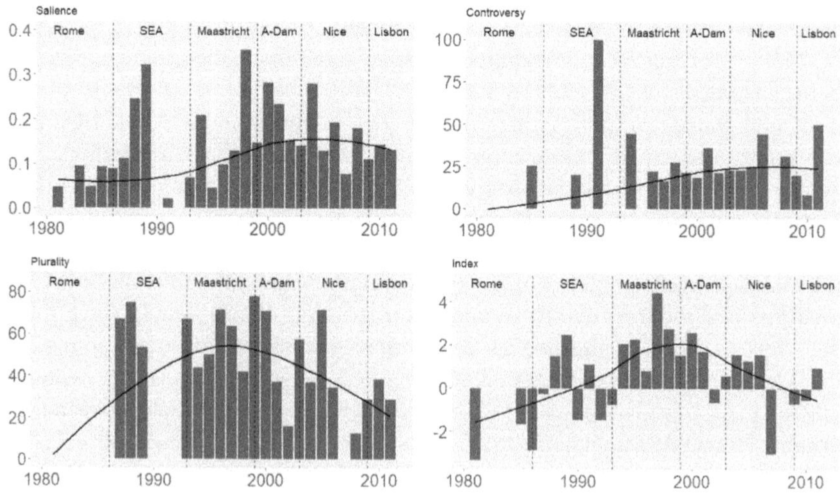

Figure 5.2 Politicization in Germany, 1981–2011

Table 5.2 Descriptive statistics for periods of European integration in Germany

Descriptive statistics	*Politicization indicators*			*Formal authority*			*Policy output*		*Mobilization %*	
	Salience	*Controversy*	*Plurality*	*Scope*	*Level*	*Overall*	*Frequency*	*Scope*	*Cosmopolitan*	*Nationalist*
1981–1986 (Treaty of Rome)[a]										
Min	0	0	0	9	1.9	17	4	0	13.9	16.9
Max	0.09	25	0	9	1.9	17	7	3		
Mean	0.06	5	0	9	1.9	17	5	2		
SD	0.03	9.3	0	0	0	0	0.94	0.69		
1987–1992 (SEA)										
Min	0	0	0	14	2.3	32	3	2	12.2	16.4
Max	0.32	100	75	14	2.3	32	28	3		
Mean	0.12	30	48.8	14	2.3	32	11	3		
SD	0.13	36.5	33.1	0	0	0	8.5	0.5		
1993–1998 (Treaty of Maastricht)										
Min	0.05	0	41.9	18	2.8	50.5	7	2	14.8	22.9
Max	0.36	44.4	71.4	18	2.8	50.5	26	3		
Mean	0.15	18.4	56.2	18	2.8	50.5	15	3		
SD	0.11	15.6	11.5	0	0	0	6.9	0.5		
1999–2011 (Treaties of Amsterdam, Nice, Lisbon)										
Min	0.08	0	0	18	3.3	58.5	15	2	1999: 4.4 2008: 10.4	7.7 8.4
Max	0.28	50	77.8	18	3.9	69.8	42	5		
Mean	0.17	27.2	39.2	18	3.5	61.3	22	4		
SD	0.03	12.5	23.5	0	0.3	4.8	6.6	0.8		

a While the Treaty of Rome was signed in 1957, my time series data on politicization only starts with the year 1981.

operationalizing components of politicization. The data result from 351 statements on EU tax governance published in 320 newspaper articles. The top-left plot shows the salience of EU tax governance, that is, the percentage of newspaper articles discussing issues of EU tax governance relative to the overall number of newspaper articles published per year. The top-right plot displays the controversy dimension of politicization, which measures the share of newspaper articles that feature a minimum of two affective statements. The bottom-left plot shows the final component of politicization. The plurality of the debate considers the share of affective statements contributed by non-executive actors. Finally, the bottom-right plot integrates these data into the politicization index, which adds up the z-scores for salience, controversy, and plurality. Vertical dashed lines mark the years of major treaty revisions.

Politicization indicators, the trajectories of EU authority and tax legislation, and the German mobilization potential, reveal a picture that is broadly in line with my theory of politicization. Although politicization indicators followed slightly different trajectories, the overall development is as expected. Salience grew strongly during the SEA and Maastricht periods, leveling off during the post-Amsterdam phase.

More specifically, although salience fluctuated after the enactment of the SEA and the Treaty of Maastricht, overall attention to EU tax governance grew substantially. On average, salience almost doubled after the enactment of the SEA and continued to increase, by almost 25 percent, after the enactment of the Treaty of Maastricht (Table 5.2). In addition, both minimum and maximum salience grew during these periods of increasing EU authority and almost constant domestic conditions. Similarly, plurality jumped to almost 49 percent subsequent to the enactment of the SEA and grew to a mean value of more than 56 percent during the Maastricht period. This strong growth of mean values was accompanied by increasing maximum and minimum values. Like salience, plurality is marked by strong ups and downs especially during the SEA phase and to a lesser extent during the Maastricht period.[5]

With the enactment of Amsterdam, this trend of growing politicization flattened quite in line with the decreasing mobilization potential.

Although the Treaties of Amsterdam, Nice, and Lisbon, as well as the EU's tax policy output, continued to increase, levels of politicization did not due to the substantially lower mobilization potential. The data reveal stagnation or even decreasing salience and plurality during this time period. While the mean value of salience grew by almost 10 percentage points, its maximum value and many annual scores of the post-Amsterdam period were substantially lower than during the Maastricht period. The slightly higher average salience during the post-Amsterdam period was mainly the result of a stabilizing and not so much of an intensifying debate on European tax governance.

For the plurality of the debate, this picture was even more pronounced. The mean value of civil society participation decreased by 17 percentage points to less than 40 percent during the post-Amsterdam period. Although the maximum score for this period of 78 percent in 1999 was slightly higher than for the previous

Ireland: rebellion of the Celtic Tiger

The Republic of Ireland is not a founding member of the EU. It joined the EU in 1973. At that time, Ireland was a small, rural, and comparatively poor country on the European periphery. EU founding members had reservations about Irish accession due to its lack of political and economic clout. Irish reasons for applying for membership in 1961 were economic in nature (Rees, 2009). While German political elites saw the European project as a way to lasting peace and stability, the Irish welcomed EU membership primarily for its economic advantages, including the common agricultural policy, the common market, and the structural funds (Laffan and O'Mahony, 2008: 30). Access to the European market and EU funds played an important role in the weak Irish economy of the 1970s. European economic support sowed the seeds for Ireland's unprecedented economic success that became known as the "Celtic Tiger" during the 1990s (Barry et al., 2001; Kirby, 2010).

This context set the tone for Irish engagement with the EU for the following 25 years. While being generally integrationist, Ireland's support for European integration was conditional on economic advantages (Laffan and O'Mahony, 2008: 42; Adshead and Tonge, 2009: 212). Economic considerations were accompanied by hopes that the country would also grow politically and socially, including the stabilization of Irish independence from the UK (O'Kelly, 2004: 515). Yet, Ireland was clearly less enthusiastic about the more political components of the European project. As a result of these reservations and the strong commitment to military neutrality – one of the leitmotifs of Irish independence (Laffan and O'Mahony, 2008: 11; Devine, 2009) – Ireland opted out of some recent steps of European integration. The Irish Republic has not adopted the Schengen acquis, which became part of the EU legal framework with the enactment of the Treaty of Amsterdam in 1999. In 2002, Ireland's military neutrality was officially recognized by the Seville Declaration, which limits Irish obligations in this issue area of European integration. In 2010, the Irish government negotiated exceptions in the field of criminal and domestic security cooperation.

Consequently, the Irish Republic is subject to less European authority than Germany. Although the scope and level of EU's formal authority grew steadily over time, this growth was weaker than in the case of Germany due to the opt-outs of Amsterdam and Lisbon. The Treaty of Rome, the SEA, and the Treaty of Maastricht had equally strong effects on Ireland. The impact of the Treaties of Amsterdam and Lisbon was slightly weaker than in German. Although these opt-outs do not directly shape the EU's tax authority, they reduce the potential for politicization via discursive spillovers. Formally, European tax legislation affects Ireland as strongly as it does Germany. Practically, EU tax governance became increasingly important for Ireland. It substantially shaped the Irish tax system, including the introduction of a VAT system, the harmonization of excises in 1972, and recent regulations of corporate income taxation.

In sum, the Irish polity is strongly affected by growing EU authority. Both formal authority and tax legislation grew over time and limited Irish sovereignty to an ever-increasing extent. The growth of formal authority was marked by strong increases during the first two periods of treaty revision and less tremendous changes during the later revision periods of Amsterdam, Nice, and Lisbon. The opt-outs of Amsterdam and Lisbon contributed to weaker growth than in the German case. The development of EU tax legislation followed a continuous trajectory. Both the frequency and scope of EU tax legislation expanded slowly but constantly. The interaction of formal authority and tax legislation should result in a constant growth of politicization levels. The strongest growth of public debate and controversy should be observable during the SEA and Maastricht periods. The less ambitious treaty reforms of Amsterdam, Nice, and Lisbon should drive a less strong growth of politicization.

The mobilization potential of the Irish society

Similar to the previous case study on the politicization of EU tax governance in Germany, I trace how and to what extent the Irish mobilization potential mediated the impact of EU's authority on the politicization of EU tax governance. Figure 5.3 shows the share, distribution, and development of cosmopolitans and nationalists. The figure plots the share of individuals holding a cosmopolitan outlook and the share of individuals holding an exclusive nationalist outlook. The vote share of radical right parties is zero due to a lack of such parties in Ireland.

The Irish mobilization potential appears to be relatively similar to the German case. Yet, it is the result of a substantially different trajectory. At the beginning of the observation period, exclusive nationalism predominated over cosmopolitism (see also O'Kelly, 2004). With a share of 18 percent, the group of Irish nationalists was more than three times larger than the group of

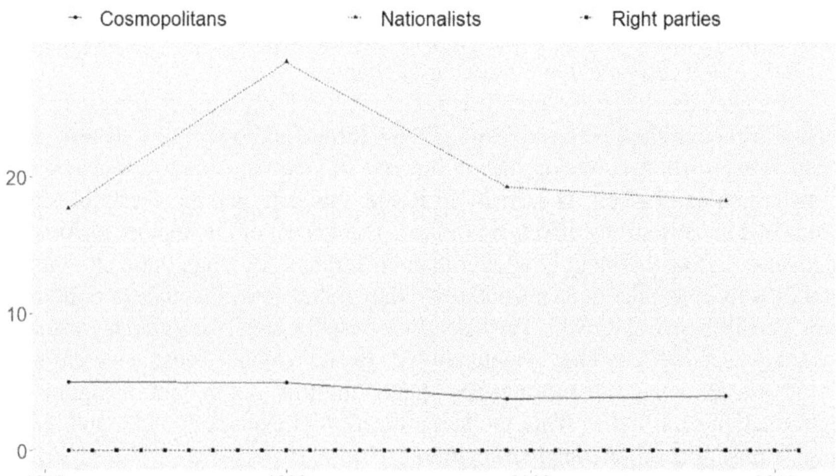

Figure 5.3 Irish mobilization potential, 1981–2011

cosmopolitans (at five percent). Due to this strong dominance of exclusive nationalism, the domestic conditions in Ireland were less favorable to the politicization of EU tax governance than in Germany, where a considerable polarization between cosmopolitans and nationalists provided a more fertile environment. The absence of radical right parties in Ireland underlined this situation. In addition, the combined share of both groups amounted to less than 25 percent of the Irish population and was consequently almost 10 percentage points lower than in the German case during the 1980s.

During the subsequent decade, the dominance of exclusive nationalism increased and resulted in even less polarization. In 1990, the share of exclusive nationalists was more than 10 percentage points higher than in 1981, whereas the share of cosmopolitans had decreased slightly. Because cosmopolitans remained a rare species, Irish society was substantially less polarized than the German population of that time. Although both populations had a similar overall mobilization potential, the skewed distribution in Ireland and weak right party mobilization imply a lower potential for the politicization of EU tax governance than in the German case.

During the following decade, the gulf between nationalists and cosmopolitans narrowed slightly due to the decreasing share of exclusive nationalists. The growth of nationalism during the 1980s was followed by a similarly strong decline by almost 10 percentage points in 1999. The level of cosmopolitanism was constant. These changes resulted in a decreasing mobilization potential by more than 10 percentage points to 23 percent and a still substantially unbalanced distribution of both groups in favor of exclusive nationalists. Due to the continued weakness of cosmopolitanism, exclusive nationalists were still five times more frequent in 1999. In comparison to the German situation during this time period, the overall Irish mobilization potential was higher because the combined share of cosmopolitans and exclusive nationalists in Germany had dropped to only 12 percent.

The 2000s were marked by stability. The share of exclusive nationalists was almost constant. In 2008 – the final data point in the survey data – the share of nationalists decreased slightly to 18 percent. Similarly, the share of cosmopolitans did not change substantially. With a share of four percent, cosmopolitans were still a marginal group. The combined share of both groups was 22 percent. The overall mobilization potential was thus almost identical to its initial level in 1981. Although this value is slightly higher than in Germany (19 percent), the strongly skewed distribution of exclusive nationalists and cosmopolitans and the weakness of radical right parties suggest that the overall mobilization potential of the Irish society was still weaker than in Germany. Contrary to the expectations of much of the modernization and Europeanization literature (Inglehart, 1970; Sinnott, 1995; Risse, 2010), Irish society remained firmly rooted in nationalism (O'Kelly, 2004; Girvin, 2010). With time, even cosmopolitanism experienced marginalization. It is still a social identity held only by a small minority. As a result, the public debate and controversy on EU tax governance should be framed in nationalist terms.

Public debate on EU tax governance in Ireland

How and to what extent did this context shape the effect of the growing formal authority and EU tax legislation on the politicization of EU tax governance in Ireland? This section traces Irish public debates across the periods of European integration and compares it to the German discussions.

Figure 5.4 plots the three components of politicization and the politicization index (see also Table 5.3). Scores for salience and controversy build on 111 newspaper articles on EU tax governance. Scores for plurality build on 197 affective statements found in these articles.

The Irish mobilization potential was predominantly nationalist. Cosmopolitans were rare and could not be expected to drive the politicization process. This situation should result in weakly growing politicization during the SEA period. Because cosmopolitans were few and exclusive nationalists weakly mobilized, the mounting authority of the EU should be accompanied by lower levels of politicization than in Germany. Despite the different mobilization potentials of both countries, the timing of the politicization process should be similar. The first shots of public debate on EU tax governance should be observable during the SEA period. With almost one-third of the population holding exclusive nationalist identities, the sheer size of this group should be sufficient to trigger the politicization process. In this vein, the SEA period constitutes a strong test for my theory of politicization. If the presence of nationalists is indeed a relevant condition for politicization, a debate framed in nationalist terms should be observable during this time period.

This development should continue during the Maastricht period. The Treaty of Maastricht was a strong push for the EU's formal authority. Although the Irish

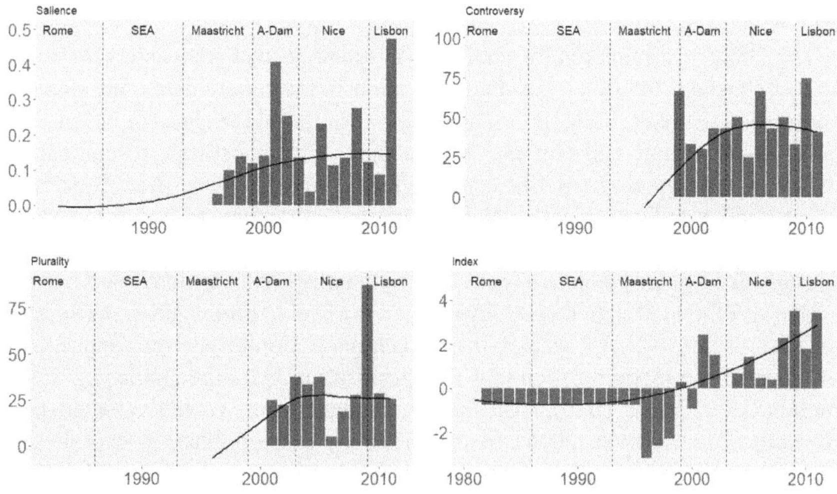

Figure 5.4 Politicization in Ireland, 1981–2011

Table 5.3 Descriptive statistics for periods of European integration in Ireland

Descriptive statistics	*Politicization indicators*			*Formal authority*			*Policy output*		*Mobilization %*	
	Salience	*Controversy*	*Plurality*	*Scope*	*Level*	*Overall*	*Frequency*	*Scope*	*Cosmopolitan*	*Nationalist*
1981–1986 (Treaty of Rome)[a]										
Min	0	0	0	9	1.9	17	4	0	5	17.7
Max	0	0	0	9	1.9	17	7	3		
Mean	0	0	0	9	1.9	17	5	2		
SD	0	0	0	0	0	0	0.94	0.69		
1987–1992 (SEA)										
Min	0	0	0	14	2.3	32	3	2	4.9	28.4
Max	0	0	0	14	2.3	32	28	3		
Mean	0	0	0	14	2.3	32	11	3		
SD	0	0	0	0	0	0	8.5	0.5		
1993–1998 (Treaty of Maastricht)										
Min	0	0	0	18	2.8	50.5	7	2	3.8	19.3
Max	0.19	0	0	18	2.8	50.5	26	3		
Mean	0.04	0	0	18	2.8	50.5	15	3		
SD	0.05	0	0	0	0	0	6.9	0.5		
1999–2011 (Treaties of Amsterdam, Nice, Lisbon)										
Min	0.03	25	0	18	3.2	58	15	2	4	18.2
Max	0.47	75	87.5	18	3.8	68.3	42	5		
Mean	0.19	46.11	26.9	18	3.5	63.3	22	4		
SD	0.12	14.68	21.4	0	0.2	4.3	6.6	0.8		

a While the Treaty of Rome was signed in 1957, my time series data on politicization only starts with the year 1981.

mobilization potential was weaker than during the SEA period and in comparison to the German situation, Maastricht can still be expected to result in growing politicization. With a share of almost 20 percent, nationalists were still strong enough to lead a substantive debate on EU tax governance.

Similar to developments in Germany, in Ireland the Maastricht period should be followed by a flattening out of politicization levels from 1999 to 2011. Because the level of EU authority grew at a more moderate pace than during the previous years – due to less ambitious treaties and Irish opt-outs – and because the share of both exclusive nationalists and cosmopolitans was stable, politicization should grow only marginally compared to the Maastricht period.

In sum, the politicization of EU tax governance in Irish public debates can be expected to be weaker than in Germany due to less polarization between nationalists and cosmopolitans and the weak mobilization of radical right parties. Because cosmopolitanism is marginal in Ireland, the debate is unlikely to be driven by an exchange of different perspectives. Rather, it should follow the path of a relatively narrow critique of EU tax governance on the ground of nationalist arguments.

These expectations are only partly met by the data. Levels of politicization followed a trajectory that does not match theoretical expectations. Especially during the SEA and the Maastricht periods (between 1987 and 1998), the level of politicization fell short of theoretical expectations. Although the strong growth of formal authority and tax policy output took place in a relatively strong nationalist context, the Irish public developed little interest. Up until the middle of the Maastricht period (1996), salience was very low. EU tax governance was not politicized at all. Even the enactment of the Treaty of Maastricht, which had a substantial impact on the German debate, and the respective Irish referendum in 1992, did not spark public controversy.[7] It took until the mid-1990s for the Irish public to discover EU tax governance – and even then, it was not until the enactment of the Treaty of Amsterdam that the debate became more controversial and plural. In comparison to the German public, the Irish were less interested in EU tax governance for most of the observation period. While less politicization in Ireland than in Germany was expected, the complete lack of newspaper coverage on EU tax governance up until 1996 is striking and can hardly be explained by the low number of cosmopolitans and the weak mobilization of radical right parties.

A more detailed analysis of individual politicization indicators reveals two main sequences of the Irish politicization process. The first sequence covers the early 1980s, the SEA period, and most of the Maastricht phase. It was largely characterized by the absence of any meaningful politicization. The second sequence, starting with the enactment of the Treaty of Amsterdam in 1999, experienced a substantial growth of salience, controversy, and plurality. It was marked by growing politicization that was similar – albeit weaker – to the German case during this period. Salience started to grow during the mid-1990s but remained weaker than in Germany. Yet, during the post-Amsterdam period, the Irish public became almost equally interested in EU tax governance as the Germans. However, the controversy of the debate did not start to grow until 1999. Until the end of the Maastricht period, the Irish debate lagged far behind the controversy of the

German debate. Subsequently, this picture changed and controversy increased to consistently high levels. During the post-Amsterdam period, the controversy of the debate was 20 percentage points higher than in Germany.

A comparably stable participation of civil society speakers emerged during the early 2000s, but fell short of plurality in Germany. Prior to this moderate upturn of civil society participation, the Irish debate was dominated by Irish executives and European officials. It resembled the conventional reporting of foreign policy.

In sum, EU tax governance became substantially politicized only during 2000. This belated politicization process was as strong as it was in Germany. Except for the lower participation of civil society speakers in the Irish debate, both debates were strikingly similar although Ireland opted-out of some of the more recent integration projects and was characterized by less favorable domestic conditions. This overview of the Irish debate shows that the strong presence of exclusive nationalists during the SEA period did not constitute a sufficient condition for the politicization of EU tax governance. Despite the strong presence of exclusive nationalists, the tension between national identity and EU tax governance remained weak and, therefore, a politicization process failed to materialize. This result corresponds to Jane O'Mahony's (2009: 429) observation that up until the Treaty of Nice and the failure of the respective referendum, Irish public opinion on European issues was characterized by a broad permissive consensus. Furthermore, the comparably strong politicization after the enactment of the Treaty of Amsterdam in 1999 indicates a rather limited explanatory capacity of modernization theory. Although the share of cosmopolitans did not grow, politicization emerged during this period. These results seem to contradict the conclusion drawn from the previous case study, in which a substantial influence of cosmopolitanism on the politicization process could be identified. By contrast, the Irish politicization process appears to be shaped by some other factor. Overall, my politicization theory does not provide a satisfactory explanation to the question as to why EU tax governance was politicized in Ireland 10 years later than in Germany. Although the SEA and the Treaty of Maastricht shaped the Irish Republic's macro-economic policy, spurring the liberalization of the economy (Leddin and Walsh, 1998: 561; Smith, 2005a: 157), EU tax governance went largely unnoticed for more than half of the observation period.

An explanation for this development can be found in the details of the Irish debates. The newspaper articles reveal that the Irish debate was strikingly less diverse than the German one. The German public took note of the whole array of European tax governance and discussed issues ranging from VAT to income taxation. Irish news coverage was much narrower, focusing primarily on income taxation. Already in 1997, descriptive newspaper articles dealt with the EU's influence on Ireland's corporate tax system, which came under pressure from the European Commission at that time. During the subsequent years, newspaper coverage of this tax area became more controversial and shaped the politicization process. Between 1997 and 2011, public debates focused strongly on corporate income taxation. Hence, the politicization of EU tax governance was first and foremost driven by controversy over the EU's activities in this area.

The major bone of contention was Ireland's preferential corporate tax rate of 10 percent for manufacturing and manufacturing services. Designed as a temporary measure to stimulate the Republic's manufacturing industry in 1980, successive governments expanded the number of sectors entitled to the lower rate as well as its duration.[8] In 1990, the preferential rate was applicable to a vast range of economic enterprises – most importantly the data processing and software industry. It was envisioned to stay in place until 2010 (Blue, 2000: 56). Over time, the policy became a cornerstone of the Republic's industrial development strategy and a key to Ireland's competitive position in the global economy (O'Hearn, 2003: 38; Smith, 2005a: 72–74). It was, thus, "deemed politically beyond challenge" (Hardiman, 2000: 828) in large segments of the population.

During the late 1990s, this corporate tax system came under scrutiny from the EU. While the European Commission approved the provisions in 1987 and allowed for extension in 1990 and 1994, the enactment of the European code of conduct for corporate taxation in 1997 changed the situation. Under pressure from German Chancellor Gerhard Schröder and British Prime Minister Tony Blair, in July 1998 the European Commission urged Ireland to bring its corporate tax system into conformity with EU rules on state aid (European Union, 1992: § 18) and the code of conduct for corporate taxation. The European Commission requested Ireland to phase out its preferential tax regime until 2010. In 2003, Ireland reacted with the introduction of a common corporate tax rate of 12.5 percent applicable to all trading profits in all sectors to protect its competitive advantage (Eggert and Haufler, 2006: 587).

This incident marked the beginning of an ongoing conflict between successive Irish governments, European institutions, and high-tax countries such as Germany and France. It triggered the politicization process in Ireland. Due to their crucial role in Ireland's economic success story, corporate taxes were an issue of pronounced national interest (Laffan, 2002: 87) and thus a particularly sensitive tax area. The expansion of the EU's tax legislation to this particular area of Irish tax policy, therefore, constituted a strong conflict with Irish preferences and set the tone for the growing politicization of EU tax governance. Attempts to harmonize corporate taxation, like former German Finance Minister Oskar Lafontaine's 1998 proposal to limit tax competition in Europe by harmonizing tax rates, or the European Commission's reoccurring initiative to implement the CCCTB, were regarded as an affront to the Irish nation itself (Allen, 2000: 84). These initiatives and EU tax legislation on corporate taxation dominated the Irish public debate on EU tax governance. Whenever proposals to increase EU authority in the field of taxation or to change the Council's decision-making procedure, abolishing the national veto on tax matters, were put on the agenda – for instance, during the negotiations on Europe's draft constitution in 2003 or the Treaty of Lisbon in 2009 – Irish politicians and civil society representatives stood firm against such limitations of Irish sovereignty.

The enactment of the code of conduct (and the resulting pressure on Ireland's corporate tax system) was the starting point for the politicization of EU tax governance. This development of the Irish public debate underlines the notion that the EU's growing authority is the key driving force behind the politicization of its tax governance. In addition, the Irish politicization process highlights the more specific post-functionalist link between nationalism and the expansion of international institutions' authority. The growing authority of international institutions is more likely to trigger nationalist backlash if it interferes with issues of strong national interest. The strong nationalist framing of the controversy on corporate taxation shows that the Irish nationalist mobilization potential was dormant as long as EU tax legislation only touched upon issues outside of this narrow set of core national interest, only to unfold rapidly when an issue of national interest was targeted.

The Irish debate during the 2000s verifies this conclusion. Initially, newspaper coverage was characterized by mounting salience and descriptive tone. Yet, it became more controversial and reached a climax in 2001 over the course of the Nice negotiations, the failure of the respective referendum, and a conflict over the government budget between the Irish government and the European Commission. The peak of salience is another indication of the strong politicizing effect of the EU's growing authority over Ireland's tax policy. It also underlines the importance of spillover effects of growing formal authority in other fields of European integration on the politicization of EU tax governance. Especially the European Commission's questioning of Ireland's 2001 budget (Smith, 2005a: 134) – in the context of European efforts to maintain monetary stability – which included cuts in private income taxes, provoked a substantive nationalist backlash against EU tax governance. Similar to the discussion on corporate taxation, Irish civil society and political elites stood together to defend national tax sovereignty against Brussels and other European capitals (see also Meyer, 2004).

The strong nationalist framing of the controversy over the European Commission's criticism of Irish plans to cut private income taxes resembled the discussions on corporate taxation. When the European Commission interfered with a particularly sensitive issue of wide national concern, it received a strong nationalist reply. Private income taxation (in particular, the progressiveness of the system) was a traditionally contested issue in the Irish Republic. For instance, in 1980 more than 700,000 people staged a general strike over income taxes. In Dublin, 300,000 went to the streets to protest the allegedly unfair distribution of the tax burden (Allen, 2000: 82). Successive governments did not approach this issue and the tax burden on low- and middle-income earners remained high (Christensen, 2013: 573–574). As a result, wide parts of the population considered the system to be utterly unfair (Hardiman, 2000). By end of the 1990s, the then-acting center-right government aspired to change this situation and began to reduce private income tax rates. But in 2001, the European Commission told the Irish that the private income tax reductions proposed in their 2001 budget were in conflict with the Broad Economic Policy Guidelines (BEPG) and could potentially threaten the stability of the economy. Similar to the European Commission's activities in the area of corporate taxation, this interference with the traditionally controversial issue of income taxation provoked a strong nationalist backlash against EU tax governance.

Subsequent to this episode, salience, controversy, and plurality stabilized on levels relatively similar to those of the German debate. This was accompanied by a slight broadening of the debate both in terms of tax areas and in terms of criteria of politicization. Clearly, the discussion on income taxation remained central and continued to be characterized by a confrontation between a coalition of Irish speakers from different camps on the one side and the EU and speakers from other European member states on the other. However, additional issues – like the European Commission's initiative to adapt VAT regulations to the rapid development of e-commerce, the introduction of an EU tax, or a tax on CO^2 emissions – were discussed more frequently between different Irish actors and in less nationalist terms. This trend of a sustained and broadening debate suggests that EU tax governance was subject to a process of politicization during the post-Amsterdam period.

The EU's interference with the Republic's income tax policies during the late 1990s and early 2000s was an important driver of this process. Yet, the picture is still incomplete because it is less obvious why the debate remained politicized over the entire post-Amsterdam period and broadened to issues beyond income taxation. The solution to this remaining puzzle is found in the wider political context. The politicization process coincided with a more general transformation of the relationship between the Irish Republic and the EU. At the time of accession, Ireland was a poor country at the periphery of the EU. This changed dramatically during the late 1990s and early 2000s when Ireland's economic turnaround made the country a wealthy and prosperous competitor for growth and employment in Europe (Laffan, 2002: 89). Access to the European market and financial transfers from Brussels contributed to Ireland's economic success story. The Republic became the Celtic Tiger, which outperformed most of its OECD neighbors (Barry et al., 2001: 537).[9] During the 2007–2013 EU budgetary period, Ireland even became a net contributor to EU funds (Laffan and O'Mahony, 2008: 49).[10] This change in Ireland's economic position marked a new era in the relationship between the Republic and the EU (Laffan and O'Mahony, 2008: 32; Adshead and Tonge, 2009: 213). It also changed the perception of European institutions within the Irish population (Rees et al., 2009: 1). The permissive consensus on European integration, which had been built around a "donor/recipient narrative" (O'Mahony, 2009: 435), began to crumble. It turned into an increasingly constraining dissensus as Ireland's economic position improved. Over the course of the Republic's emancipation from European economic support, both elite and public commitment to Ireland's role as a constructive member of the EU became contested. Although EU membership was still perceived as a matter of vital national interest, the role of the Republic in Europe and with it EU tax governance became increasingly controversial issues in party politics (Benoit, 2009) and the broader public. The failed referenda on the Treaty of Nice in 2001 (Garry et al., 2005) and the Treaty of Lisbon in 2008 (O'Mahony, 2009) are the most visible indicators of this transformation, which set the stage for the politicization of EU tax governance. The politicization of EU tax governance in Ireland was not only shaped by the mobilization of cosmopolitans and nationalists but also by the profound change of the Irish Republic's position within the multi-level system of European governance.

Overall, the twofold sequence of the Irish debate on EU tax governance suggests three core conclusions. First, EU tax legislation has become a more common component of Irish public debate. Although EU tax governance is not one of the most important issues on the public agenda, the topic has become more visible and controversial within a broader segment of the population. However, this process began much later in Ireland than in Germany, where politicization was already visible during the SEA period and especially during the Maastricht period. Furthermore, the Irish politicization process differs from the German case in terms of broadness. While the German public discussed a broad variety of tax areas, the Irish focused particularly on corporate and private income taxation. Finally, the German link between domestic and European tax issues is not present in Ireland. A "Europeanization" of national tax issues did not take place.

Second, my theory of politicization can only partly illuminate the Irish politicization process and the differences between the Irish and German debates. On the one hand, the crucial relevance of the growing political authority of international institutions is further corroborated and specified by the Irish case. It shows that the expansion of EU authority to particularly sensitive areas of wide national concern spurs politicization framed in strong nationalist terms. The Irish case demonstrates the complex interaction between different forms of authority and even non-binding agreements on politicization. The politicization process was mainly triggered by the European Commission's activities in the areas of corporate and private income taxes. While these activities expanded EU authority to an additional area of taxation, the European Commission's interventions neither resulted from a change of its formal tax mandate nor from legally binding tax legislation. Rather, the European Commission built its cases on increased formal authority in the field of competition, state aid, and monetary policy, as well as on the non-binding code of conduct for corporate taxation. On the other hand, the mobilization potential of nationalists and cosmopolitans is only one part of the puzzle. Neither post-functionalism nor modernization theory can explain why the Irish public became more interested in EU tax governance only during the 2000s.

Third, in combination with the lack of any substantive nationalist backlash against the Treaty of Maastricht and its potential implications for tax policy, these developments point to an explanatory factor that has been neglected so far: the relationship between a country and an international institution. This was not an issue in Germany because it is a core member and driving force of European integration. Yet, the Irish case suggests that dependence on EU financial support in combination with a successful improvement of living conditions hampered the politicization process. Because the first decades of Irish membership in the EU were characterized by a donor–recipient relationship in which Ireland was grateful for European economic support, EU authority was rarely questioned in public (Benoit, 2009: 449). When this situation changed, due to Ireland's economic success, Ireland–EU relations became more of a partnership among equals. As a result, the politicization of EU tax governance grew further. As the EU attempted to regulate Ireland's corporate tax system – thus endangering its model of economic growth – the assumption that the EU had a positive impact on economic well-being and growth (Diez Medrano, 2003: 26) was challenged.

More generally, this finding suggests not only that politicization processes are conditioned by domestic mobilization potentials but also that socio-economic considerations play a role. In the Irish case, the socio-cultural cleavage between cosmopolitans and nationalists overlapped with the economic dimension of political conflict. While the Irish debate was framed in strong nationalist terms, it cannot be denied that the European Commission's attacks on the Irish corporate tax system have had important implications for Ireland's economic success, which depends considerably on a low corporate tax rate. The effects of cultural and economic mobilization are difficult to disentangle on the basis of this particular episode of politicization. However, the fact that the Irish debate continued to grow even after this conflict on corporate taxation was over suggests that mobilization potentials were still a relevant factor conditioning the Irish politicization process. In sum, the recipe for the politicization of EU tax governance in Ireland during the late 1990s and 2000s incorporates the EU's expansion of authority to sensitive issues of wide public concern and a substantial change in the relationship between the Irish Republic and the EU.

Switzerland: the critical outsider

The final case study of this chapter turns to Switzerland, a country that many experts consider to be one of the great anomalies of European integration (Vahl and Grolimund, 2006: 15; Church, 2007: 2). Located at the heart of Western Europe and surrounded by EU member states, Switzerland has chosen to stay out of the EU. Nevertheless, Switzerland is closely integrated with the EU not only economically but also in terms of political cooperation and coordination. Close ties of bilateral agreements and unilateral adaptations to EU legislation amount to a centralization of political authority over Swiss policies at the European level that is similar to, although considerably weaker than, the formal EU members Germany and Ireland. This section provides an overview of Swiss–European relations since the signing of the Treaty of Rome. It demonstrates that the level and scope of EU's "external governance" (see Lavenex and Schimmelfennig, 2009) in Switzerland can be classified in terms of Tanja Börzel's (2005: 221) typology of degrees of centralization (see Table 4.1).

Switzerland's relationship with the EU can be divided into two periods. First, a long period (1957–1993), during which the EU did not have formal authority over Swiss policy. Second, a more recent phase of enhanced coordination (1994–2011) during which Swiss legislation became "eurocompatible" (Kux, 1998: 10; Kriesi and Trechsel, 2008: 182; Gava and Varone, 2014; Linder, 2014) indirectly via unilateral implementation of EU legislation and directly via bilateral treaties concluded during this period (Sciarini et al., 2004: 355).[11]

The creation of the EU demanded that the Swiss react to avoid isolation. Switzerland was not eager to become a member of the newly created institution, due to its fears of external interference with the core principles of Swiss politics: federalism, direct democracy, and neutrality (Dardanelli, 2007; Ganser and Kreis, 2007; Treschel, 2007). Yet, it was also not willing to stand on the sidelines of European integration and lose its economic status (Gstöhl, 2002: 534). The Swiss solution, a multilateral free trade agreement, failed in 1958. Similarly, in 1963 loose negotiations on accession ran into technical and political problems that derailed the process. After this period of disappointed hopes and frustration, the Swiss reverted to a passive stance. Only accession negotiations between the EU and Denmark, UK, Norway, and Ireland brought the Swiss back to the negation table. These negotiations led to a narrow bilateral free trade agreement on industrial goods. The agreement provided Swiss exporters with better access to the European market but did not substantially affect Swiss policy, let alone Swiss political institutions (Dupont and Sciarini, 2001: 220). Due to its intergovernmental nature and limitation to specific sectors, the agreement did not fundamentally alter Switzerland–EU relations. There was only a very limited transfer of political authority to the European level.

The free trade agreement was followed by a long period of stagnation. Swiss involvement in the European integration process remained narrow for most of the 1970s and 1980s (Kriesi and Trechsel, 2008: 174).[12] This situation could have changed with the enactment of the SEA in 1986. The creation of the single European market brought new momentum to Switzerland–EU relations. It initiated negotiations between EFTA countries and the EU on the establishment of a European Economic Area (EEA; Dupont and Sciarini, 2001: 220).[13] Although this treaty was signed in 1992, the renewed multilateral approach eventually resulted in failure.[14] Because the Swiss government could not mobilize sufficient public support for the agreement in the mandatory referendum, it failed in December 1992 (Treschel, 2007: 40–42) and the agreement had to be abandoned. After this repeated failure of the multilateral approach, Swiss plans for a formal application for accession were "frozen" and the country entered a period of enhanced bilateral integration and unilateral adaption. This relationship still persists and shapes the Switzerland–EU relationship.

The beginning of this period, which made Switzerland one of the most strongly integrated non-members of the EU (Vahl and Grolimund, 2006: 6), coincides with the beginning of my time-series data on Swiss public debate. It starts in 1994 with the opening of the bilateral negations on a set of seven sector agreements. Initiated by a Swiss proposal to take up negations after the failure of the EEA agreement, bilateral negotiations were ready to commence in December 1994. After more than four years of cumbersome negotiations, the deal (Bilateral I) was concluded and ready for ratification (Dupont and Sciarini, 2007). The Swiss ratification process was complex, involving a popular referendum and the approval by the Federal Assembly, the Parliament, and the Federal Council (Vahl and Grolimund, 2006: 19–21). It took another four years before the agreement finally entered into force in 2002. In addition to the provisions on trade already agreed upon in 1972, Bilateral I included legislation on road and air transport, market access for agricultural products, the free movement of persons, technical barriers to trade, and public procurement. These individual regulations increased the scope and the level of EU external authority substantially because the content of individual agreements was mainly based on the EU's acquis communautaire (Goetschel, 2007: 180). The agreements were managed by so-called Joint Committees. These bodies are composed of EU and Swiss representatives and take decisions by consensus. They meet at least once a year and are responsible for the implemention of the agreements, the resolution of conflicts between the parties, and the exchange of information (Vahl and Grolimund, 2006: 34–41). In combination, the centrality of EU legislation and the competences of the Joint Committees come close to intergovernmental coordination, that is, institutionalized decision-making procedures in which decisions in specific policy areas are taken by unanimity and in which supranational institutions do not hold further competencies. Consequently, the EU's formal external authority quadrupled with the enactment of Bilateral I. Although Switzerland still held a formal veto over European external governance, the enactment of Bilateral I constituted a substantial change in Switzerland–EU relations that should trigger a politicization of EU tax governance in the Swiss public.[15]

The second set of agreements (Bilateral II) increased Europe's formal external authority further (Afonso and Maggetti, 2007). These treaties extended the scope of Switzerland–EU relations to six additional policy areas. Negotiations began before Bilateral I entered into force to take up a number of leftovers from Bilateral I and the Swiss requests to participate in the Schengen and Dublin Agreements. In June 2001, the EU accepted negotiations because of its own interest in concluding additional agreements on a system of cross-border taxation of savings and on increased cooperation in the fight against tax fraud (Kriesi and Trechsel, 2008: 180). These agreements were signed in 2004, after long and difficult negotiations on the more sensitive issues of savings taxation, tax fraud, and Schengen/Dublin (Afonso and Maggetti, 2007: 216–213). They came into force in 2005.[16] Similar to Bilateral I, individual sector agreements of Bilateral II were managed by Joint Committees. Consequently, the level of EU external authority over policy areas included in the agreement was similar to the policy areas regulated under Bilateral I. The increased scope of the agreements expanded EU authority by more than 50 percent. Today, Switzerland–EU relations include a broad variety of issues ranging from economic relations, and energy and transport, to education and taxation (for an overview see Appendix 3). Hanspeter Kriesi and Alexander Treschel (2008: 187) conclude that this state of Switzerland–EU relations can be characterized as "customized quasi-membership" that subjects the Swiss to a considerable degree of European authority. Nevertheless, formal EU authority is still much lower than in Germany and Ireland. Consequently, levels of politicization should be considerably lower.

Similarly, the amount of EU tax legislation extended to Switzerland was limited. The Swiss tax system is less strongly shaped by EU legislation than are the tax systems of the formal EU members Germany and Ireland. The Swiss system is a complex, multi-level affair that involves both the cantonal and the federal level. More encompassing reforms are difficult to achieve due to the multitude of veto players and the fact that the overall structure is enshrined in the Swiss constitution. The system requires a referendum to be changed. Because of this high-level status, taxation is an utterly political issue with potential implications for direct democracy, federalism, and national sovereignty (Church et al., 2007: 137). This situation constitutes an ideal breeding ground for the politicization of EU tax governance because taxation is generally more sensitive in Switzerland than in Germany and Ireland. Before I address the Swiss politicization potential and the actual debate in more detail subsequent sections, I review respective EU tax legislation.

Most European provisions shaping the Swiss tax system are included in the bilateral agreements.[17] Yet, the first legislation with implications for Swiss corporate taxation was already included in the 1972 free trade agreement. Article 23 of this agreement states that "any public aid which distorts or threatens to distort competition by favouring certain undertakings or the production of certain goods" is "incompatible with the proper functioning of the Agreement" (EU-Switzerland, 1972). While the Swiss still argue that these provisions do not include taxation, in 2005 the European Commission referred to this article when it questioned a number of cantonal corporate tax regimes, such as the preferential rates for holding companies granted in Zug and Schwyz (Vahl and Grolimund, 2006: 99; Church et al., 2007: 136). In addition to this controversial regulation, the agreements in Bilateral II include important legislation. Most prominently, a complete sector agreement is dedicated to the EU's directive on the taxation of savings income. As one of the most controversial and sensitive issues during the negotiations of Bilateral II (Afonso and Maggetti, 2007: 216; Kriesi and Trechsel, 2008: 180), this agreement established Switzerland's participation in the directive. The conclusion of the agreement was essential for the directive as a whole because EU member states Austria, Belgium, and Luxembourg insisted that they would agree to the directive only if Switzerland and other low-tax countries (including Andorra, Liechtenstein, Monaco, and San Marino) would also participate. They argued that the exclusion of these countries would disadvantage European countries and undermine the effectiveness of the directive because loopholes in neighboring countries' taxation systems would make it easy to bypass the European directive (Afonso and Maggetti, 2007: 216). Due to these difficult conditions, negotiations on the sectoral agreement lasted more than a year. They were concluded in June 2003 and entered into force in 2005. The agreement obliges the Swiss to introduce a withholding tax on savings or to exchange relevant information with EU member states. Furthermore, the agreement provides for an exchange of information in cases of tax fraud and Swiss participation in the directive on taxation of interest and royalty payments between companies. Consequently, Switzerland participates in the two binding directives of the EU's package on income taxation passed in 2003 (Cattoir, 2007). Finally, Bilateral II includes agreements on avoiding double taxation of former EU officials residing in Switzerland, mutual administrative and legal assistance in cases of tax fraud and tax offenses in the realm of indirect taxes (customs duties, VAT, and specific excises), and the exemption of Switzerland from potential obligations for legal assistance with regard to the evasion of direct taxation under the Schengen acquis (Vahl and Grolimund, 2006: 45).

In sum, the Swiss case is characterized by milder and less direct impact of EU authority. While both formal authority and tax legislation grew over time and do limit Swiss national sovereignty to an increasing extent, this effect is substantially weaker than in the formal member states of Germany and Ireland. In particular, the development of formal authority is marked by a long period of stagnation between 1957 and 1992 and a relatively weak growth with the enactment of Bilateral I and II during the early 2000s. The development of EU tax legislation is directly connected to these bilateral treaties and is limited to a few but important legislative acts in the area of direct taxation and cooperation in cases of fraud on indirect taxes. Taken together, the interaction of both formal authority and tax policy output should contribute to a mild politicization of EU tax governance during the early 2000s. The strongest growth of politicization should be observable around 2005, when Bilateral II was enacted.

The politicization potential of the Swiss society

In this section I turn to the Swiss mobilization potential. I analyze the share of nationalists and cosmopolitans in the Swiss population and the polarization between these two groups. The period of analysis does not stretch from 1981 to 2011 but starts in 1994 due to the limited availability of newspaper content for earlier periods. Figure 5.5 shows the share of individuals holding a cosmopolitan outlook, the share of individuals holding an exclusive nationalist outlook, and the vote share of radical right parties in national elections (see Table 5.4 for descriptive statistics).

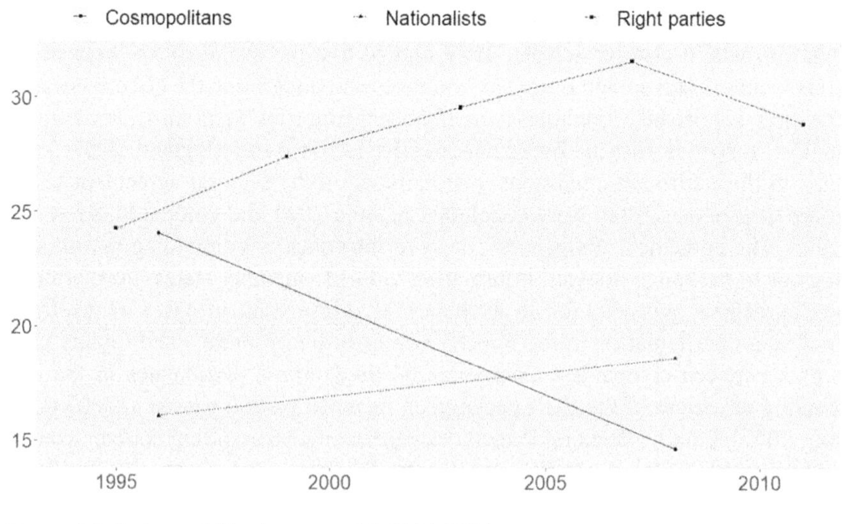

Figure 5.5 Swiss mobilization potential, 1994–2011

Table 5.4 Descriptive statistics for periods of European integration in Switzerland

Descriptive statistics	*Politicization indicators*			*Formal authority*			*Mobilization %*	
	Salience	*Controversy*	*Plurality*	*Scope*	*Level*	*Overall*	*Cosmopolitan*	*Nationalist*
1994–2001 (Bilateral Trade Agreement)								
Min	0.02	0	0	2	1	2	24.1	16.1
Max	0.21	33.3	100	2	1	2		
Mean	0.12	8.9	44.1	2	1	2		
SD	0.06	12.6	42.3	0	0	0		
2002–2004 (Bilateral I)								
Min	0.11	18.2	40	8	1	8	NA	NA
Max	0.34	42.9	52	8	1	8		
Mean	0.21	31.5	46.4	8	1	8		
SD	0.1	10.2	4.9	0	0	0		
2005–2011 (Bilateral II)								
Min	0.08	11.1	0	14	1	14	14.6	18.6
Max	0.24	40	72.7	14	1	14		
Mean	0.16	26.4	32.7	14	1	14		
SD	0.06	11.1	24.5	0	0	0		

The data suggest that the Swiss mobilization potential was high and relatively constant over the entire observation period. In 1996, the cumulative share of cosmopolitans and exclusive nationalists amounted to more than 40 percent of the population. This value constitutes the highest mobilization potential both in comparison to the subsequent scores for Switzerland and to Germany and Ireland. It suggests a higher likelihood of politicization. Although the mobilization potential decreased over time to one-third of the population, a comparison with Ireland and Germany reveals that this score is still substantial and close to the highest observed values for the other two countries.

Figure 5.5 shows that the high overall politicization potential resulted from a pattern similar to the German case, where the shares of cosmopolitans and exclusive nationalists were equally distributed. Swiss cosmopolitans made up almost one-quarter of the population (24.1 percent). The share of exclusive nationalists (16.1 percent) was only slightly smaller. The comparably high shares of both groups indicate a strong politicization potential. As almost half of the Swiss population held either exclusive nationalist or cosmopolitan identities, Swiss politics was characterized by strong polarization on the issue of internationalization (see also Kriesi et al., 2008: 152; Kriesi and Trechsel, 2008: 88) and European integration (see also Church, 2007: 2).

Over the course of the subsequent decade, this situation was relatively stable. The overall mobilization potential decreased slightly. Yet, a closer look at the development of both groups reveals important changes. During the late 1990s, cosmopolitans constituted the larger of both groups, but in 2008 this situation was reversed. Between 1996 and 2008 the share of cosmopolitans decreased by almost 10 percentage points to 15 percent, whereas the share of exclusive nationalists grew to 19 percent. As a result, exclusive nationalists even started to dominate during the Bilateral II period.

Furthermore, radical right parties were strong. Their high vote shares of 24 percent in 1995 increased to 32 percent in 2007. In 2011, the election result of 30 percent for radical right parties was almost similar. This development was linked to the rise of the Swiss People's Party (Schweizerische Volkspartei, SVP) during the 1990s (Stämpfli, 2007).[18] Although radical right parties were elected to the Swiss Parliament even during the 1980s and early 1990s, the SVP was able to dominate the political agenda, to absorb the electorate of small protest parties, and to lure voters away from mainstream parties (Linder, 2013: 194). The importance of the SVP for the Swiss mobilization potential is underlined by its archetypical behavior. SVP campaigns appealed to exclusive nationalist sentiments against internationalization. With the help of popular initiatives – for instance, the initiative against the EEA in 1992 and xenophobic campaigns – the SVP was particularly successful in presenting itself as a guardian of national sovereignty, neutrality, federalism, and direct democracy against outside predators like the EU (Stämpfli, 2007: 86) and other supranational institutions, which in Switzerland are traditionally seen as a threat to independence and self-determination (Gstöhl, 2002: 543; Linder, 2013: 200). Consequently, the growing share of nationalists might even underestimate the nationalist mobilization potential. While the survey data indicate a share of less than 20 percent, the vote share of the SVP exceeded this number since the 1999 election and came even close to 30 percent in 2007. Furthermore, the SVP's appeal to the principles of direct democracy, federalism, and neutrality – which are often considered to belong to the historical core of Swiss national identity (Gstöhl, 2002: 514) – and the repeated claim that these values are under attack due to the growing authority of international institutions points to a high mobilization potential of Swiss exclusive nationalists.

Overall, the initial predominance of cosmopolitans during the mid-1990s was undermined by a growing group of highly mobilized exclusive nationalists. While the difference in size between both groups did not come close to the skewed distribution in Ireland, the conversion of the ranking is still remarkable and exacerbated by the strength of radical right parties. As a result, the Swiss situation was characterized by a pronounced polarization between the two groups. The Swiss mobilization potential was, thus, higher than in Germany and Ireland.

Public debate on EU tax governance in Switzerland

This section compares the periods of expanding EU external governance to probe whether the strong Swiss mobilization potential reinforced the interaction effect of the EU's growing formal authority and tax legislation on the politicization process. In addition to the within-case comparison, the results of the case studies on Germany and Ireland are used for cross-case comparison.

Figure 5.6 plots the three dimensions of politicization and the politicization index. Scores for salience and controversy build on a total of 147 newspaper articles on EU tax governance for the period between 1994 and 2011. Scores for plurality build on 159 affective statements. Newspaper articles are taken from the

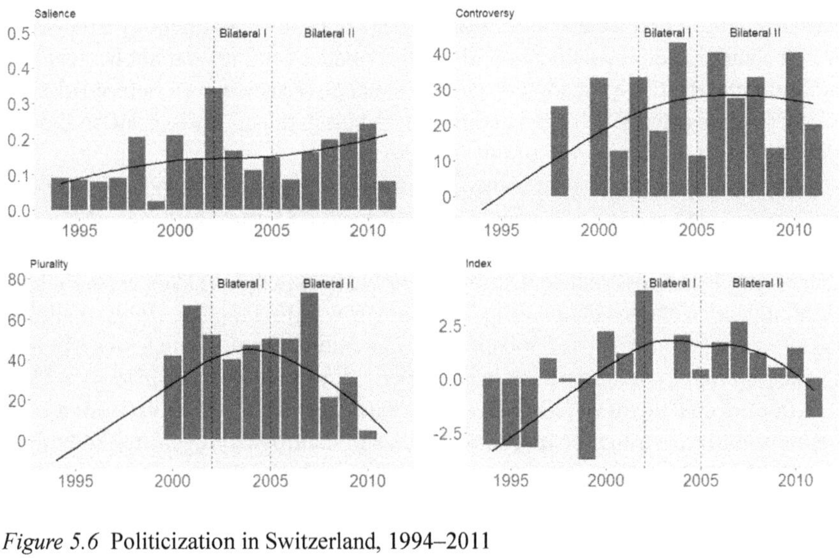

Figure 5.6 Politicization in Switzerland, 1994–2011

NZZ, for which data are available from 1994 onwards and the *TA*, for which data are available since 2000.

The overall Swiss mobilization potential was strong. It built on large groups of cosmopolitans and nationalists. The latter was strongly mobilized by radical right parties. This situation amounted to a polarization between both groups that was stronger than in German and Ireland. However, the first period of Switzerland–EU relations (1994–2001) was characterized by weak and informal ties. Despite the free trade agreement of 1972 and a set of sectoral agreements, the formal authority of the EU and its influence on taxation were limited compared to Germany and Ireland. It did not constitute a strong driver of politicization. Overall, the Swiss case was marked by favorable socio-cultural conditions and a weak driving force of politicization during the second half of the 1990s. This constellation suggests a rather weak politicization. During the Bilateral I period, EU authority increased slightly and the mobilization potential remained almost stable. This should result in growing politicization. This trajectory of growing politicization should continue over the course of the Bilateral II period (2005–2011). Bilateral II extended the scope of EU authority and introduced a number of significant tax policies. Although the Swiss mobilization potential was weaker than during the Bilateral I period, the Bilateral II agreements should still result in growing politicization.

In sum, the level of the politicization of EU tax governance in Switzerland should be lower than in Germany and Ireland. Although the strong mobilization potential of Swiss cosmopolitans, exclusive nationalist, and in particular the dominance of the radical right SVP should amplify the effect of EU authority, this authority was more limited than in Germany and Ireland. During the Bilateral II period, which increased both formal EU authority and tax legislation, levels of politicization should come closer to those in Ireland and Germany.

The inspection of politicization indicators reveals that these expectations are partially met. As expected politicization grew with the enactment of Bilateral I. Yet, the anticipated intensification of public debate after 2005 cannot be noted. In addition, the relatively steady debate on EU tax governance even before Bilateral I is striking because EU formal authority was marginal and tax legislation did not directly affect the Swiss during this time period.

More specifically, the data show that already between 1994 and 2001 EU tax governance was salient and controversial for a broad array of actors. Although salience was not exceptionally high during these years, there was a constant debate on EU tax governance. During the early 2000s, salience even grew slightly. Similarly, controversy and plurality began to grow during the late 1990s. A similar picture emerges as regards the controversy of public debate, which was lower at the beginning of the time period but also grew during the early 2000s.

After the enactment of Bilateral I, this trend continued. All politicization indicators stabilized on higher levels. Salience and controversy even reached maximum values. During this period, salience almost doubled to scores higher than in Germany and Ireland. In 2002, salience peaked at a level that came close to the German maximum score observed in 1998 and was only slightly lower than the Irish maximum in 2011. Although the subsequent years were marked by lower salience, scores no longer dropped to the low values of the previous period. In a similar vein, the mean value of controversy more than tripled. In 2004, controversy peaked at a share of 42.9 percent and approached the maximum values seen in Germany and Ireland.

While plurality did not peak during the Bilateral I period, the development of the indicator matched this general impression. Civil society speakers became a constant voice in the debate and contributed around 50 percent of all affective statements. Similar to the German and Irish debates, civil society speakers accounted for the largest share of affective statements.

In sum, all three politicization components point to an intensification of politicization during the Bilateral I period. Although this development matches theoretical expectations, the strength of politicization was higher than anticipated. Taking into account the comparably low level of formal authority and the lack of EU tax legislation affecting the Swiss, the level of politicization almost similar to Germany and Ireland is remarkable and demands a more detailed analysis of the textual material.

The Bilateral II period (during which the mean values of all three politicization components were lower than during the Bilateral I period) suggests a similar conclusion. This development does not fit the theoretical expectations because the Swiss mobilization potential was only marginally lower and both formal authority and EU tax legislation in particular grew with the enactment of Bilateral II. Clearly, salience and controversy decreased only slightly, but the drop in plurality was substantial. This decline of civil society participation began after a peak in 2007. In 2008 civil society speakers began to withdraw from the debate, and they had disappeared completely by the end of the observation period. These developments point to a substantial decline of politicization to levels similar to or lower than those in Germany and Ireland during the 2000s. While the similar levels of politicization during this period in all three countries are compatible with the theoretical expectations, the trend of less politicization during the Bilateral II period is difficult to explain with the help of the quantitative information. Hence, I turn to a qualitative reading of the textual material.

The first period was characterized by news coverage that took the position of an outside observer. The majority of articles described potential implications of the Treaty of Maastricht and the EMU for European tax governance. These articles frequently reflected the content of controversial debates within European member states, including Germany. Clear assessments of EU tax governance from a Swiss perspective were, however, very rare. Those few statements that did take a position were critical and sometimes even fearful in tone. They postulated that Swiss tax sovereignty might fall victim to the efforts of European high-tax countries to harmonize taxation not only within the EU but also beyond its borders. Despite these few critical voices, the unexpectedly high values of controversy during this time period resulted mainly from an observer perspective that described conflicts between EU members and not the controversial examination of EU tax governance in the Swiss public.

One interesting exception to this general result is a reoccurring discussion on the Swiss VAT rate. This issue acquired a European dimension because Switzerland introduced an Euro-compatible VAT system in 1995 but set a rate significantly below the European threshold. The few newspaper articles on this issue reveal a clear conflict between pro-Europeans, who argued that the introduction of a VAT should be accompanied by a rate in conformity with EU standards, and nationalists, who feared that the implementation of the new system was the beginning of the end of Swiss tax sovereignty. This controversy is noteworthy because it demonstrates that not only the EU's external governance but also unilateral adaption has the potential to spur the politicization of EU tax governance.

Another exception to the generally unpoliticized debate during the 1990s was the newspaper coverage on the start of Austria's European Council presidency in 1998. Because the Austrian government announced that it would make the fight against HTC within and beyond European borders one of the top priorities for its presidency, a few articles openly criticized Europe's quest for tax harmonization and potential infringements with Swiss banking secrecy.

With the Feira European Council of June 2000, this picture changed and the tone of the Swiss debate became more critical, although the debate partly maintained an observer perspective. The reason for this transformation lies in the events in Feira, where European member states solved the long-standing conflict on the savings directive. The compromise reached in Feira included the exchange of information on cross-border interest payments and the condition that equivalent measures would be adopted by six non-member states, including Switzerland, and by Dutch and British dependent or associated territories (Cattoir, 2007: 7–10).[19]

This decision set off alarm bells among Swiss executives, the press, and bankers. It triggered a politicization process that was shaped by nationalist concerns about potential restrictions on banking secrecy. The potential exchange of information on interest payments attracted considerable attention and provoked a critical nationalist debate. The key message was clear: the savings directive must not be allowed to restrict Swiss banking secrecy. Although it is a crucial element of the success of the Swiss financial sector (Emmenegger, 2014), banking secrecy is often considered to be more than just an economic issue. For many Swiss, it is part of their national identity (Guex, 2000; Church et al., 2007: 127). Hence, my conjecture that a specific conflict between EU tax policies and national identity is an essential driver of nationalist politicization is confirmed by the strong reaction of the Swiss public to the EU's demand for information exchange.

The subsequent years underline this result. The Swiss debate between 2001 and 2004 was dominated by a controversy over the savings directive and the defense of banking secrecy. The 2002 peak in salience and the growing controversy and plurality of the debate during this period were almost exclusively driven by Switzerland–EU negotiations about the question of whether Switzerland should be allowed to implement a withholding tax instead of the exchange of information (Afonso and Maggetti, 2007: 217; Church et al., 2007: 143–144). The close coverage of this episode was mainly framed in exclusive nationalist terms. Cosmopolitan arguments were marginalized, despite the relatively large share of cosmopolitans in Switzerland. A broad variety of speakers claimed that banking secrecy and the commitment to tax competition were not only economic assets but also constituted an essential component of Swiss national identity.

The strong focus on the savings directive during the Bilateral I period provides additional support for the hypothesis that not only the increasing formal authority of international institutions but also their policies are an important driver of politicization. Similar to the Irish case, particular policies and their potential effects on the national tax system shaped the Swiss debate. In both cases, public debates were not primarily driven by growing formal authority but reacted mainly to the expansion of EU tax governance towards sensitive areas of wide national concern. This conclusion is underlined by the fact that the overarching context of the enactment of Bilateral I and negotiations on Bilateral II was rarely mentioned in discussions on the savings directive.

Furthermore, the sustained focus on the savings tax directive supports my more specific interpretation of the post-functionalist explanation. It demonstrates that nationalist identities may constitute the breeding ground for the politicization of international institutions if international policies conflict with specific elements of national identity. In the Swiss case, this specific element was the long-standing commitment to banking secrecy and the related protection of the privacy of individuals (Guex, 2000). These values stood in direct conflict with the EU's savings directive and the demand for information exchange. The importance of this specification of post-functionalism can also be seen from the fact that Swiss participation in the directive on taxation of interest and royalty payments between companies and cooperation with European institutions in cases of VAT fraud – both negotiated during the same time period – received no attention in the Swiss public. If exclusive nationalism per se was an important catalyst of politicization, these extensions of EU tax legislation should have been politicization as well.

This interpretation is further supported by the development of the Swiss debate between 2004 and 2011. After several years of tough negotiations on the savings directive and equally heated public debate, the Swiss government achieved an important breakthrough in June 2003. The EU had finally accepted a withholding tax instead of information exchange. This success translated quickly into less public controversy. While the savings directive was by far the dominant issue during the early 2000s, attention for the directive dropped substantially as soon as information exchange and respective restrictions of banking secrecy were off the table. In 2004 – even before the directive was enacted – the Swiss public had already lost interest. Public debates turned to other issues such as corporate taxation, which gained attention due to the European Commission's renewed CCCTB initiative and because of the European Commission's 2005 crackdown on preferential corporate tax rates offered by Swiss cantons. Related public discussions took off quickly but remained less controversial and plural. Despite the potential economic consequence of a stricter regulation of the Swiss corporate tax system, this debate was only short-lived. European demands were answered with good advice on the advantages of tax competition and provoked considerably less nationalist concerns than the savings directive.

This situation changed slightly with the financial crisis of 2008. But former German Finance Minister Peer Steinbrück's critique of the Swiss tax system and its role as a tax haven evolved into a bilateral Swiss–German conflict in which EU tax governance played only a marginal role. Between 2008 and 2011, the Swiss debate was, thus, again characterized by an observer perspective that only rarely engaged critically with EU tax governance.

The qualitative interpretation of the Swiss debate sheds light on the causal mechanisms that drive politicization, mobilization potential, and international authority. Contrary to initial expectations, Swiss public debate was only marginally driven by the growing scope of European authority over Swiss policy. The early and late years of the analyzed time period showed few signs of a substantial and sustained politicization. During these years, the Swiss took the position of an interested observer. Even the enactment of Bilateral II had little influence on the debate. Only direct contact with EU tax governance – that is, with the EU's savings tax directive – changed this situation for a limited time period. Contrary to the German and Irish cases, EU tax governance has not become an issue of regular debate. In line with its role as a closely associated partner of the EU, the Swiss public was rather generally interested in European tax policy. Politicization remained conditional on one crucial factor: the direct activation of nationalist identity. Exclusive nationalist mobilization potentials lay dormant as long as EU tax governance did not interfere with issues of broad national concern. In line with the results of the previous case studies, the early Swiss debate had a cosmopolitan problem-solving tone. This changed radically when the EU demanded information exchange on capital income taxation. This specific policy created a strong conflict between Swiss national identity and EU tax legislation that radical right parties could easily exploit. A strong nationalist backlash was the result. The comparison of the Swiss case to Germany and Ireland illustrates the importance of a conflict between specific configurations of national identity and international policy. Although the share of German nationalists was similar or at times even higher than in Switzerland, nationalist resentments against European integration in general only played a subordinate role in the German debate.

In conclusion, the Swiss case matches a more specific reading of my theory of politicization. The overall level of politicization in Switzerland was lower than in Germany and Ireland, where European formal authority and the frequency of European tax legislation were much higher. Although the quantitative indicators seem to imply that politicization levels were quite similar across countries, a qualitative analysis of the Swiss debate demonstrates that a large share of affective statements in the sample simply reported on conflicts between EU members. They did not assess EU tax governance from a Swiss perspective. Hence, the institutionalist perspective was largely confirmed by the Swiss case. Furthermore, the strong politicization of the savings directive demonstrates the expected conditioning effect of domestic context. While the early years of the Swiss discussion mirrored the cosmopolitan framing of debates in Germany, the controversy on the savings directive was dominated by strongly mobilized nationalists and their concern for the Swiss banking secrecy, as a matter of national identity and economic concern. Similar to the Irish politicization process, economic considerations did feed into this strong episode of nationalist politicization. While the debate was indeed dominated by arguments about national identity, the potential economic implications of the savings directive cannot be denied. Clearly, Swiss banking secrecy is an important condition of the success of the Swiss financial industry (Palan, 2002; Steinlin and Trampusch, 2012). Cultural and economic politicization is, therefore, difficult to disentangle. As in Ireland, the conditioning effects of both dimensions of conflict overlap.

Conclusion: comparison across countries

This chapter probes the explanatory power of my theory of politicization. It extends Chapter 4 on the explanatory power of international authority through an analysis of cross-country variance and the conditioning effect of domestic contexts on politicization. The chapter examines how national mobilization potentials shape politicization. My theory suggests that specific groups of a national population – that is, exclusive nationalists and cosmopolitans – are particularly important in spurring public debates on international institutions. Varying shares of these groups in different countries mediate the effect of political authority and thus help to explain different politicization process across countries.

I compare the politicization of European tax governance in three countries that are subject to different levels of European authority and tax governance, and that are characterized by varying mobilization potentials. Table 5.5 summarizes the three case studies. It ranks the strength of the EU's formal authority and tax legislation in the three countries and their different mobilization potentials. In addition, the table provides information about the conflict between national identity and

Table 5.5 Cross-country comparison

Explanatory factors	*Germany*	*Ireland*	*Switzerland*
Formal authority	High and increasing	High and increasing	Low and slightly increasing
Tax legislation	Frequent and increasing	Frequent and increasing	Rare
Mobilization potential	Medium (substantial shares of cosmopolitans and exclusive nationalist, weak mobilization)	Medium (substantial share of exclusive nationalists, weak mobilization)	High (substantial shares of cosmopolitans and exclusive nationalists, high mobilization)
Conflict between national identity and EU tax legislation	Low (taxation or related issues are not an important component of national identity; national identity favors international integration)	Medium (private and corporate income taxes are of particular relevance)	High (taxation and banking secrecy are issues of wide national concern)
Economic standing	Strong (high-tax country)	Weak but improving (low-tax country)	Strong (low-tax country)
Politicization level	Constantly growing politicization with a strong cosmopolitan framing	Politicization starts in the 2000s with a strong nationalist framing	No stable politicization, single issue focus with a strong nationalist framing

EU tax legislation and the economic standing of the selected countries, because both factors appear to play important roles in the specific national politicization processes.

In sum, the results of all three case studies underline the core conclusion of Chapter 4: the interaction effect between formal authority and tax legislation is the driving force of politicization. Furthermore, the case studies support my expectations for how domestic context shapes politicization. The results also point to a more specific link between national mobilization potentials and the expansion of EU tax governance. The in-depth analysis of the three country cases shows that differences in international authority result in considerably different levels, changes, and patterns of politicization. The politicization of EU tax governance is most pronounced in Germany (see Figure 5.7 for an overview). Although mean and maximum values for politicization indicators point to relatively similar levels of salience, controversy, and plurality in all three countries, a more detailed analysis of the debates indicates that the German public meets the politicization criteria best. Despite some stagnation towards the end of the observation period, the German debate was characterized by a lively and sustained problem-solving debate on a broad set of EU tax policies. The German public critically examined the full portfolio of EU tax legislation, ranging from the harmonization of VAT and excises to more recent initiatives in the area of private and corporate income taxation. In the case of withholding taxes on capital income, public opposition against the introduction of this tax in 1989 forced the German government to abolish it and put a hold on larger plans to implement such a tax on a European scale.

In Ireland, the politicization of EU tax governance began almost one decade later than in Germany and focused on a much narrower set of issues. The Irish public was mainly concerned with issues of private and corporate income taxation. Other issues were largely ignored. Contrary to the German politicization process, the Irish debate on income taxation was more strongly framed as a nationalist legitimacy debate.

This strong focus on a limited set of issues and the legitimacy of EU tax governance was even more pronounced in the Swiss debate. Yet for most of the observation period, the public of this non-member state was more of an interested spectator. A strong politicization was triggered by Switzerland–EU negotiations on the savings tax directive only during the early 2000s. As a result, a continuous politicization of EU tax governance can be noted in Germany and to a weaker extent in Ireland. In Switzerland, I note short episodes of politicization in the form of nationalist legitimacy debates but no sustained politicization of EU tax governance in general.

These results are broadly in line with the institutionalist part of the theory. Yet, the considerable differences between the levels, changes, and patterns of politicization in the three countries cannot fully be explained by varying international authority. The questions of why the Irish politicization process set in only 10 years later than in Germany, why the Irish debate was much narrower than in Germany, and why the Swiss public reacted strongly to the savings directive but ignored

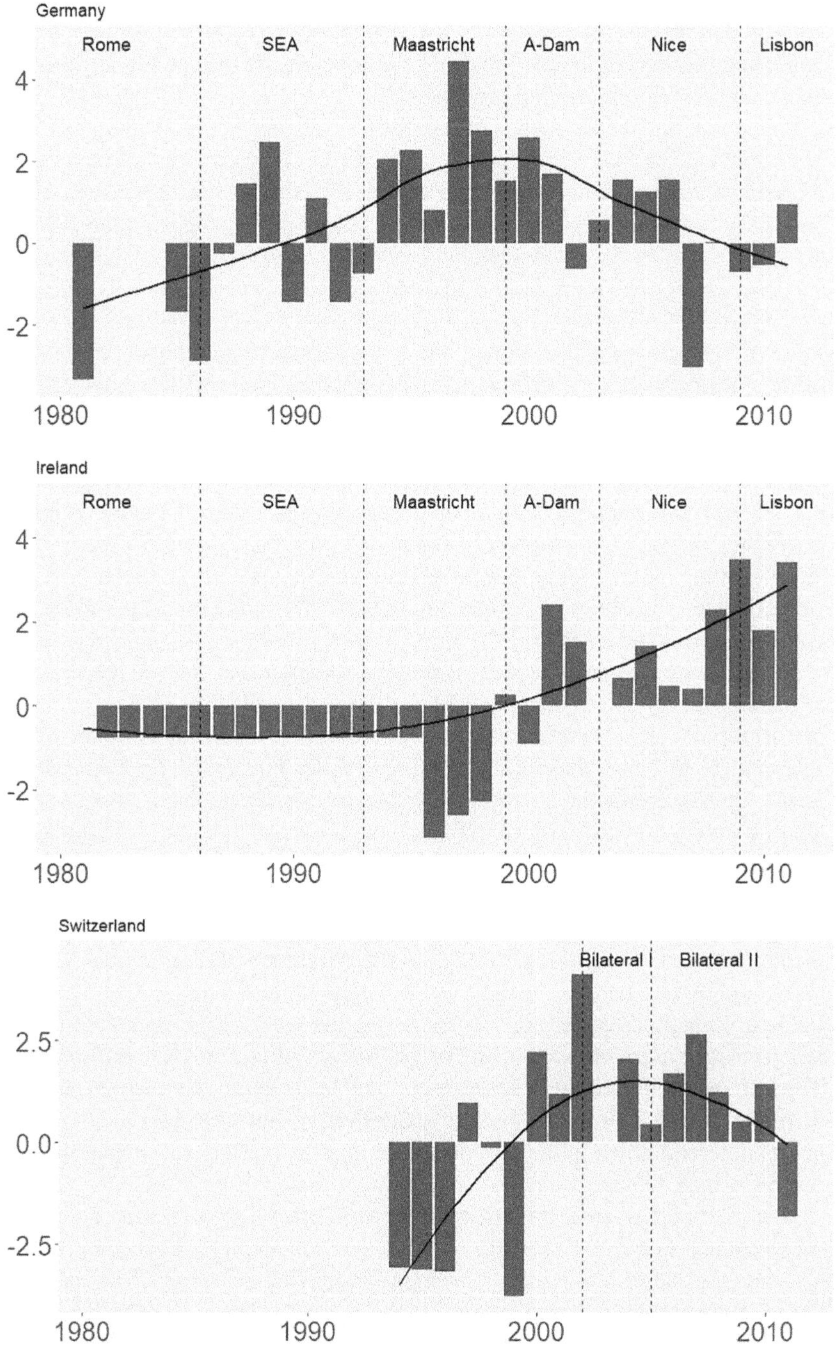

Figure 5.7 Politicization index across countries, 1981–2011

other extensions of EU tax legislation to the Swiss tax system demand a more country-specific explanation. My theory of politicization aims for exactly this kind of explanation. By pointing to the idea that national mobilization potentials moderate the effect of international authority, it specifies the conditions that shape country-specific politicization processes.

In general, this theory sheds light on the differentiated politicization of EU tax governance in Germany, Ireland, and Switzerland. A comparison between the two EU member states demonstrates that higher levels of politicization in Germany and the considerably broader spectrum of issues under consideration were the results of the more favorable German mobilization potential. The German public was characterized by a substantial polarization between cosmopolitans and exclusive nationalists. Although both groups were only weakly mobilized, the overall share of both groups and the much higher number of cosmopolitans explains the differences between both countries. The German debate was characterized by a cosmopolitan problem-solving discussion on how more European cooperation in taxation can stabilize the monetary union and how tax cooperation and harmonization can help to achieve other goals, like climate protection. By contrast, the lack of a substantial cosmopolitan group in Ireland shaped a more nationalist legitimacy debate that was mainly concerned with the European Commission's attacks on the Irish system of corporate and private taxation. In this debate, considerations on the future of Europe and the stability of the monetary union were only of marginal relevance.

Yet, questions remain: why did the relatively similar shares of exclusive nationalists in Germany and Ireland play out so differently, and why did the higher share of cosmopolitans in Switzerland not contribute to a more cosmopolitan debate? The answer to these questions is a more-specific interaction between national identity and international authority. All three cases indicate that a strong national identity conflicts with European tax governance under specific conditions only. To trigger a substantial nationalist backlash, EU tax legislation must extend to issue areas of wide national concern and thus create a conflict between national identity and European aspirations. In Ireland, these issues are found in the area of income taxation. Private income taxation was a traditionally controversial issue in Ireland; corporate taxation became increasingly important due to its core role for the Irish Republic's economic success during the 1990s. Both issues are particularly sensitive areas of taxation and of nationalist cultural and economic concern. The European Commission's activities in both areas during the early 2000s were, therefore, met by a strong nationalist backlash that cannot be observed in the context of other initiatives of the European Commission and that is completely absent in the German debate.

A similar picture emerges in the Swiss case. Strong politicization began only in the context of Europe's savings tax directive. This policy was accompanied by a strong episode of politicization because it extended the scope of EU tax legislation to a particularly sensitive area of the Swiss tax systems: banking secrecy. Since World War II, banking secrecy has obtained a totemic position in the minds of many Swiss. Strongly connected to national values – including personal freedom and privacy – and the economic success of the Swiss financial industry, banking secrecy is an important component of Swiss national identity. Hence, the European attempt to limit it and establish a regime of information exchange on capital earnings created a strong conflict between European aspirations and Swiss national identity. The result was a strong nationalist backlash. This effect was further amplified by the strength of radical right parties in Switzerland. The SVP in particular used the opportunities provided by the conflict between the savings tax directive, national identity, and economic preferences to politicize EU tax governance.

In Germany, these episodes of strong nationalist legitimacy debates cannot be observed. Although the share of exclusive nationalists is similar to Ireland and Switzerland, and although German tax revenues could suffer from European tax competition, the lack of a strong conflict between German national identity and EU tax legislation left the nationalist mobilization potential dormant. Due to the lessons of German history, even German nationalists are convinced that closer international integration will help to prevent renewed German desires for power. Strong nationalist arguments are difficult to make not only in the case of EU tax legislation but more generally in the context of international integration. Therefore, the considerable share of German exclusive nationalists did not play the important role their high number would suggest.

Finally, the Irish politicization process was triggered by the European Commission's attack on the Irish private and corporate tax system. Over the course of the 2000s, it became broader and more generally interested in the EU tax governance. This trajectory points to an additional explanatory variable not part of my theory. The perception of the national economic and social model seems to be an important variable that helps to explain the differentiated politicization of EU tax governance. With Germany and Switzerland, the country sample encompasses two countries whose populations are particularly proud of their countries' economic and social achievements. In the German context, Juan Diez Medrano (2003: 61) observes that many of his interviewees saw Germany as superior to the rest of Europe in terms of work ethic, standards of living, and social benefits. They, therefore, preferred an EU shaped along the German model. Similarly, the Swiss narrative of the "third way" and Swiss specificity (Sciarini and Dupont, 2001) contribute to a pronounced self-confidence that makes the Swiss population more skeptical of European governance. This situation was different in Ireland. The early period of analysis revealed a common understanding that Ireland's quest for economic and societal modernization can strongly profit from European integration (Laffan and O'Mahony, 2008; Rees, 2009). Contrary to the Swiss and Germans, Irish citizens were not at all convinced of the superiority of their national economic and social model. Rather, they stood in awe of the European economic model and thus did not politicize European integration during the 1980s. The Irish economic success story changed this situation. Irish self-confidence started to grow. As a result, the Irish population also began to question European integration in general and European tax governance more specifically.

Notes

1 Small countries enjoy competitive advantages as regards the link between tax base and tax rate. They are likely to profit from international tax competition whereas large countries are potential losers (Kanbur and Keen, 1993).
2 Equally parsimonious and even more precise question items on exclusive nationalism provided by the Eurobarometer, the European Election Survey (EES), or the International Social Survey Programme (ISSP) frequently applied in European Integration research (Schild, 2001; Hooghe and Marks, 2004; Hooghe and Marks, 2005; Garry and Tilley, 2009) do not cover Switzerland or the entire time period (for an overview of survey sources see Kittilson, 2007). WVS and EVS datasets comprise of a total of four waves covering a time span between 1981 and 2008.
3 Since both EVS and WVS data indicate this strong decrease from 1997 to 1999 and similarly low values are observable in 2008, measurement error seems to be an unlikely source of this strong transformation of the German society.
4 The previous chapter demonstrated that politicization is frequently characterized by issue attention cycles induced by the interaction of formal treaty revisions and tax policy output. Hence a steady increase is unlikely.
5 Note that these fluctuations are to some extent the result of low absolute numbers of articles in the sample.
6 The low number of relevant articles makes the interpretation of descriptive statistics difficult. The high mean value of controversy (30 percent) during the SEA period results from four controversial articles and should, thus, not be overestimated.
7 Due to a ruling of the Irish Supreme Court, referenda are mandatory for the enactment of constitutional changes to the European institutional structure (O'Mahony, 2009). These referenda are a potentially important opportunity structure for the politicization of the EU (De Wilde and Zürn, 2012: 139–142).
8 See Ireland's Finance Act No 14, Ch. VI (Republic of Ireland, 1980).
9 In addition to EU benefits, higher foreign direct investment especially from the US, the stabilization of public finances, improvement in competitiveness, the better qualification of the labor force, and a social partnership process – institutionalizing wage bargaining between government, employers, and trade union resulting in an explicit trade off of tax cuts for wage moderation – contributed to this development (Smith, 2005a: Ch. 3).
10 Until then Ireland had been a net beneficiary of EU funds.
11 The exact number of bilateral agreements is difficult to determine. Including all amendments and updates their count easily amounts to more than 100. The number of substantial agreements is considerably lower (Vahl and Grolimund, 2006: 22).
12 Although two more bilateral agreements on trade in clocks and watches (1974) and on trade in soups (1985) were concluded, the EU's political authority did not grow fundamentally during this period.
13 The European Free Trade Association (EFTA) is a free trade organization that operates parallel to the EU. The founding members were Austria, Denmark, Norway, Portugal, Sweden, Switzerland, and the United Kingdom.
14 The bilateral agreements on trade in non-agricultural and processed agricultural goods (1986), trade in electronic data systems (1989), and the carriage of goods (1990) signed during this period constitute minor amendments to the 1972 free trade agreement. Yet, they did do not increase the scope or level of EU authority.
15 This de jure right is severely limited de facto because of the so-called guillotine clause and the dependence of Swiss economic success on bilateral integration. Because the principle of parallelism – enshrined in the clause – ensures that all agreements come to an end, if any one of them is terminated, it is highly unlikely for Switzerland to opt-out of these agreements (Lavenex et al., 2009: 819).
16 By 2009 most of the agreements were implemented and a successful referendum on Schengen/Dublin was conducted in 2005 (all other sector agreements did not require a referendum).

17 More indirect effects of EU tax governance on the Swiss tax system are the replacement of the turnover tax by an EU-compatible VAT in 1995 (approved by referendum in 1993) and the introduction of a Heavy Goods Vehicle (HGV) tax in 2001 (approved by referendum in 1998) in reaction to the transport agreements included in Bilateral I (Vahl and Grolimund, 2006: 67).

18 The SVP's success cannot be overestimated. It even managed to increase its vote share above the share of exclusive nationalists in Switzerland.

19 The initial list included Andorra, Liechtenstein, Monaco, San Marino, Switzerland, and the United States. But negotiations with the US failed quickly. Since June 2005, Anguilla, British Virgin Islands, Cayman Islands, Guernsey, Isle of Man, Jersey, Montserrat and Aruba, Netherlands Antilles, and the Turks and Caicos Islands have implemented the directive.

References

Adshead, M. and Tonge, J. 2009. *Politics in Ireland: Convergence and Divergence in a Two-Polity Island*, Basingstoke: Palgrave Macmillan.

Afonso, A. and Maggetti, M. 2007. Bilaterals II: Reaching the Limits of the Swiss Third Way? *In:* Church, C. (ed.) *Switzerland and the European Union*, Oxon: Routledge.

Allen, K. 2000. *The Celtic Tiger: The Myth of Social Partnership in Ireland*, Manchester: Manchester University Press.

Banchoff, T. 1997. German Policy Towards the European Union: The Effects of Historical Memory. *German Politics*, 6, 60–76.

Barry, F., Bradly, J. and Hannan, A. 2001. The Single Market, the Structural Funds and Ireland's Recent Economic Growth. *Journal of Common Market Studies*, 39, 537–552.

Benoit, K. 2009. Irish Political Parties and Policy Stances on European Integration. *Irish Political Studies*, 24, 447–466.

Blue, J. R. 2000. The Celtic Tiger Roars Defiantly: Corporation Tax in Ireland and Competition Within the European Union. *Duke Journal of Comparative & International Law*, 10, 443–468.

Börzel, T. A. 2005. Mind the Gap! European Integration Between Level and Scope. *Journal of European Public Policy*, 12, 217–236.

Bulmer, S. and Paterson, W. E. 2010. Germany and the European Union. *International Affairs*, 86, 1051–1073.

Bundeswahlleiter. 2013. *Ergebnisse der Bundestagswahlen.* http://www.bundeswahlleiter.de/de/bundestagswahlen/fruehere_bundestagswahlen/

Cattoir, P. 2007. A History of the "Tax Package": The Principles and Issues Underlying the Community Approach. *European Commission Taxation Papers*, 10, 1–25.

Christensen, J. 2013. Bureaucracies, Neoliberal Ideas, and Tax Reform in New Zealand and Ireland. *Governance*, 26, 563–584.

Church, C. 2007. Introduction. *In:* Church, C. (ed.) *Switzerland and the European Union*, Oxon: Routledge.

Church, C., Severin, C. and Hurni, B. 2007. Sectors, Structures, Suspicions: The Financial and Other Aspects of Swiss Economic Relations with the EU. *In:* Church, C. (ed.) *Switzerland and the European Union*, Oxon: Routledge.

Dardanelli, P. 2007. Federalism: Institutional Adaptation and Symbolic Constraints. *In:* Church, C. (ed.) *Switzerland and the European Union*, Oxon: Routledge.

Das Schweizer Parlament. 2013. *Parlamentswahlen.* http://www.parlament.ch/d/wahlen-abstimmungen/parlamentswahlen/Seiten/default.aspx

Devine, K. 2009. Irish Political Parties' Attitudes Towards Neutrality and the Evolution of the EU's Foreign, Security and Defence Policies. *Irish Political Studies*, 24, 467–490.

De Wilde, P. and Zürn, M. 2012. Can the Politicization of European Integration Be Reversed? *Journal of Common Market Studies*, 50, 137–153.

Diez Medrano, J. 2003. *Framing Europe: Attitudes Towards European Integration in Germany, Spain, and the United Kingdom*, Princeton: Princeton University Press.

Dupont, C. and Sciarini, P. 2001. Switzerland and the European Integration Process: Engagement Without Marriage. *West European Politics*, 24, 211–232.

Dupont, C. and Sciarini, P. 2007. Back to the Future: The First Round of Bilateral Negotiations With the EU. *In:* Church, C. (ed.) *Switzerland and the European Union*, Oxon: Routledge.

Eggert, W. and Haufler, A. 2006. Company Tax Coordination Cum Tax Rate Competition in the European Union. *Public Finance Analysis*, 62, 579–601.

Emmenegger, P. 2014. The Politics of Financial Intransparency: The Case of Swiss Banking Secrecy. *Swiss Political Science Review*, 20, 146–164.

European Union. 1992. *The Maastricht Treaty*, Brussels: European Union.

EU-Switzerland. 1972. *Agreement Between the European Economic Community and the Swiss Confederation*, Brussels: European Union.

Furia, P. A. 2005. Global Citizenship, Anyone? Cosmopolitanism, Privilege and Public Opinion. *Global Society*, 19, 331–359.

Ganser, D. and Kreis, G. 2007. Swiss Neutrality: Incompatible With EU Membership? *In:* Church, C. (ed.) *Switzerland and the European Union*, Oxon: Routledge.

Garry, J., Marsh, M. and Sinnott, R. 2005. "Second-Order" Versus "Issue-Voting" Effects in EU Referrendums: Evidence From the Irish Nice Treaty Referendums. *European Union Politics*, 6, 201–221.

Garry, J. and Tilley, J. 2009. The Macroeconomic Factors Conditioning the Impact of Identity on Attitudes Towards the EU. *European Union Politics*, 10, 361–379.

Gava, R. and Varone, F. 2014. The EU's Footprint in Swiss Policy Change: A Quantitative Assessment of Primary and Secondary Legislation (1999–2012). *Swiss Political Science Review*, 20, 216–222.

Genschel, P. 2002. *Steuerwettbewerb und Steuerharmonisierung in der Europäischen Union*, Frankfurt a.M.: Campus.

Genschel, P., Lierse, H. and Seelkopf, L. 2016. Dictators Don't Compete: Autocracy, Democracy, and Tax Competition. *Review of International Political Economy*, 23, 290–315.

Genschel, P. and Seelkopf, L. 2016. Did They Learn to Tax? Taxation Trends Outside the OECD. *Review of International Political Economy*, 23, 316–344.

Gerring, J. 2007. *Case Study Research: Principles and Practices*, Cambridge: Cambridge University Press.

Girvin, B. 2010. Becoming European: National Identity, Sovereignty and Europeanisation in Irish Political Culture. *In:* McCall, C. and Wilson, T. M. (eds.) *Europeanisation and Hibernicisation: Ireland and Europe*, Amsterdam: Rodopi.

Goetschel, L. 2007. The Wider Setting of Swiss Foreign Policy. *In:* Church, C. (ed.) *Switzerland and the European Union*, Oxon: Routledge.

Gstöhl, S. 2002. Scandinavia and Switzerland: Small, Successful and Stubborn Towards the EU. *Journal of European Public Policy*, 9, 529–549.

Guex, S. 2000. The Origins of Swiss Banking Secrecy and Its Repercussions for Swiss Federal Policy. *The Business History Review*, 74, 237–266.

Hardiman, N. 2000. Taxing the Poor: The Politics of Income Taxation in Ireland. *Policy Studies Journal*, 28, 815–842.

Hooghe, L. and Marks, G. 2004. Does Identity or Economic Rationality Drive Opinion on European Integration? *PS: Political Science and Politics*, 37, 415–420.

Hooghe, L. and Marks, G. 2005. Calculation, Community and Cues. *European Union Politics*, 6, 419–443.

Inglehart, R. 1970. Public Opinion and Regional Integration. *International Organization*, 24, 764–795.

Jung, K. J. 2008. Growing Supranational Identities in a Globalising World? A Multilevel Analysis of the World Value Survey. *European Journal of Political Research*, 47, 578–609.

Kanbur, R. and Keen, M. 1993. Jeux Sans Frontièrs: Tax Competition and Tax Coordination When Countries Differ in Size. *American Economic Review*, 83, 877–892.

Katzenstein, P. (ed.) 1997. *Tamed Power: Germany in Europe*, Ithaca: Cornell University Press.

Kirby, P. 2010. *Celtic Tiger in Collapse*, Basingstoke: Palgrave Macmillan.

Kittilson, M. C. 2007. Research Resources in Comparative Political Behaviour. *In:* Dalton, R. J. and Klingemann, H.-D. (eds.) *The Oxford Handbook of Political Behavior*, Oxford: Oxford University Press.

Kriesi, H., Grande, E., Lachat, R., Dolezal, M., Bornschier, S. and Frey, T. 2008. *West European Politics in the Age of Globalization*, Cambridge: Cambridge University Press.

Kriesi, H. and Trechsel, A. H. 2008. *The Politics of Switzerland: Continuity and Change in a Consensus Democracy*, Cambridge: Cambridge University Press.

Kux, S. 1998. Zwischen Isolation und autonomer Anpassung: Die Schweiz im integrationspolitischen Abseits? *ZEI Discussion Paper of the Center for European Integration Studies*, C3/1998, 1–36.

Laffan, B. 2002. Ireland and the European Union. *In:* Crotty, W. and Schmitt, D. E. (eds.) *Ireland on the World Stage*, Harlow: Longman.

Laffan, B. and O'Mahony, J. 2008. *Ireland and the European Union*, Basingstoke: Palgrave Macmillan.

Lavenex, S., Lehmkuhl, D. and Wichmann, N. 2009. Modes of External Governance: A Cross-National and Cross-Sectoral Comparison. *Journal of European Public Policy*, 16, 813–833.

Lavenex, S. and Schimmelfennig, F. 2009. EU Rules Beyond EU Borders: Theorizing External Governance in European Politics. *Journal of European Public Policy*, 16, 791–812.

Leddin, A. and Walsh, B. 1998. *The Macro-Economy of Ireland*, Dublin: Gill & Macmillan.

Lightfoot, S. and Luckin, D. 2000. The 1999 Ecological Tax Reform Law. *German Politics*, 9, 139–144.

Linder, W. 2013. Switzerland and the EU: The Puzzling Effects of Europeanisation Without Institutionalisation. *Contemporary Politics*, 19, 190–202.

Linder, W. 2014. Swiss Legislation in the Era of Globalisation: A Quantitative Assessment of Federal Legislation (1983–2007). *Swiss Political Science Review*, 20, 223–231.

Meyer, C. 2004. The Hard Side of Soft Policy Co-Ordination in EMU: The Impact of Peer Pressure on Publicized Opinion in the Case of Germany and Ireland. *Journal of European Public Policy*, 11, 814–831.

Mudde, C. 2007. *Populist Right Parties in Europe*, Cambridge: Cambridge University Press.

Norris, P. 2000. Global Governance and Cosmopolitan Citizens. *In:* Nye, J. S. and Donahue, J. D. (eds.) *Governance in a Globalizing World*, Washington, DC: Brooking Institution Press.

Norris, P. 2005. *Radical Right: Voters and Parties in the Electoral Market*, Cambridge: Cambridge University Press.

O'Hearn, D. 2003. Macroeconomic Policy in the Celtic Tiger: A Critical Reassessment. *In:* Coulter, C. and Coleman, S. (eds.) *The End of History? Critical Approaches to the Celtic Tiger*, Manchester: Manchester University Press.

O'Kelly, C. 2004. Politics of Identity – V: Being Irish. *Government and Opposition*, 39, 504–520.

O'Mahony, J. 2009. Ireland's EU Referendum Experience. *Irish Political Studies*, 24, 429–446.

Palan, R. 2002. Tax Havens and the Commercialization of State Sovereignty. *International Organization*, 56, 151–176.

Paterson, W. E. 2010. Does Germany Still Have a European Vocation? *German Politics*, 19, 41–52.

Rees, N. 2009. The Irish Economy and Europe. *In:* Rees, N., Quinn, B. and Connaughton, B. (eds.) *Europeanization and New Patterns of Governance in Ireland*, Manchester: Manchester University Press.

Rees, N., Quinn, B. and Connaughton, B. 2009. Ireland and the European Union. *In:* Rees, N., Quinn, B. and Connaughton, B. (eds.) *Europeanisation and New Patterns of Governance in Ireland*, Manchester: Manchester University Press.

Republic of Ireland. 1980. Finance Act No. 14. http://www.irishstatutebook.ie/eli/1980/act/14/enacted/en/html

Risse, T. 2010. *A Community of Europeans? Transnational Identities and Public Spheres*, Ithaca: Cornell University Press.

Roudometof, V. 2005. Transnationalism, Cosmopolitanism and Glocalization. *Current Sociology*, 53, 113–135.

Schild, J. 2001. National v. European Identities? French and Germans in the European Multi-Level System. *Journal of Common Market Studies*, 39, 331–351.

Sciarini, P. and Dupont, C. 2001. Example, Exception or Both? Swiss National Identity in Perspective. *In:* Cederman, L.-E. (ed.) *Constructing Europe's Identity: The External Dimension*, Boulder: Lynne Rienner.

Sciarini, P., Fischer, A. and Nicolet, S. 2004. How Europe Hits Home: Evidence From the Swiss Case. *Journal of European Public Policy*, 11, 353–378.

Sinnott, R. 1995. Bringing Public Opinion Back In. *In:* Niedermayer, O. and Sinnott, R. (eds.) *Public Opinion and Internationalized Governance*, Oxford: Oxford University Press.

Smith, J.-A. 2005a. *Showcasing Globalisation*, Manchester: Manchester University Press.

Smith, M. P. 2005b. Introduction: From Modell Deutschland to Model Europa: Europe in Germany and Germany in Europe. *German Politics*, 14, 275–282.

Stämpfli, R. 2007. Populism in Switzerland and the EU: Form *Vox Populi* to *Vox Mediae*. *In:* Church, C. (ed.) *Switzerland and the European Union*, Oxon: Routledge.

Statham, P. and Trenz, H.-J. 2013. *The Politicization of Europe: Contesting the Constitution in the Mass Media*, London: Routledge.

Steinlin, S. and Trampusch, C. 2012. Increasing Vulnerability: Financial Regulation in Switzerland. *In:* Mayntz, R. (ed.) *Crisis and Control*, Frankfurt a.M.: Campus.

Treschel, A. H. 2007. Direct Democracy and European Integration: A Limited Obstacle? *In:* Church, C. (ed.) *Switzerland and the European Union*, Oxon: Routledge.

Vahl, M. and Grolimund, N. 2006. *Integration without Membership: Switzerland's Bilateral Agreements with the European Union*, Brussels: Centre for European Studies.

Zimmer, M. 1999. From the National State to the Rational State and Back? An Exercise in Understanding Politics and Identity in Germany in the Twentieth Century. *German Politics*, 8, 21–42.

6 Conclusion

The varied politicization of global tax governance

Until recently, international politics were considered the preserve of political elites. In the world of security specialists, establishment pundits, and international bureaucrats, international affairs were regarded as high diplomacy rather than town-hall politics. This divide between a publicly contested sphere of national politics and the elite-driven game of IR – which was long taken for granted in International Relations and European integration research (Steffek, 2007; Nullmeier et al., 2010: 23–27) – becomes increasingly blurred because of the politicization of international authority (Zürn, 2018). A mounting number of political protests directly address international institutions and headlines on the riots in Seattle (1999) and Genoa (2001) have remained in memory (Gronau et al., 2009). Moreover, globally organized campaigns such as the International Campaign to Ban Landmines (ICBL) – which target international institutions such as the UN – catch the attention of millions of people, lead to the establishment of international treaties, and may even win the Nobel Peace Prize (Cameron, 2002).

Although there seems to be a general agreement that international institutions have become politicized since the end of the 1980s, our understanding of the determinants of levels of politicization changes at specific points in time, and the way in which public debates unfold is still underdeveloped and fragmented. The growing literature on the politicization of international institutions has identified a set of potential explanations for these developments, which range from the transfer of political authority to international institutions (institutionalist perspective) to more society-based approaches (modernization theory and post-functionalism). However, the explanatory power of these approaches and their specific application are still the subjects of controversy. Although this can be partly explained by differing conceptions of politicization, the debate also reflects inadequacies in the available data and a lack of long-term systematic comparative analysis of the complementary explanatory power of these approaches.

The empirical chapters of this book address this controversy by asking how the formal transfer of political authority to international institutions and the exercise of this authority interact with country-specific mobilization potentials. The analyses provide substantial empirical evidence that the politicization of global tax governance is indeed driven by the growing scope and level of international authority, and by the respective tax policy output of the EU and the OECD. The growing political authority of these institutions has contributed to mounting public salience, controversy, and plurality of global tax governance in the quality press of Germany, Ireland, Switzerland. The empirical chapters demonstrate that this process is neither linear over time nor similar across countries. Rather, authority transfer appears to result in recurring episodes of politicization, which are driven by a complex interaction of formal authority and tax legislation, and which differ across countries according to the specific constellation of cosmopolitan and exclusive nationalist agents of politicization.

In the following sections, I summarize this argument of the complementary explanatory power of the institutionalist approach and the more society-based perspectives of post-functionalism and modernization theory. The chapter proceeds in four steps. First, I analyze the overall level of politicization across time, institutions, and countries to show how international authority and tax legislation interact as a driving force of politicization. Second, I discuss the specific trajectories of politicization processes to demonstrate how the overall levels of politicization and its specific timing is shaped by the complex interaction of formal authority, tax policy output, and national mobilization potentials. Third, I turn to the actual content of national debates to demonstrate how these interactions are channeled into substantially different patterns of politicization. Finally, I conclude with a discussion of the broader empirical and theoretical implications of my findings and the generalizability of these results to other areas of global governance.

The levels of politicization across time, institutions, and countries

The public salience of global tax governance grew significantly over time. This mounting visibility is the basis of the politicization process. The second component of politicization is the controversy of the debate. Although controversy did not increase as strongly as salience, the growing number of evaluations and claims indicates that global tax governance has become more contested. The respective indicator is thus in line with the propositions that mounting public debate also becomes increasingly controversial over time. The data on the plurality of the debate underline this diagnosis of politicization. Speakers from outside of national governments have dominated the discussions over the entire time period. Non-executive speakers have played an important role since the early 1980s. Together with national and international executives, they have pushed global tax governance on the public agenda.

The comparison of the levels of politicization across time and institutions indicates that authority transfer and the exercise of this authority are indeed the main drivers of this politicization process. The considerably higher levels of politicization of EU tax governance in comparison to the OECD and the substantial increases of the levels of the politicization of both institutions surrounding the expansion of formal authority and tax legislation show that the analyzed publics are indeed sensitive to authority shifts. They react with more attention, higher controversy, and a diversification of the actors voicing their views. While the level and scope of OECD authority remained relatively stable over time, both aspects of political authority increased in the EU case. As a result, I observe increasing politicization of EU tax governance, whereas OECD tax governance has remained largely invisible. This trend continued over the entire observation period. Today, EU tax governance has become a regular feature of public debates. OECD tax governance – except for some scattered discussions of the initiative to prevent HTC – is largely not politicized.

The comparison between the politicization of EU and OECD tax governance also clarifies the interaction effect between formal authority transfer and the exercise of this authority via tax legislation as the driving force of politicization. The substantial difference between the politicization of EU tax governance and the largely absent politicization of OECD tax governance is mainly the result of the interaction between policy output and formal authority. At the time of their foundation, the OECD and the EU started with a relatively similar scope and level of formal authority. Both institutions were active in a relatively similar number of issue areas in which the level of their authority barely exceeded intergovernmental coordination. In addition, their tax policy output was not fundamentally different. The EU issued limited legislation in the field of VAT and excises. The similarly limited tax policy output of the OECD was exclusively concerned with coordinating national corporate and private income tax systems. As a result, the politicization of both institutions was marginal and the differences between both debates were small. This picture has changed substantially with the enactment of the SEA. The strongly diverging levels of politicization of EU tax governance, in comparison to the OECD during this period, highlight the important effect of formal authority on politicization. The formal authority of European institutions experienced strong growth with the enactment of the SEA, while the frequency and scope of policy output remained low. Politicization, however, started to grow, and the SEA period experienced the first episode of the politicization of EU tax governance. By contrast, the formal authority of the OECD did not change over the course of the observation period. The only changes in the authority of the institution resulted from changes in tax policy output. As the politicization of these policies was considerably weaker than of EU tax governance, the OECD case shows that a strong politicization is more likely, if growing policy output is accompanied by a transfer of formal authority.

The more recent episodes of both institutions' policies to curb international tax competition provide additional evidence for this interaction between formal authority and policy output as a driver of politicization. Although both policies had similar aims, were initiated during similar time periods, and used comparably weak enforcement mechanisms, the EU initiative was much more politicized than the OECD policy. Consequently, high formal authority appears to be a precondition for strong politicization processes of specific policies. This result is underlined by a qualitative reading of the material. The debates show that there was a much stronger public debate on the non-binding EU code of conduct on harmful tax practices than on the relatively strong OECD initiative on HTC. Hence, only the combination of policy output and international authority leads to substantial politicization. The absence of one of the two components is likely to limit politicization to weak and short-lived episodes.

These results regarding the crucial explanatory power of the institutionalist perspective are corroborated by the cross-country comparison. Overall, the level of politicization was highest in Germany, a founding member of the EU that has not opted-out of major integration steps. In Ireland, an accession country that has withdrawn from some of the more recent steps of European integration, the overall level of politicization was lower than in Germany and emerged almost one decade later. Switzerland, by contrast, is integrated with European institutions via a set of bilateral treaties and unilateral adaptation only. Here, the public mainly assumed the role of an interested spectator. A politicization of EU tax governance can be observed only during the early 2000s negotiations on Swiss participation in the EU savings tax directive. In sum, this threefold comparison across institutions, countries, and over time provides substantial evidence in support of the institutionalist perspective on politicization.

The timing of the politicization process

This book addressed the question of how international authority, policy output, and national mobilization potentials shape the timing of politicization, which so far has been largely unexplored. A direct sequence – in which mounting international authority and policy output result in increasing politicization – is just one plausible scenario. It is similarly plausible that politicization precedes increasing international authority because public debates are not only interested in the results of political processes but also in the processes themselves. In this scenario, a major treaty revision that expands the scope and level of international authority, or the growing policy output by an institution, does not contribute only to the politicization of the institution at the moment of legal enactment or ratification. Rather, these events change public debate much earlier because the decision-making process and potential policy alternatives are debated even before legal enactment. Finally, politicization could also come with a considerable time lag. Here, increasing formal authority or policy output is initially not recognized by the public – but as soon as outcomes become more visible, debates start to grow and increase the level of politicization.

Most generally, my analysis shows that the mid-1990s were crucial for the politicization of global tax governance. The salience and the controversy of the debate were marked by strong increases during this time period. The changes in both indicators were considerably weaker before and after this phase. This ratchet-like effect of relatively little politicization during the 1980s pronounced growth during the mid-1990s, and a subsequent stabilization of the debate during the 2000s was mainly shaped by the politicization of EU tax governance. More specifically, the timing of the debates shows that the enactment of the Treaty of Maastricht was a critical juncture for the politicization process. During this period, the level of politicization grew to unprecedented highs that subsequently were rarely undercut. This trajectory of the debate provides additional evidence in support of the interaction of formal authority transfer and tax policy output. The SEA and in particular the Treaty of Maastricht increased the formal authority of European institutions substantially and transformed the nature of the EU from an economic union into a more political one (Marks and Steenbergen, 2004: 258; Garry and Tilley, 2009: 375). EU tax policy output increased in a more linear fashion. As a result, this time period was characterized by the substantial growth of politicization.

Furthermore, the EU case demonstrates that politicization processes do not necessarily follow simple mechanistic cause–effect temporal sequences. Rather, politicization appears to be characterized by cycles that follow different temporal sequences. Public debates on EU tax governance were periodical, flared up under specific conditions, and were more diffuse than a close reading of the institutionalist approach would imply. At times, discussions were anticipatory and accompanied early stage policy initiatives. At other times, discussions arose with a substantial time lag. These debates were not limited to specific policies or treaty revisions, but instead they dealt with a variety of issues ranging from demand for more or less formal tax authority to policy debates linked to actual policies or even to issues that were not on the political agenda. Here, international authority mainly had a discursive spillover effect. In particular, the SEA and the Maastricht period show that the increasing authority of the EU contributed to the politicization of tax governance because economic integration and the EMU were seen to depend on more strongly integrated European tax governance.

The patterns of politicization across countries

As regards the conditions under which international authority and policy output drive politicization, national politicization patterns lend support to the general expectations of post-functionalism and modernization theory. However, the results also point to a more specific link between national mobilization potentials and the expansion of international authority. In general, modernization theory and post-functionalism appear to shed additional light on the politicization of EU tax governance in Germany, Ireland, and Switzerland. A comparison between the two EU member states Germany and Ireland demonstrates that higher levels of politicization in Germany and the considerably broader spectrum of issues under consideration were shaped by the more favorable German mobilization potential. In Germany, socio-cultural conditions were characterized by a substantial polarization between cosmopolitans and exclusive nationalists. Although both groups were only weakly mobilized, their overall share and the much higher number of cosmopolitans explains the differences between both countries.

This contrast between the German and the Irish discussions is fully in line with modernization theory and its expectation of more politicization in the form of problem-solving debates in countries with a higher share of cosmopolitans. Yet, the specifics of all three politicization processes in terms of timing and content can be explained only by a more specific application of post-functionalism. The specificities of all three cases point to the idea that a strong national identity conflicts with European tax governance under specific conditions only. To trigger a substantial nationalist backlash, EU tax legislation must extend to issue areas of wide national concern and, thus, create a strong conflict between national identity, economic preference, and European aspirations.

In Ireland, this conflict was found in the area of income taxation. Private income taxation is a traditionally controversial issue in Ireland (Allen, 2000: 82; Christensen et al., 2013: 573–574). Corporate taxation emerged as a sensitive issue only due to its core role in Ireland's economic success during the 1990s (Hardiman, 2000: 828; O'Hearn, 2003: 38; Smith, 2005: 72–74). Irrespective of their historical roots, both areas of taxation were particularly sensitive and of nationalist concern. The European Commission's activities in both areas during the early 2000s were therefore accompanied by a strong nationalist backlash, which cannot be observed in the context of other initiatives of the European Commission and which was completely absent in the German debate.

A similar picture emerges from the Swiss public debate, where a strong episode of nationalist politicization unfolded in the context of Europe's savings directive. This European tax policy was accompanied by a strong nationalist episode of politicization because it extended the scope of EU tax legislation to the particularly sensitive area of banking secrecy. For many Swiss, this institution has held a totemic position since World War II. Because banking secrecy is of high economic importance and is connected to other important elements of Swiss national identity, including personal freedom and privacy, it has itself become an important component of Swiss identity. Hence, the European attempt to regulate this particular tax area and establish a regime of information exchange on capital earnings created a strong tension between European aspirations and Swiss national identity. This, in turn, triggered a strong nationalist politicization episode. This effect was amplified by the strength of the radical right SVP in Switzerland. While the role of radical right parties was marginal in Germany and Ireland, the Swiss case was strongly shaped by such parties. The SVP in particular used the opportunities provided by the tension between the savings tax directive and national identity to mobilize opposition to EU tax governance.

In the German debate, these episodes of strong nationalist politicization were not present. Although the share of exclusive nationalists was similar to that in Ireland and Switzerland, the lack of a strong conflict between German national identity and EU tax legislation left the nationalist mobilization potential lay dormant. A more cosmopolitan politicization process unfolded. Due to the lessons of German history, even German nationalists are largely convinced that close international integration will help to prevent renewed German desires for great power. Not only in the case of EU tax legislation, but also more generally in the context of international integration, strong nationalist arguments are considered inappropriate. Therefore, the considerable share of German exclusive nationalists did not play the role their high number would suggest.

Finally, the Irish politicization process was clearly triggered by the European Commission's attack on the Irish private and corporate tax system. Subsequently, this debate became broader and more generally interested in EU tax governance.

This trajectory points to the conjecture that the perception of the national socio-economic model in comparison to the European model constitutes an important variable that helps in the understanding of the varied politicization within and across countries.

In Germany and Switzerland, citizens are particularly proud of their countries' economic and social achievements. Many Germans consider their country to be superior to the rest of Europe because of its work ethic, standards of living, and social benefits. They prefer the EU to follow the German socio-economic model. Similarly, the Swiss narrative of the "third way" and Swiss specificity builds on pronounced self-confidence and translates into a more Eurosceptic atmosphere. This situation appears to constitute an important background condition for the politicization processes in both countries. In Ireland the situation was different. The early observation period was characterized by a common understanding that Ireland's quest for economic and societal modernization profited from European integration.

Contrary to the Swiss and Germans, Irish citizens were not at all convinced of the superiority of their socio-economic model. Rather, they used the European model as an inspiration. During the 1980s, politicization was rare and public debate marked by permissive consensus. This situation changed with Irish economic success during the 1990s, when Irish self-confidence started to grow. The Irish population also became more critical of European integration in general and of European tax governance more specifically. This result points to the rather unexplored idea that the political space, in which the politicization of international institutions unfolds, is not only structured along a socio-cultural but also along an economic dimension. Similar to domestic political spaces (Kriesi et al., 2008; Kriesi et al., 2012), "international political spaces" may also assume this two-dimensional structure, in which economic and socio-cultural conflicts shape public debates and specific levels, changes, and patterns of politicization.

Empirical and theoretical implications

What does international authority imply for the world's citizens who have long been accustomed to the nation-state? How do they respond to authorities who are not created by constitutions, who are not located in formal governmental structures, and whose legitimacy may be in flux? The answers of this book can be summarized as follows.

The recipe for a strong politicization of global tax governance consists of an international institution with strong formal authority, a broad and frequent tax policy output, and a high share of cosmopolitans and exclusive nationalists in a given population. In other words, the emergence of political authority beyond the nation-state has different implications for citizens according to their socio-cultural and economic situations and perceptions. This overall result corroborates my integrated theory of politicization. The empirics also point to a specific form of the preparation of these ingredients not detailed in the initial model.

First, formal authority and policy output interact in a specific way. As the politicization of EU tax governance shows, the increasing formal authority of European institutions sets the stage on which tax governance becomes politicized. Although formal authority in the area of taxation did not grow over time, European integration in other areas – for instance, in the form of EMU – contributed to the politicization of EU tax governance via discursive spillover effects. The rising tide of growing formal authority appears to lift the boat of EU tax governance with it. In other words, growing formal authority and tax policy output may spark public controversy in isolation. Yet, a strong and sustained politicization is considerably more likely if policy output acquires a higher visibility through growing international authority.

Second, the country case studies show that it is not only the share of cosmopolitans and exclusive nationalists that shapes the levels, changes, and patterns of politicization, but also the relative distribution of both groups and their mobilization. As indicated by the politicization of EU tax governance in Switzerland, this mobilization is crucial for exclusive nationalists. Their role in the politicization process is clearly linked to the presence of radical right parties mobilizing fears for the loss of national sovereignty, identity, and economic well-being.

Finally, the post-functionalist explanation is further specified by the empirical results, which show that exclusive nationalists become agents of politicization only if international authority – either in the form of formal authority or in the form of policy output – conflicts with country-specific elements of national identity. This more precise understanding of post-functionalism is supported by all three country case studies. Such a specific conflict between national identity and EU tax governance was absent in Germany, where taxation is not a particularly important element of national identity and where even exclusive nationalists agree to international integration due to German history. By contrast, specific identity conflicts triggered strong episodes of politicization in Ireland and Switzerland.

In this context, the interaction between formal authority transfer and tax policy output is particularly important. It has implications for the EU decision-making processes. Public debates reacted not only to major treaty revisions – as often assumed by EU public opinion research (McLaren, 2006) – but also to legislative output. It is plausible to expect that international decision-making bodies such as the European Commission and the members of the European Council take public debate into account in their day-to-day policy-making and not only during the negation of major treaty reforms.

The empirical case studies show that room for maneuver for political elites decreased in the area of global taxation. As the public becomes more aware of global tax governance and its implications, political elites can be expected to become more careful in taking this public scrutiny into account. More specifically, it is likely that the politicization of EU tax governance in Germany and Ireland and to a lesser extent also in Switzerland will make both European actors and national governments more aware of the increased public contestation of EU tax governance.

The question of whether these developments will result in more responsive EU tax governance because the European Commission and national governments are forced to take a broader set of preferences into account or in even less responsive tax governance because the European Commission and national governments react to politicization by shielding EU tax governance from public scrutiny is not the subject of this book. However, some informed speculation is warranted. Taking into account the rather complex nature of politicization, concerted strategies of shielding global tax governance from public scrutiny appear to be difficult to implement. First, the empirical case studies have shown that levels, changes, and patterns of politicization vary across countries. This cross-country variation implies that both national governments and international institutions are confronted with different strategic environments (Schmidtke, 2018). While some governments are haunted by public scrutiny and demand for more or maybe less international cooperation, other governments may be less constrained by public scrutiny. Clearly, this situation transforms the nature of the game and may even decrease the chances of international cooperation altogether; but whether governments and international institutions are able to implement common shielding strategies under these conditions is questionable at best.

Second, the temporal variation of the politicization process makes coordinated shielding mechanisms even less likely. As politicization does not follow a single temporal sequence but instead sometimes emerges during negotiation processes, and at other times only years after legal enactment of major treaties or specific policies, politicization processes appear to be beyond the control of political elites. It may be possible to design and cover authority transfer during the phase of negotiation and implementation. The outcomes of these changes are difficult to control and may spur politicization even years after legal enactment. Furthermore, the ratchet-like trajectory of the politicization of EU tax governance suggests that issues of international cooperation, once they have appeared on the public agenda, are there to stay or are at least difficult to remove. As soon as an issue like EU tax governance makes it to the public agenda, the development of public debates is partly beyond the control of political elites and shielding strategies become difficult to implement (Schattschneider, 1960).

In sum, the varied nature of the politicization of global tax governance seems to constitute a substantial impediment to concerted shielding mechanisms of national governments and international institutions. Hence, I expect the politicization of global tax governance to grow and exert an increasing influence on the politics of global taxation.

To what extent can the empirical findings on the varied nature of the politicization of global tax governance, its causes, and the more speculative comments on the potential effects of this politicization be generalized? What can we learn from this case study about the politicization of international institutions more generally? How do citizens react to the emergence of political authority beyond the nation-state? Global tax governance is a typical case of global governance due to the limited distributive consequences of this regulatory field. However, the selected organizations and their activities in the field of taxation are extreme rather than typical cases of IOs. The level and scope of political authority centralized at the European level are unparalleled among IOs. The OECD is a rather weak IO. Despite its large staff and budget, compliance mechanisms are limited and OECD authority is mainly of an expertocratic nature. As a result, the generalizability of my empirical findings to other international institutions is limited. In addition, the presented results should not be interpreted as the final word on the causes of politicization, nor are the potential consequences sketched earlier likely to be similar for other trajectories of politicization. However, providing such definitive answers by testing a well-developed explanatory model is beyond the intended purpose of this study. Designed as a theory-developing exercise, the book outlined a route towards an integrated and fine-grained understanding of the multi-dimensional varieties of politicization. Consequently, the main results of a complex interaction between formal authority transfer and policy output on the one hand and national socio-cultural and economic mobilization potentials, on the other hand, stand out for a more systematic examination on the basis of a larger, more encompassing, and representative set of international institutions and countries.

References

Allen, K. 2000. *The Celtic Tiger: The Myth of Social Partnership in Ireland*, Manchester: Manchester University Press.

Cameron, M. 2002. Global Civil Society and the Ottawa Process: Lessons From the Movement to Ban Anti-Personnel Mines. *In:* Cooper, A., English, J. and Thakur, R. (eds.) *Enhancing Global Governance: Towards a New Diplomacy*? Tokyo: United Nations University Press.

Christensen, J. G., Klemmensen, R. and Ostrup, N. 2013. Politicization and the Replacement of Top Civil Servants in Denmark. *Governance*, 27, 215–241.

Garry, J. and Tilley, J. 2009. The Macroeconomic Factors Conditioning the Impact of Identity on Attitudes Towards the EU. *European Union Politics*, 10, 361–379.

Gronau, J., Nonhoff, M. and Nullmeier, F. 2009. Spiele ohne Brot: Die Legitimitätskrise der G8. *Leviathan*, 37, 117–143.

Hardiman, N. 2000. Taxing the Poor: The Politics of Income Taxation in Ireland. *Policy Studies Journal*, 28, 815–842.

Kriesi, H., Grande, E., Dolezal, M., Helbling, M., Höglinger, D., Hutter, S. and Wüest, B. 2012. *Political Conflict in Western Europe*, Cambridge: Cambridge University Press.

Kriesi, H., Grande, E., Lachat, R., Dolezal, M., Bornschier, S. and Frey, T. 2008. *West European Politics in the Age of Globalization*, Cambridge: Cambridge University Press.

Marks, G. and Steenbergen, M. R. (eds.) 2004. *European Integration and Political Conflict*, Cambridge: Cambridge University Press.

McLaren, L. M. 2006. *Identity, Interests and Attitudes to European Integration*, Basingstoke: Palgrave Macmillan.

Nullmeier, F., Biegoń, D., Gronau, J., Nonhoff, M., Schmidtke, H. and Schneider, S. 2010. *Prekäre Legitimitäten: Rechtfertigung von Herrschaft in der postnationalen Konstellation*, Frankfurt a.M.: Campus.

O'Hearn, D. 2003. Macroeconomic Policy in the Celtic Tiger: A Critical Reassessment. *In:* Coulter, C. and Coleman, S. (eds.) *The End of History? Critical Approaches to the Celtic Tiger*, Manchester: Manchester University Press.

Schattschneider, E. 1960. *The Semisovereign People: A Realist's View of Democracy in America*, New York: Harcourt College Publications.
Schmidtke, H. 2018. Elite Legitimation and Delegitimation of International Organizations in the Media: Patterns and Explanations. *Review of International Organizations*, Online First: https://doi.org/10.1007/s11558-018-9320-9.
Smith, J.-A. 2005. *Showcasing Globalisation*, Manchester: Manchester University Press.
Steffek, J. 2007. Legitimacy in International Relations: From State Compliance to Citizen Consensus. *In:* Hurrelmann, A., Schneider, S. and Steffek, J. (eds.) *Legitimacy in an Age of Global Politics*, Basingstoke: Palgrave Macmillan.
Zürn, M. 2018. *A Theory of Global Governance: Authority, Legitimacy, and Contestation*, Oxford: Oxford University Press.

Appendices

Appendix 1

Level and scope of formal authority, 1981–2011

Figure A1 provides a graphic representation of authority indicators over time. The top plot displays the overall authority in terms of the sum of individual policy scores. The middle plot shows the mean level of authority, that is, the total authority score divided by the number of issue areas in which the institutions are active. The bottom plot shows the issue scope of both institutions, that is, the number of issue areas in which they exercise authority. Data on the EU are taken from Dirk Leuffen and colleagues (2013). Data on the OECD are my own.

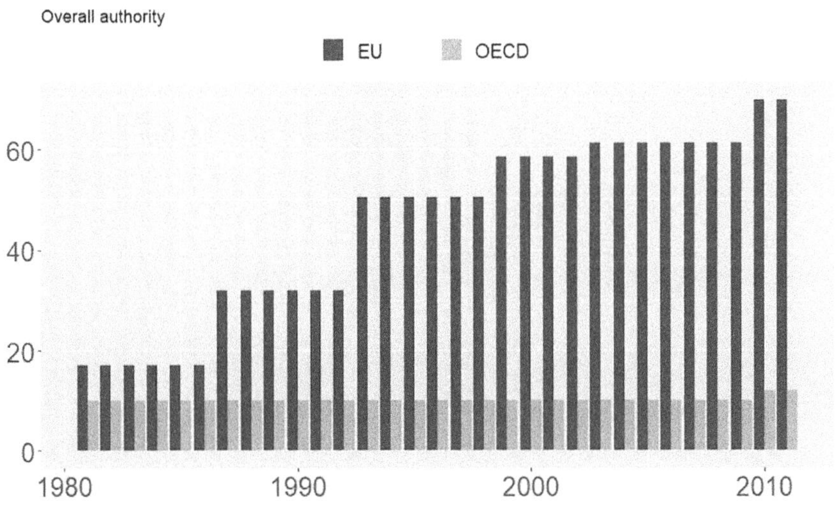

Figure A1 Level and scope of formal authority, 1981–2011

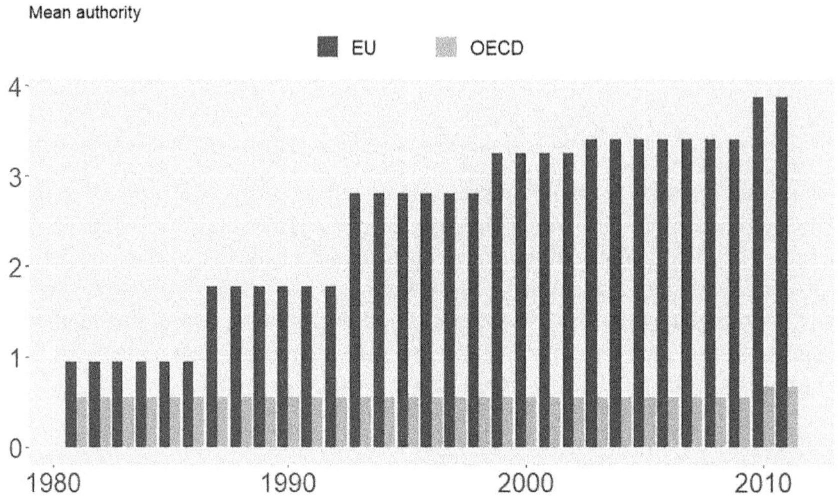

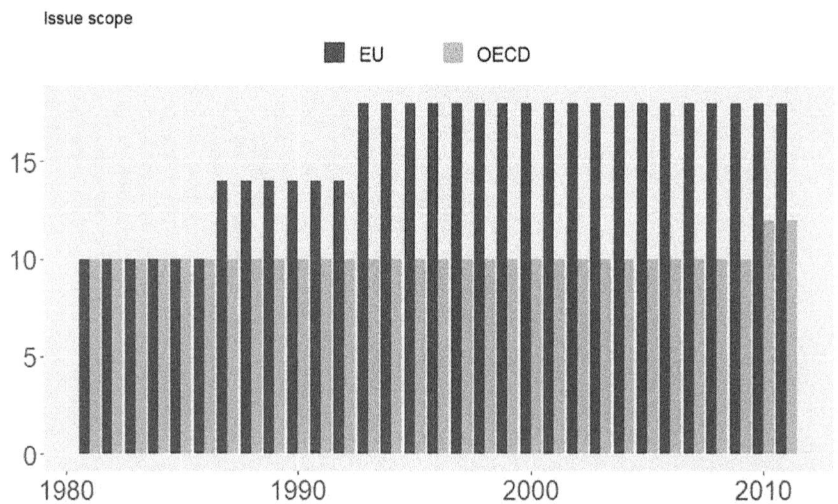

Figure A1 (Continued)

Appendix 2

Formal political authority of EU and OECD, 1981–2011

Table A1 Formal political authority of the EU and OECD, 1981–2011

Issue area	*1981 Treaty of Rome (1958)*		*1987 Single European Act (1986)*		*1993 Maastricht Treaty (1992)*		*1999 Amsterdam Treaty (1997)*		*2003 Nice Treaty (2001)*		*2010 Treaty of Lisbon (2009)*	
	EU	*OECD*	*EU*	*OECD*	*EU*	*OECD*	*EU*	*OECD*	*EU*	*OECD*	*EU*	*OECD*
Security and defense	0	0	1	0	1.5	0	2	0	2	0	2.5	0
Economic external relations	1.5	0	1.5	0	3.5	0	3.5	0	3.5	0	3.5	0
Criminal and domestic security	0	0	0	0	1	0	2	0	3	0	4	0
Civil law	0	0	0	0	3	0	3.5	0	4	0	4	0
Macro-economic policy and employment	1.5	1	1.5	1	1.5	1	3.5	1	3.5	1	3.5	1
Monetary policy	1	0	1	0	4	0	5	0	5	0	5	0
Taxation	1.5	1	1.5	1	1.5	1	1.5	1	1.5	1	1.5	1
Economic freedoms	2	1	4	1	4.5	1	4.5	1	4.5	1	4.5	1
Competition and industry	2	1	2	1	3	1	3	1	4	1	4	1
Environment and consumer protection	0	1	3	1	3.75	1	3.75	1	3.75	1	3.75	1
Occupational health and safety standards	0	0	4	0	4	0	4.5	0	4.5	0	4.5	1

(*Continued*)

Table A1 (Continued)

Issue area	*1981 Treaty of Rome (1958)*		*1987 Single European Act (1986)*		*1993 Maastricht Treaty (1992)*		*1999 Amsterdam Treaty (1997)*		*2003 Nice Treaty (2001)*		*2010 Treaty of Lisbon (2009)*	
	EU	*OECD*	*EU*	*OECD*	*EU*	*OECD*	*EU*	*OECD*	*EU*	*OECD*	*EU*	*OECD*
Energy and transport	2	0	2	0	2	0	2	0	2	0	4	1
Labor	1	1	1	1	3.5	1	4	1	4	1	4	1
Culture	0	0	0	0	1	0	1	0	1	0	4.5	0
Welfare	0	1	0	1	3	1	4	1	4	1	4	1
Research and development	0	1	3.5	1	3.5	1	4	1	4	1	4	1
Agriculture	3	1	3	1	3	1	3	1	3	1	4.5	1
Territorial, economic, and social cohesion	1.5	1	3	1	3.25	1	3.75	1	4	1	4	1
Total	17	10	32	10	50.5	10	58.5	10	61.25	10	69.75	12

Appendix 3

EU formal external authority in Switzerland

Table A2 shows EU authority for individual issue areas. Authority classification uses Tanja Börzel's (2005) scale, which was presented in Chapter 4.

Table A2 EU formal external authority in Switzerland

Issue area	*1972 Free Trade Agreement*	*2002 Bilateral I (1998)*	*2005 Bilateral II (2004)*
Security and defense	0	0	0
Economic external relations	1	1	1
Criminal and domestic security	0	1	1
Civil law	0	0	0
Macro-economic policy and employment	0	1	1
Monetary policy	0	0	0
Taxation	0	0	1
Economic freedoms	0	1	2
Competition and industry	1	1	1
Environment and consumer protection	0	1	1
Occupational health and safety standards	0	0	0
Energy and transport	0	1	1
Labor	0	0	1
Culture	0	0	1
Welfare	0	0	1
Research and development	0	1	1
Agriculture	0	1	1
Territorial, economic, and social cohesion	0	0	1
Total	2	9	15

Appendix 4
Codebook

To explore the levels and patterns of the politicization of global tax governance, a sample of newspaper articles is collected and examined. Newspaper articles are included in the sample if they contain at least one statement that refers to the activities of the EU or the OECD in the field of tax governance. The unit of analysis is, thus, acts of political communication that deal with global tax governance that can be identified and described with the help of a stylized grammar:

Object of discussion: OECD or EU as a whole, without further specifications, core political institutions of the organizations, and actors part of the organization

Issue area: Global tax governance, that is, issues of international tax cooperation, tax harmonization, tax competition, or any other international effects of tax governance. Newspaper articles are selected if one of these objects is mentioned in the context of taxation. This also includes proposals made by them or directed at them, judicial affairs such as European Court of Justice rulings on national taxation, the administration of conflicts between different tax systems – that is, the representation of European tax interests versus US interests in World Trade Organization (WTO) dispute settlements. News articles must explicitly name the issue area of taxation and the OECD or the EU. Articles dealing with "the European", "the West" or similar objects which might point to the EU or the OECD but are not clear about this distinction are not selected.

Example: "Ireland is leading opposition to the tax strategy being developed by the commission and has warned that harmonising the base would inevitably lead to the harmonisation of corporate tax rates, the rock upon which Ireland's economic success is founded" (*IT*, 14 December 2006).

The linguistic form of pertinent statements and particular grammatical functions of its elements may not exactly correspond to this structure, hence the elements of a statement are not necessarily integrated into a single sentence or paragraph. They may have various grammatical functions and be spread over several sentences or even paragraphs but must be recognizable as components of an argumentative unit. The reformulation of statements in the earlier-mentioned categories of the object of discussion and issue area must be possible without distorting or over-interpreting the meaning of the text from which statements are taken. The following two sections first describe the sampling and text selection strategies, then explain individual codes, coding rules, and their application.

Sampling

To compare levels and patterns of politicization across international institutions and countries on the basis of a manageable but still representative text corpus, a multistage sampling strategy is applied to the basic population of respective news coverage in Germany, Ireland, and Switzerland. At the first stage, a purposive decision was taken and the analysis limited to two quality newspapers per selected country.

The number of pertinent articles is further reduced with the help of the stratified random sampling technique of constructed weeks. Four constructed weeks per year and newspaper are selected. The "constructed week" approach refers to a series of six week-days (one Monday, one Tuesday, excluding Sundays) that correspond to randomly selected non-consecutive dates.

The procedure implies three levels of stratification. First, the selected time span is split into years, because years represent a natural planning cycle for media and political debates. Second, the selected years are split into four equal periods of three months each (January to March, April to June, July to September, and October to December) to account for possible seasonal variation of coverage (for instance, regular times of elections, budgetary debates, etc.). Finally, a constructed week is drawn from each period to represent weekly production cycles of daily newspapers (newspapers vary in thickness on the basis of advertising, which is determined by the day of the week).

With the help of a random number generator, one Monday is chosen from among all of the Mondays in each three-month period, one Tuesday from among

Table A3 Newspaper characteristics and data availability

Newspaper (Country)	*Political orientation*	*Circulation size*[a]	*Daily news hole*[b]	*Data availability*[c]
SZ (Germany)	Center-left	429,476	192	1995–2011
FAZ (Germany)	Center-right	384,895	192	1981–2011
II (Ireland)	Center-left	134,836	91	2003–2011
IT (Ireland)	Center-right	99,347	116	1982–2011
TA (Switzerland)	Center-left	210,665	127	1999–2011
NZZ (Switzerland)	Center-right	154,707	120	1994–2011

a Circulation size refers to average circulation over the period of analysis reported by the newspaper

b "News hole" refers to the average number of news articles per day over one randomly constructed week for the entire period of analyses.

c Data availability indicates the period of time over which newspapers are available at online databases.

all of the Tuesdays in each three-month period, etc. This procedure results in one constructed month for each year, with each week representing a different period of the year. It is repeated independently for every year and newspaper to guarantee the randomness of the samples.

Text retrieval

The text corpus drawn from this sample contains the digital version of articles dealing with the tax governance of the EU or the OECD. Newspaper articles are provided by the online data bank Factiva and are stored in RTF files. No distinction is made between news articles, news analyses, commentaries, editorials or other kinds of material. All articles in a newspaper are treated equally.

Constructing an appropriate information extraction system for this task aims at reconciling the goals of recall and precision. The former goal refers to depicting newspaper coverage of EU and OECD tax governance as comprehensively as possible and is thus concerned with reducing the number of false negatives to the lowest possible number. The latter objective intends to reduce the additional workload following from a large number of false positives. Hence the first methodological challenge is to design an information extraction system that is capable of doing just that. As pertinent statements are often complex and may take an almost infinite number of linguistic forms, it proved difficult to perform this task by means of a fully automated search routine. While it is absolutely possible to create a very broad and open search routine that is capable of extracting almost all pertinent articles, it proved to be more difficult to reduce the number of false positives to a manageable number by solely applying an automated search. Hence I use a twofold selection procedure that combines automated and manual (interpretative) steps.

Step 1: automated search routine

In the first step, newspaper articles are preselected with the help of an automated search routine. The primary objective of this stage is to retrieve as many pertinent articles from the data bank as possible. Search routines are constructed similarly for each country but differ slightly among the two German-speaking countries and the English-speaking country. The reason for these slight differences is a peculiarity of the German language and a technical limitation of the data bank: the German and English languages differ in the way different taxes are denoted. The English language uses a combination of separate words such as "income tax", "corporate tax", "valued-added tax". The German language creates proper names by using compound words such as *Einkommensteuer*, *Unternehmensteuer*, or *Mehrwertsteuer* (*Steuer* = tax). This complicates the design of cross-linguistically comparable search routines because Factiva does not feature left truncation of search terms. While right truncation is available, implying that a search for the term "tax*" retrieves all continuations of the word "tax" (such as taxation, taxes, taxi, etc.), search terms ending on "tax" but beginning differently cannot be retrieved in a similar way. Because the German routines need to take this issue into account they differ slightly from the English ones.

Digital newspaper databases feature Boolean operators, which provide the toolkit for the construction of search routines by connecting a variety of search terms. Based on extensive testing for recall and precision, the search routines shown in Table A4, which combine search batteries on the objects of discussion (EU/OECD) and issue area (global tax governance), are used.

Table A4 Search strings

Language/ Institution	*Search string*
German EU	(steuer* or Mehrwertsteuer* or Besteuer* or Umsatzsteuer* or Einkommensteuer* or Einkommenssteuer or Unternehmenssteuer* or Unternehmensteuer* or Unternehmensbesteuer* or Körperschaftssteuer* or Körperschaftsteuer or Zinssteuer* or Quellensteuer* or Europasteuer* or Ökosteuer* or Mineralölsteuer* or Doppelbesteuer*) near6 (europ* or EU or E.U. or EuGh*)
German EU FAZ[a]	(steuer* or Mehrwertsteuer* or Besteuer* or Umsatzsteuer* or Einkommensteuer* or Einkommenssteuer or Unternehmenssteuer* or Unternehmensteuer* or Unternehmensbesteuer* or Körperschaftssteuer* or Körperschaftsteuer or Zinssteuer* or Quellensteuer* or) and (europ* or EU or E.U. or EuGh*)/ (Europasteuer* or Ökosteuer* or Mineralölsteuer* or Doppelbesteuer*) and (europ* or EU or E.U. or EuGh*)
English EU	tax* near6 (europ* or EU or E.U.)
German OECD	(Steuer* or Besteuer* or Mehrwertsteuer* or Gewerbesteuer* or Körperschaftsteuer* or Einkommensteuer* or Einkommenssteuer* or Doppelbesteuer* or Unternehmensteuer or Unternehmenssteuer* or Finanztransaktionssteuer* or Ökosteuer*) near6 (internat* or glob* or "Organisation für wirtschaftliche Zusammenarbeit und Entwicklung" or OECD*)
German OECD FAZ	(steuer* or Besteuer* or Mehrwertsteuer* or Gewerbesteuer* or Körperschaftsteuer* or Einkommensteuer* or Einkommenssteuer* or Doppelbesteuer* or Unternehmensteuer or Unternehmenssteuer*) and ("Organisation für wirtschaftliche Zusammenarbeit und Entwicklung" or OECD* or O.E.C.D*)/(Finanztransaktionssteuer* or Ökosteuer*) and ("Organisation für wirtschaftliche Zusammenarbeit und Entwicklung" or OECD* or O.E.C.D*)
English OECD	tax* near6 (internat* or glob* or OECD* or O.E.C.D.* or "Organisation for Economic Co-operation and Development" or "Organisation for Economic Cooperation and Development")

a FAZ is not part of Factiva or Lexis Nexis but provides its own database, which cannot handle longer search routines and complex operators. Hence the search routine was split into two parts and the NEAR operator was substituted by the AND operator. To guarantee comparability, the proximity of search terms was checked through human coding in the selection process.

Table A5 Articles on the EU found by the routines, full year

Year	*SZ*	*FAZ*[a]	*NZZ*	*TA*	*II*	*IT*
1981		9,551				
1982		9,353				1
1983		9,992				0
1984		9,790				1
1985		10,659				0
1986		11,165				0
1987		11,366				0
1988		12,798				0
1989		15,279				3
1990		16,622				5
1991		17,354				9
1992		18,386				3
1993		13,773				11
1994		17,397	58			40
1995	41	19,095	48			33
1996	144	20,790	85			62
1997	112	21,575	102			113
1998	350	23,636	101			160
1999	240	27,844	121			127
2000	308	29,009	124	35		133
2001	188	29,295	137	32		146
2002	136	26,050	196	106		173
2003	164	23,718	163	82		160
2004	183	26,217	165	109	104	141
2005	215	24,734	121	70	123	120
2006	263	24,133	132	81	84	128
2007	255	22,765	245	123	90	122
2008	291	22,812	239	164	105	182
2009	327	20,294	167	128	62	168
2010	220	20,717	232	91	81	159
2011	469	23,165	181	87	112	228
Total	3,906	2,865,210	2,617	1,108	761	2,428

a The high scores for the FAZ result from the limited availability of Boolean operators in the FAZ database. The NEAR operator is not available. Search results were adjusted subsequently by eliminating all articles in which the NEAR6 condition is not fulfilled.

Table A6 Articles on the OECD found by the routines, full year

Year	*SZ*	*FAZ*[a]	*NZZ*	*TA*	*II*	*IT*
1981		17				
1982		21				0
1983		16				0
1984		19				0
1985		27				0
1986		25				0
1987		32				1
1988		36				0
1989		29				1
1990		31				7
1991		37				11
1992		44				8
1993		40				15
1994		47	35			22
1995	14	64	49			15
1996	49	54	55			20
1997	73	88	65			26
1998	97	97	75			44
1999	83	115	107			34
2000	105	93	110	17		42
2001	70	97	88	21		47
2002	58	96	101	38		34
2003	54	75	97	33		47
2004	61	97	103	28	30	32
2005	98	84	85	36	24	40
2006	108	77	106	40	31	53
2007	116	84	99	46	18	36
2008	108	124	159	70	36	61
2009	211	184	308	156	66	116
2010	83	141	309	62	29	81
2011	95	134	159	67	20	75
Total	1,483	2,125	2,110	614	254	868

a Note that the high scores for FAZ result from the limited availability of Boolean operators in the FAZ database. The NEAR operator is not available there. Search results were adjusted subsequently by eliminating all articles in which the NEAR6 condition is not fulfilled.

Table A7 Articles on the EU found by the routines, four constructed weeks

Year	*SZ*	*FAZ*[a]	*NZZ*	*TA*	*II*	*IT*
1981		54				0
1982		45				0
1983		61				0
1984		59				0
1985		71				0
1986		69				0
1987		75				0
1988		106				0
1989		137				0
1990		101				0
1991		122				0
1992		116				0
1993		108				0
1994		138	5			2
1995		152	3			2
1996	3	182	6	4		6
1997	4	189	6	2		6
1998	27	259	6	10		8
1999	11	237	3	6		4
2000	19	268	13	2	3	4
2001	16	220	14	3	7	15
2002	10	209	22	6	12	14
2003	13	225	15	4	4	15
2004	16	239	9	10	2	6
2005	15	223	12	11	8	10
2006	25	240	7	6	5	10
2007	24	202	16	4	6	9
2008	24	157	12	2	3	13
2009	22	176	6	10	7	7
2010	16	209	14	6	12	9
2011	27	219	8	5	10	27
Total	248	4,868	177	69	57	167

a Note that the high scores for FAZ result from the limited availability of Boolean operators in the FAZ database. The NEAR operator is not available there. Search results were adjusted subsequently by eliminating all articles in which the NEAR6 condition is not fulfilled. In general, search results for the entire year and the four constructed weeks are highly correlated. This indicates the representatives of the constructed weeks.

Table A8 Articles on the OECD found by the routines, four constructed weeks

Year	*SZ*	*FAZ*[a]	*NZZ*	*TA*	*II*	*IT*
1981		1				
1982		1				0
1983		0				0
1984		1				0
1985		4				0
1986		1				0
1987		3				0
1988		6				0
1989		3				0
1990		1				0
1991		3				0
1992		2				2
1993		1				0
1994		4	2			2
1995	0	6	6			4
1996	2	9	7			2
1997	2	5	5	0		1
1998	3	9	8	0		3
1999	8	7	7	0		2
2000	3	2	8	5		0
2001	2	7	8	1		5
2002	5	1	10	2		2
2003	3	5	8	2	1	4
2004	4	4	6	3	0	3
2005	5	5	4	2	4	3
2006	6	2	12	4	4	3
2007	5	4	9	4	0	2
2008	6	4	7	8	4	1
2009	9	12	26	7	9	9
2010	5	11	26	8	6	10
2011	4	8	9		1	6
Total	72	135	165	51	29	64

a Note that the high scores for FAZ result from the limited availability of Boolean operators in the FAZ database. The NEAR operator is not available there. Search results were adjusted subsequently by eliminating all articles in which the NEAR6 condition is not fulfilled.

Step 2: identification of pertinent articles

The obtained corpora are subsequently browsed manually to sort out irrelevant articles. Decisions on text selection are made on the basis of entire articles. Articles found by the search routines are fully read and scanned for pertinent statements. As soon as one possibly pertinent statement is found, the article is stored in a separate RTF file for all pertinent articles. Articles are considered pertinent and included in the sample if they contain one or more pertinent statement. The following rules are applied in the selection process.

1 Articles are pertinent whenever they are related to international tax governance and the EU or the OECD.
2 This has to be explicit. No assumptions about implicit content are made by "reading between the lines". Wherever the reference to the policy field or the organization remains unclear, the article is discarded from the analysis.
3 Statements under consideration may stretch over several sentences and are not limited to single paragraphs. This might, for instance, be the case when one of the selected organizations is discussed in one paragraph in a non-tax-related context and is referred to by a pronoun in a subsequent paragraph which deals with tax issues.

Table A9 Sample articles on the EU (pertinent articles after the selection process)

Year	*SZ*	*FAZ*	*NZZ*	*TA*	*II*	*IT*
1981		2				0
1982		0				0
1983		4				0
1984		2				0
1985		4				0
1986		4				0
1987		5				0
1988		11				0
1989		15				0
1990		0				0
1991		1				0
1992		0				0
1993		3				0
1994		9	2			0
1995	1	1	2			0
1996	1	8	2			1
1997	1	11	2	0		3
1998	13	20	4	0		4
1999	5	9	1	0		3
2000	7	20	7	2		3
2001	10	12	8	0		10
2002	3	11	15	9		7
2003	6	7	9	2	0	7
2004	10	16	5	2	1	1
2005	7	5	8	1	6	6
2006	9	9	3	2	1	5
2007	4	3	8	3	2	5
2008	12	4	7	8	4	10
2009	5	5	5	10	2	4
2010	5	8	10	5	2	2
2011	8	4	2	3	3	19
Total	107	213	100	47	21	90

Table A10 Sample articles on the OECD (pertinent articles after the selection process)

Year	*SZ*	*FAZ*	*NZZ*	*TA*	*II*	*IT*
1981		0				
1982		0				0
1983		0				0
1984		0				0
1985		0				0
1986		0				0
1987		0				0
1988		0				0
1989		0				0
1990		0				0
1991		0				0
1992		0				0
1993		0				0
1994		0	0			0
1995	0	0	0			0
1996	0	0	0			0
1997	1	2	0			0
1998	0	3	1			0
1999	1	1	1	0		1
2000	0	3	1	0		0
2001	0	0	1	0		0
2002	1	4	3	1		1
2003	0	0	3	1	0	0
2004	0	3	4	1	0	0
2005	0	1	4	1	0	1
2006	0	2	0	0	0	1
2007	0	0	4	1	1	1
2008	0	0	5	2	1	0
2009	4	7	15	3	2	1
2010	1	2	8	4	1	0
2011	1	2	4	0	0	0
Total	9	31	54	14	5	6

Subsequent to the final text selection, irrelevant articles are deleted. The remaining data files are prepared for and imported to MaxQDA. MaxQDA is a text-analysis software, which offers the opportunity to create a data matrix that can be exported to statistical software packages.

Variables and coding rules

Variable **STYPE**

The next step is to determine whether the article contains evaluative statements or claims relating to international tax governance activities of the EU or the OECD.[1]

If the article contains no statements that fall into these two categories, it is coded on the article level only.

1 Claim
2 Evaluative
3 None of the above

Rules to determine the character of the statement

Claims

1 A claim consists of the expression of a political demand, proposal, or call to action through some form of physical or verbal action or the attribution of such action to a claimant, regardless of the form this expression takes (statement, violence, etc.) and regardless of the nature of the speaker.
2 A claim is composed of up to six elements:

  a CLAIMANT: The speaker making the claim (Who makes the claim?)
  Variables: SPEAKER, SPNAME, SPORIG
  b FORM of the claim (How is the claim inserted in the public sphere?)
  Variables: SFORM
  c The ADDRESSEE of the claim (At whom is the claim directed?)
  Variables: SADDRESSEE, SADDORIG
  d The substantive ISSUE of the claim (What is the claim about?)
  Variables: SISSUE
  e TARGET: Who or what would be affected by the claim if it is realized?
  Variables: STARGET
  f The JUSTIFICATION for a claim (Why should this action be undertaken?)
  Variable: SPATTERN

In grammatical terms, such claims can be written as a CLAIMANT-ACTION-ADDRESSEE-ACTION-OBJECT-JUSTIFICATION clause sequence: an actor, the claimant, undertakes some sort of action in the public sphere (or this action is publicly attributed to the actor) to get another actor, the addressee, to do or leave something (the target) affecting the interests of a third actor (the addressee) and provides a justification for why this should be done. Empirically, claims are frequently not as differentiated as the grammar suggests and several claim elements are missing. The only information always needed for coding is information on the FORM (some sort of act in the public sphere has to be identifiable), ADDRESSEE or TARGET, CLAIMANT, and ISSUE, which allows determining whether the claim relates to tax governance activities of the EU or the OECD.

ADDRESSEE is the EU or the OECD, some of its major institutional elements (see Variable SADRESSEE) or group of actors such as the member states that are asked to do something about or within the organization. It is, however, possible that a claim deals with one of the organizations but does not name a particular addressee. In these cases, the TARGET of the claim must be the EU or the OECD or some of their major institutional elements (see Variable STARGET).

ISSUE must be related to the tax governance activities of the two organizations (see Variable SISSUE)

While it may be the case that some elements are missing, it is also possible that a statement contains a variety of different forms of one element. The claim "Mrs. X and Mrs. Y asked the European member states to push the European Commission and the Council for stronger tax harmonization and tax coordination" mirrors such a case. With Mrs. X and Mrs. Y, it contains two claimants; the European Commission and the Council are two targets, and tax harmonization and coordination are two issue contexts. Such complex statements are split into simpler ones which contain exactly one form of the given elements and coded this way. For the present example, this procedure results in the following eight claims:

Mrs. X asked the European member states to push the European Commission for stronger tax harmonization.

Mrs. X asked the European member states to push the Council for stronger tax harmonization.

Mrs. X asked the European member states to push the European Commission for stronger tax coordination.

Mrs. X asked the European member states to push the EU-Council for stronger tax coordination.

Mrs. Y asked the European member states to push the European Commission for stronger tax harmonization.

Mrs. Y asked the European member states to push the Council for stronger tax harmonization.

Mrs. Y asked the European member states to push the European Commission for stronger tax coordination.

Mrs. Y asked the European member states to push the Council for stronger tax coordination.

3 An instance of a claim must be (a) the result of the purposive action of a speaker or the attribution of such action to the speaker and (b) to qualify as a claim, a statement must include a reference to an ongoing or past physical or verbal act in public or an attribution of such an act to a speaker. This implies that direct demands, proposals, or calls to action and attributions of such demands, proposals, or calls to action to a speaker by the media or by other actors do count as a claim.

Example: "ATTAC, who wants the EU to introduce the Tobin tax" (attribution of a claim by ATTAC directed at the EU)

Example: "ATTAC, who says they want the EU to introduce the Tobin tax" (direct claim by ATTAC directed at the EU)

Both statements count as a claim by ATTAC and are coded similarly.

4 Statements by journalists, guest commentators, or other authors are also coded because the publication of the article is regarded as the action so that verbs indicating action or the attribution of action are not required.
5 Speculations about the opinions or actions of others are not coded. For instance, a journalist's statement that the German government will probably soon push the EU for more tax harmonization is neither a claim by the German government (it has not done anything yet) nor by the journalist because statements about what others will do are not claims.

Evaluations

1 Statements are coded as evaluative if they evaluate negatively or positively the EU or one of its components, core institutions, authorities, or policies in the field of tax governance, and in doing so, draw on a normative pattern of evaluation. The same is true for the OECD. This can be formalized in the following evaluation grammar:

   Evaluation object (EO) involved in global tax governance – (b) evaluation as positive or negative – because of (c) evaluation pattern (EP)

   An evaluative statement must, as a minimum, contain an EO and an EP or else an EO and an evaluation of it. Thus a statement may either omit an explicit formulation of the evaluation if the evaluation of the EO is already implied in the EP or the statement may omit an explicit formulation of an EP if a clear evaluation is present. As both variations can be transformed into the evaluation grammar, they are considered to be evaluations.

   Example: EU tax governance is bad (EP missing)

   Example: EU tax governance is completely ineffective (evaluation implied in the EP)

   If both a clear evaluation and an evaluation pattern are absent, a statement cannot be coded as an evaluation.

   Similar to claims, evaluative statements can also appear in more complex forms that contain a variety of different forms of particular elements of the grammar. In these situations, complex statements are split into simpler ones which contain exactly one form of the present elements and coded in this way (for details and examples see the section on claims)

2 Statements are coded as evaluative if an object of evaluation is referred to by a pronoun in the paragraph under consideration but can be clearly identified in the preceding or subsequent paragraphs.
3 Statements are coded as evaluative if abstract principles or elements of the EU or OECD are evaluated but there is no clear reference to the organizations as such.
4 Statements are coded as evaluative if the evaluative character can be derived from (a) the use of clearly value-laden adjectives, often in a superlative form; (b) the use of adjectives in a comparative form, if the comparison implies an evaluation of the present state of an EO.

5 Statements are coded as evaluative if they are backed by survey data that refer to public evaluations of political activities of the selected organizations in the field of tax governance. Such statements are coded as a positive and a negative evaluation.
6 No assumptions about implicit evaluations are made by "reading between the lines".
7 Statements are considered non-evaluative if they simply describe or explain the activities of the selected organizations in the field of tax governance or make factual statements related to this issue area. This includes, for instance, reports on activities and trends, etc.
8 Statements are not coded if evaluations are implicit or hidden in some rhetorical figure such as rhetorical questions, whose answer is not made explicit, or weak forms of irony.
9 Statements are also not coded as evaluative if the consequences of some future course of action are described in prognostic statements, but there is no explicit reference to the organization, its components, or its policies.

The coding procedure starts with formal and technical variables that do not create interpretative challenges. For articles that do not include claims and/or evaluations, coding is limited to these technical variables which are then coded on the article level. Articles that contain claims and/or valuations are coded on the statement level. All variables are numeric except when otherwise indicated.

Technical variables

Variable **SID**

A unique number is assigned to every statement for identification purposes. The first digit of the eight-digit identification number indicates from which newspaper the article was taken. The following four digits are a serial numbering of all articles from the respective newspapers. Numbering starts with the first article in terms of year of appearance. The remaining three digits identify in a serial numbering the statement in a specific article, starting with the first pertinent statement in a given article.

1. xxxx.xxx *Neue Zürcher Zeitung* (NZZ)
2. xxxx.xxx *Tagesanzeiger* (TA)
3. xxxx.xxx *Irish Independent* (II)
4. xxxx.xxx *Irish Times* (IT)
5. xxxx.xxx *Süddeutsche Zeitung* (SZ)
6. xxxx.xxx *Frankfurter Allgemeine Zeitung* (FAZ)

If the article does not contain claims or evaluations and is thus only coded on the article level, the final three digits are filled in as 000.

Example: 10001001 This SID identifies the newspaper NZZ (**1**0001001), the very first article from it (1**0001**001), and the very first coded statement in this article (10001**001**).

Variable **AHEAD** (string variable)
The main headline of the article in which the statement occurs is taken automatically and transferred to the data matrix by MAXQDA
Variable **ADAY**
The publication day of newspaper issue (1–31)
Variable **AMONTH**
The publication month of newspaper issue (1–12)
Variable **AYEAR**
The publication year of newspaper issue (two digits, 90 = 1990, 99 = 1999, 2000 = 00, 2010 = 10)
Variable **AFRPAGE**
Is the pertinent article reported on the front page of the paper? Articles that begin on page 1 are coded as front-page articles. If the information is missing, articles are coded as 3.

1 No
2 Yes
3 Unknown

Variable **AORG**

Does the article deal with the EU, its components, authorities, or policies or is it concerned with OECD activities, or both?

1 EU
2 OECD
3 Both
4 Unclear

If the article does not contain claims or evaluations, coding ends at this point.
If the article does contain claims or evaluations, the following rules apply.

Statement level

CLAIMS: If a statement was coded as a claim under the STYPE variable, the following variables and coding rules apply.

Variable **SLEVEL**

Claims are defined to contain a reference to the activities of the EU or the OECD in the field of tax governance. Such statements may relate to different system levels: the polity, the politics, or the policy aspect of such activities. Often, system levels intermingle in a single statement. If this is the case and it cannot be clearly decided which aspect is dominant, the highest level is coded. Hence if there is, for instance, a mixture of reference to polity and policy, the statement is coded to be on the polity level.

1 Polity (the organizational structure of the institution)
2 Politics (the processes of decision-making)
3 Policy (the results of the decision-making process, but also intermediate results such as proposals, verdicts, debates, or statements)
9 Unclear

1 A statement is coded as polity if it relates to the institutional set-up or the legal system of the EU or the OECD.
2 A statement is coded as politics if it relates to the political process within this institutional set-up of the EU or the OECD. It refers particularly to the decision-making procedures and this process of coming to mutually binding decisions.
3 A statement is coded as policy if it relates to a course or principle of action adopted or proposed by the EU or the OECD.

CLAIMANT: **The speaker making the claim (Who makes the claim?)**

Variable **SPEAKER**

This variable asks for the speaker of a statement. In newspaper articles, this can be the author of the article – the journalist – or any other person who is quoted or referred to as having said something or to holding some opinion. If there are two or more speakers uttering the same claim, this results in the statement being coded separately for every speaker. If the speaker is a group of people that cannot be differentiated, then this results in the claim being coded once.

10 Journalist
20 Holder of national political office
30 Holder of international political office
40 Civil society speaker (non-economy)
50 Economic speaker (representative of private companies; representatives of economic associations)
60 Other collective categories (the people, the Germans, . . .)
70 National politician (not an active member of the government or holder of another national political office)
90 Unclear

Variable **SPNAME** (string variable)

The name of the speaker is noted in the following format: Last Name, First Name. If no information on the name is given in the article, this is type UNKNOWN. If the statement is by more than one person, for instance, by two journalists in a co-authored article, all author names are noted (Last Name, First Name/ Last Name, First Name/ Last Name, First Name . . .) If it is not a person but a group, country, etc., note the word that is given there (for instance, Germany, Bundesbank, ATTAC, etc.).

Variable **SPORIG**

This variable refers to the country of origin of the coded speaker (if known).

1 Switzerland
2 Ireland
3 Germany
4 United States of America
5 Other EU country
6 Other Western/ OECD non-EU countries
7 Non-Western countries
8 Several speakers of different Groups (for instance, the Europeans)
9 Unclear
10 Unknown and to be researched (only for prominent political speakers of which the name is given in the article)

Variable **SPPARTY** (string variable)

If **SPEAKER** = 20/30/70 the abbreviation of the political party where a given speaker holds membership is noted as a string variable.

Variable **SFORM**

FORM of the claim (How is the claim inserted in the public sphere?)

1 Verbal statements

Demands and proposals uttered in non-specified statements, press conferences, interviews, public speeches, public letters, newspaper articles, other publications, publicity campaigns, polls, or research presentations

2 Direct-democratic action

Demands and proposals uttered in a referendum, initiative, or petition

3 Protest

Demands and proposals uttered in a public assembly, march, (violent) demonstration, boycott, strike, blockade, occupation, or violent attack

4 Judicial Action

Demands and proposals uttered in a criminal lawsuit, civil lawsuit, administrative lawsuit, constitutional lawsuit, or other judicial activities.

5 Attribution

Refers to all claims that are marked by a clear active form but where the author of the article or somebody quoted in the article attributes a particular claim to a claimant.

Note: if there are several forms of action, the following priority rules apply: (a) protest forms have priority; (b) the category of verbal statements is only used if none of the other categories applies.

ADDRESSEE of the claim (At whom is the claim directed?)

Variable **SADDRESSEE**

The addressee of the claim denotes the actor who is held responsible for implementing the claim or at whom the claim is directly addressed in form of a call or appeal to do or not to do something. Addressees are defined by their discursive relation to the claimant. They are the objects of demand, or, in other words, they are the actors to whom the claimant relates in the public discourse. If there is more than one ADDRESSEE of the claim, this results in coding additional statements (see general rules on claim identification).

EU/OECD

10 Organization as whole, without further specifications
20 Core principles of the organizations
30 Core political institutions of the organization
40 Genuine actors of the organization
50 National actors participating in the organization
60 Unclear
70 Other IO

10 Organization as whole

Examples (German):

- EU: *Die EU, die Europäische Union*
- OECD: *Die OECD, die Organisation für wirtschaftliche Zusammenarbeit und Entwicklung*

Examples (English):

- EU: The EU, the European Union
- OECD: The OECD, the Organisation for Economic Co-operation and Development

20 Core principles of the organizations

Examples (German):

- EU: *Demokratie, wirtschaftliche Integration, Stabilität*
- OECD: *Wirtschaftliche Entwicklung und Zusammenarbeit*

Examples (English):

- EU: Democracy, economic integration, stability
- OECD: Economic development, open cooperation

30 Core political institutions of the organization

Examples (German):

- EU: *Rat, Kommission, Parlament*
- OECD: *Rat, Sekretariat, Ausschüsse und Arbeitsgruppen*

Examples (English):

- EU: Council, Commission, Parliament
- OECD: Council Secretariat, Committees and Working Groups

40 Genuine actors of the organization (such as Bureaucrats)

Examples (German):

- EU: *Präsident der Kommission, Präsident des Rats, Bürokraten, Parlamentarier*
- OECD: *General-Sekretär, Bürokraten*

Examples (English):

- EU: President of Commission, President of the Council, Bureaucrats, Parliamentarians
- OECD: Secretary-General, Bureaucrats

50 National actors participating in the organization (individual member state or group of member states)
60 Unclear
70 Other IO

Variable SADDORIG (coded only when SADDRESSEE is 50)
This variable refers to the country of origin of the coded speaker (if known).

1 Switzerland
2 Ireland
3 Germany
4 United States of America

5 Other EU country
6 Other Western/ OECD non-EU countries
7 Non-Western countries
8 Several speakers of different countries (for instance, the Europeans)
9 Unclear
10 Unknown and to be researched (only for prominent political speakers of which the name is given in the article)

Variable **STARGET**

Who or what would be affected by the claim if it is realized? To be a pertinent claim the target must be the EU or the OECD or one of its sub-elements. If there is more than one TARGET of the claim, then this results in coding additional statements (see general rules on claim identification).

10 Organization as whole, without further specifications
20 Core principles of the organizations/constitutional treaties
30 Core political institutions of the organization
40 Genuine actors of the organization
50 National actors participating in the organization
60 Political regulations authored by the respective organization (such as regulations, directives, and decisions by the EU) constituting treaties are excluded from this category as they are part of the above categories

For clarifications and examples see Variable **SADDRESSEE**.

Substantive ISSUE of the claim (What is the claim about)
Variable: **SISSUE**

This aspect is fixed because the claim must be related to tax governance activities of the EU or the OECD. However, international tax governance can be subdivided according to a variety of types of governance. If there is more than one ISSUE of the claim, then this results in coding additional statements (see general rules on claim identification).

1 Harmonization (adaptation of national law through hard or soft measures)
2 Coordination (measures that do not change national law but contribute to international exchange of information, the collaboration of tax offices, etc.)
3 Tax competition (competition between states for investment by means of taxation)
4 Judicial activity (the review of national tax law by the ECJ, tax conflicts with external actors, for instance, at the WTO)

5 Creation of a new tax
6 Unspecific/general tax policy

The category unspecific is a residual category that should only be used if no other category applies.

Variable: **STAX**

Which area of taxation/tax type is addressed in the claim?

11 Private income and profits
12 Private capital gains
21 Corporate income and profits
22 Corporate capital gains
31 Property taxes (including capital duties, financial transaction taxes)
41 VAT or other sales taxes
51 Excise (including taxes on specific goods, energy taxation; excluding fees, customs duties)
61 other indirect (for instance, taxes on cars other than VAT)
62 other direct
71 Unspecific/several

Variable: **SPATTERN**

This variable denotes the normative basis or the evaluation criterion on which a claim is based. Following the theoretical considerations of the project, six categories are provided: nationalist input, cosmopolitan input, nationalist output, cosmopolitan output, no pattern, other/none of the above.

A first distinction is made between input and output criteria. Input criteria refer to the process of decision-making. Such criteria are mainly concerned with the questions of which actors are involved in decision-making and which procedures are followed. Output criteria deal with the decision itself, that is, the result of the decision-making process. Such criteria are mainly concerned with the quality and consequences of political action. The distinction between these two categories is first to be made when coding the evaluation pattern. They can, in general, be applied to all evaluation levels and objects.

A second distinction is made between cosmopolitan and nationalist criteria. Nationalist criteria evaluate the quality of international political processes (input) and its results (output) against the backdrop of national or state interests. States are the dominant category. As regards the input side, nationalist patterns evaluate political processes with respect to the question of whether all states concerned could participate in the process, whether no state had been coerced to accept a rule, etc. Nationalist input criteria refer to traditional valuation criteria that focus on state and nation. Similarly, nationalist output criteria refer to the question of

Table A11 Claims criteria

	Nationalist	*Cosmopolitan*
Input	Nationalist input (10) National sovereignty Participation of nation states Legal sovereignty Credibility State equality Capability/Agency	Cosmopolitan input (20) Participation also of non-state actors Deliberation/Moderation Transparency Accountability Charismatic/Expertocratic Leadership
Output	Nationalist output (30) Effectiveness/Efficiency in terms of state interests National distributive justice Protection of human rights (national) Contribution to the national public good	Cosmopolitan output (40) Effectiveness/Efficiency in terms of sub/transnational interest Distributive justice Protection of human rights Contribution to the public good Democratic empowerment

whether a rule or international policy is a good result for one or more nation-states. Again the core question to be answered when differentiating between nationalist and cosmopolitan criteria is whether the valuation centers on the nation-state and its interest or whether a larger constituency beyond national borders is taken as a point of reference. The categories and comprehensive list of respective arguments are summarized in Table A11.

50 No pattern
60 Other/none of the above

If there is more than one PATTERN for the claim, this results in coding additional statements (see general rules on claim identification).

EVALUATIONS: if a statement was coded as an EVALUATION under the STYPE variable, the following variables and coding rules apply.

Variable **SLEVEL**

Evaluations are defined to contain a reference to the activities of the EU or the OECD in the field of tax governance. Such statements may relate to different system levels: the polity, the politics, or the policy aspect of such activities. Often system levels intermingle in a single statement. If this is the case and it cannot be clearly decided which aspect is dominant, the highest level is coded. If there is, for instance, a mixture of reference to polity and policy, the statement is coded to be on the polity level.

1 Polity (the organizational structure of the institution)
2 Politics (the processes of decision-making)

3 Policy (the results of the decision-making process, but also intermediate results such as proposals, verdicts, debates, or statements)
10 Unclear

1 A statement is coded as polity if it relates to the institutional set-up or the legal system of the EU or the OECD.
2 A statement is coded as politics if it relates to the political process within this institutional set-up of the EU or the OECD. It refers particularly to the decision-making procedures and this process of coming to mutually binding decisions.
3 A statement is coded as policy if it relates to a course or principle of action adopted or proposed by the EU or the OECD.

SPEAKER: the speaker making the evaluation (Who makes the evaluation?)

Variable **SPEAKER**

This variable asks for the speaker of a statement. In newspaper articles, this can be the author of the article – the journalist – or any other person that is quoted or referred to as having said something or to holding some opinion. If there are two or more speakers uttering the same evaluation this results in the statement being coded separately for every speaker. If the speaker is a group of people that cannot be differentiated, this results in the evaluation being coded once.

10 Journalist
20 Holder of national political office
30 Holder of international political office
40 Civil society speaker (non-economy)
50 Economic speaker (representative of private companies, representatives of economic associations)
60 Other collective categories (the people, the Germans, . . .)
70 National politician (not an active member of the government or holder of another national political office)
90 Unclear

Variable **SPNAME** (string variable)

The name of the speaker is noted in the following format: Last Name, First Name. If no information on the name is given in the article type UNKNOWN. If the statement is by more than one person, for instance, by two journalists in a co-authored article, all author names are noted (Last Name, First Name/ Last Name, First Name, etc.) If it is not a person but a group, country, etc. note the word which is given there (for instance, Germany, Bundesbank, ATTAC, etc.).

Variable **SPORIG**

This variable refers to the country of origin of the coded speaker (if known).

1 Switzerland
2 Ireland
3 Germany
4 United States of America
5 Other EU countries
6 Other Western/ OECD non-EU countries
7 Non-Western countries
8 Several speakers of different groups (for instance, the Europeans)
9 Unclear
10 Unknown and to be researched (only for prominent political speakers of which the name is given in the article)

Variable **SPPARTY** (string variable)

If SPEAKER = 20/30/70 the abbreviation of the political party where a given speaker holds membership is noted as a string variable.

FORM of the evaluation (How is the evaluation inserted in the public sphere?)

Variable **SFORM**

1 Verbal statements

Evaluations uttered in non-specified statements, press conferences, interviews, public speeches, public letters, newspaper articles, other publications, publicity campaigns, polls, or research presentations

2 Direct-democratic action

Evaluations uttered in a referendum, initiative, or petition

3 Protest

Evaluations uttered in a public assembly, march, (violent) demonstration, boycott, strike, blockade, occupation, or violent attack

6 Judicial Action

Evaluations uttered in a criminal lawsuit, civil lawsuit, administrative lawsuit, constitutional lawsuit, or other judicial activities

7 Attribution

Refers to all evaluations that are marked by a clear active form but where the author of the article or somebody quoted in the article attributes an evaluation to a speaker

Note: If there are several forms of action, the following priority rules apply: (a) protest forms have priority; (b) the category of verbal statements is only used if none of the other categories applies.

Variable **SOBJECT**

This variable relates to the particular aspect of the EU or the OECD evaluated in a statement.

10 Organization as whole, without further specifications
20 Core principles of the organizations
30 Core political institutions of the organization
40 Genuine actors of the organization
50 National actors participating in the organization
60 Unclear

10 Organization as whole

Examples (German):

- EU: *Die EU, die Europäische Union*
- OECD: *Die OECD, die Organisation für wirtschaftliche Zusammenarbeit und Entwicklung*

Examples (English):

- EU: The EU, the European Union
- OECD: The OECD, the Organisation for Economic Co-operation and Development

20 Core principles of the organizations

Examples (German):

- EU: *Demokratie, wirtschaftliche Integration, Stabilität*
- OECD: *Wirtschaftliche Entwicklung und Zusammenarbeit*

Examples (English):

- EU: Democracy, economic integration, stability
- OECD: Economic development, open cooperation

30 Core political institutions of the organization

Examples (German):

- EU: *Rat, Kommission, Parlament*
- OECD: *Rat, Sekretariat, Ausschüsse und Arbeitsgruppen*

Examples (English):

- EU: Council, Commission, Parliament
- OECD: Council Secretariat, Committees and Working Groups

40 Genuine actors of the organization

Examples (German):

- EU: *Präsident der Kommission, Präsident des Rats, Bürokraten, Parlamentarier*
- OECD: *General-Sekretär, Bürokraten*

Examples (English):

- EU: President of Commission, President of the Council, Bureaucrats, Parliamentarians
- OECD: Secretary-General, Bureaucrats

50 National actors participating in the organization (individual member state or group of member states)
60 Unclear

Variable: **SISSUE**

This aspect is fixed because the claim must be related to tax governance activities of the EU or the OECD. However, global tax governance can be subdivided according to a variety of types of governance. If there is more than one ISSUE of the claim, then this results in coding additional statements (see general rules on claim identification).

1 Harmonization (adaptation of national law through hard or soft measures)
2 Coordination (measures that do not change national law but contribute to international exchange of information, the collaboration of tax offices, etc.)
3 Tax competition (competition between states for investment by means of taxation)
4 Judicial activity (the review of national tax law by the ECJ, tax conflicts with external actors, for instance, at the WTO)
5 Creation of a new tax
6 Unspecific/general tax policy

The category unspecific is a residual category that should only be used if no other category applies.

Variable: **STAX**

Which area of taxation/tax type is addressed in the claim?

11 Private income and profits
12 Private capital gains
21 Corporate income and profits
22 Corporate capital gains
31 Property taxes (including capital duties, financial transaction taxes)

41 VAT or other sales taxes
51 Excise (including taxes on specific goods, energy taxation; excluding fees, customs duties)
61 Other indirect (for, instance, taxes on cars other than VAT)
62 Other direct
71 Unspecific/several

Variable: **SEVAL**

The thrust of the evaluation

1 Positive evaluation
2 Negative evaluation

Variable: **SPATTERN**

This variable denotes the normative basis or the evaluation criterion on which an evaluation is based. Following the theoretical considerations of the project six categories are provided: nationalist input, cosmopolitan input, nationalist output, cosmopolitan output, no pattern, other/none of the above.

A first distinction is made between input and output criteria. Input criteria refer to the process of decision-making. Such criteria are mainly concerned with the questions of which actors are involved in decision-making and which procedures are followed. Output criteria deal with the decision itself, that is, the result of the decision-making process. Such criteria are mainly concerned with the quality and consequences of political action. The distinction between these two categories is first to be made when coding the evaluation pattern. They can, in general, be applied to all evaluation levels and objects.

A second distinction is made between cosmopolitan and nationalist criteria. Nationalist criteria evaluate the quality of international political processes (input) and their results (output) against the backdrop of national or state interests. States are the dominant category. As regards the input side, nationalist patterns evaluate political processes with respect to the question of whether all states concerned could participate in the process, whether no state had been coerced to accept a rule, etc. Nationalist input criteria refer to rather traditional valuation criteria that are focused on state and nation. Similarly, nationalist output criteria refer to the question of whether a rule or international policy is a good result for one or more nation-states. Again the core question to be answered when differentiating between nationalist and cosmopolitan criteria is whether the valuation centers on the nation-state and its interest or whether a larger constituency beyond national borders is taken as a point of reference. The categories and comprehensive list of respective arguments are summarized in Table A12.

Table A12 Evaluation criteria

	Nationalist	*Cosmopolitan*
Input	Nationalist input (10) National sovereignty Participation of nation states Legal sovereignty Credibility State equality Capability/agency	Cosmopolitan input (20) Participation also of non-state actors Deliberation/moderation Transparency Accountability Charismatic/expertocratic Leadership
Output	Nationalist input (30) Effectiveness/efficiency in terms of state interests National distributive justice Protection of human rights (national) Contribution to the national public good	Cosmopolitan input (40) Effectiveness/efficiency in terms of sub/transnational interest Distributive justice Protection of human rights Contribution to the public good Democratic empowerment

50 No pattern
60 Other/none of the above

If there is more than one PATTERN for the evaluation, this results in coding additional statements (see general rules on claim identification).

Note

1 Coding rules for the claims analysis are based on (Koopmans and Statham, 1999) and (Koopmans, 2002).

References

Börzel, T. 2005. Mind the Gap! European Integration Between Level and Scope. *Journal of European Public Policy*, 12, 217–236.

Koopmans, R. 2002. *Codebook for the Analysis of Political Mobilisation and Communication in European Public Spheres*, 15 April 2002 ed. https://europub.wzb.eu/Data/Codebooks%20 questionnaires/D2-1-claims-codebook.pdf

Koopmans, R. and Statham, P. 1999. Political Claims Analysis: Integrating Protest Event and Political Discourse Approaches. *Mobilization: An International Quarterly*, 4, 203–221.

Leuffen, D., Rittberger, B. and Schimmelfennig, F. 2013. *Differentiated Integration: Explaining Variation in the European Union*, Basingstoke: Palgrave Macmillan.

Index

Note: **Boldface** page references indicate tables. *Italic* references indicate figures.

For Product Safety Concerns and Information please contact our EU
representative GPSR@taylorandfrancis.com
Taylor & Francis Verlag GmbH, Kaufingerstraße 24, 80331 München, Germany

www.ingramcontent.com/pod-product-compliance
Ingram Content Group UK Ltd.
Pitfield, Milton Keynes, MK11 3LW, UK
UKHW022129190926
475702UK00013B/1718
* 9 7 8 1 0 3 2 0 9 3 7 7 2 *